MASTERING LAND USE AND ZONING

CAROLINA ACADEMIC PRESS MASTERING SERIES

RUSSELL WEAVER, SERIES EDITOR

For other titles, please go to caplaw.com.

Mastering Administrative Law, Second Edition
Linda D. Jellum

Mastering Adoption Law and Policy
Cynthia Hawkins DeBose

Mastering Alternative Dispute Resolution
Kelly M. Feeley, James A. Sheehan

Mastering Appellate Advocacy and Process, Second Edition
Donna C. Looper, George W. Kuney

Mastering Art Law, Second Edition
Herbert Lazerow

Mastering Civil Procedure, Fourth Edition
David Charles Hricik

Mastering Constitutional Law, Second Edition
John C. Knechtle, Christopher J. Roederer

Mastering Contract Law
Irma S. Russell, Barbara K. Bucholtz

Mastering Corporate Tax, Second Edition
Gail Levin Richmond, Reginald Mombrun, Felicia Branch

Mastering Corporations and Other Business Entities, Second Edition
Lee Harris

Mastering Criminal Law, Third Edition
Ellen S. Podgor, Cynthia E. Jones, Peter J. Henning, Neil P. Cohen, Sanjay K. Chhablani

Mastering Criminal Procedure, Volume 1: The Investigative Stage, Third Edition
Peter J. Henning, Cynthia E. Jones, Ellen S. Podgor,
Karen McDonald Henning, Sanjay K. Chhablani

Mastering Criminal Procedure, Volume 2: The Adjudicatory Stage, Third Edition
Peter J. Henning, Cynthia E. Jones, Ellen S. Podgor,
Karen McDonald Henning, Sanjay K. Chhablani

Mastering Elder Law, Third Edition
Ralph C. Brashier

Mastering Employment Discrimination Law, Third Edition
Jeffrey M. Hirsch, Joseph A. Seiner, Sandra F. Sperino

Mastering Environmental Law
Joel A. Mintz, Tracy D. Hester

Mastering Evidence, Second Edition
Richard Lorren Jolly

Mastering Family Law, Second Edition
April Carroll Meldrum

Mastering First Amendment Law
John C. Knechtle

Mastering Income Tax, Second Edition
Gail Levin Richmond, Christopher M. Pietruszkiewicz

Mastering International Sales Law
Herbert Lazerow

Mastering Interviewing and Counseling
Kelly M. Feeley, Rebecca C. Morgan

Mastering Labor Law, Second Edition
Anne Marie Lofaso, Joseph E. Slater, Jeffrey M. Hirsch

Mastering Land Use and Zoning
Robin Paul Malloy

Mastering Legal Analysis and Communication
David T. Ritchie

Mastering Legal Analysis and Drafting, Second Edition
George W. Kuney, Donna C. Looper

Mastering Legislation, Regulation, and Statutory Interpretation, Third Edition
Linda D. Jellum

Mastering Native American Law, Third Edition
Angelique Wambdi EagleWoman, Stacy L. Leeds

Mastering Negotiable Instruments (UCC Articles 3 and 4) and Other Payment Systems, Second Edition
Michael D. Floyd

Mastering Negotiation
Michael R. Fowler

Mastering Partnership Taxation
Stuart Lazar

Mastering Products Liability, Second Edition
Tim Kaye

Mastering Professional Responsibility, Second Edition
Grace M. Giesel

Mastering Property Law, Second Edition
Darryl C. Wilson

Mastering Sales
Colin P. Marks, Jeremy Kidd

Mastering Secured Transactions: UCC Article 9, Third Edition
Grace M. Giesel

Mastering Tort Law, Third Edition
Russell L. Weaver, Edward C. Martin, Andrew R. Klein, Paul J. Zwier, II, John H. Bauman

Mastering Trademark and Unfair Competition Law, Second Edition
Lars S. Smith, Llewellyn Joseph Gibbons

Mastering Trusts and Estates, Second Edition
Gail Levin Richmond

MASTERING LAND USE AND ZONING

Robin Paul Malloy

E.I. WHITE CHAIR AND DISTINGUISHED PROFESSOR OF LAW
SENIOR FELLOW, BURTON BLATT INSTITUTE FOR
DISABILITY LAW AND POLICY
KAUFFMAN PROFESSOR OF ENTREPRENEURSHIP AND INNOVATION
SYRACUSE UNIVERSITY COLLEGE OF LAW

CAROLINA ACADEMIC PRESS
Durham, North Carolina

Library of Congress Cataloging in Publication Data

Names: Malloy, Robin Paul, 1956- author
Title: Mastering land use and zoning / Robin Paul Malloy.
Description: Durham, North Carolina : Carolina Academic Press, 2026. | Series: Mastering series | Includes bibliographical references and index.
Identifiers: LCCN 2026009693 | ISBN 9781531032982 paperback | ISBN 9781531032999 ebook
Subjects: LCSH: Land use — Law and legislation — United States | Zoning law — United States
Classification: LCC KF5698 .M263 2026
LC record available at https://lccn.loc.gov/2026009693

Carolina Academic Press, LLC
700 Kent Street
Durham, NC 27701
Telephone (919) 489-7486
www.cap-press.com

Printed in the United States of America

For my grandchildren

TABLE OF CONTENTS

TABLE OF CASES

TABLE OF STATUTES AND REGULATIONS

TABLE OF DIAGRAMS

SERIES EDITOR'S FOREWORD

The Carolina Academic Press Mastering Series is designed to provide you with a tool that will enable you to easily and efficiently "master" the substance and content of law school courses. Throughout the series, the focus is on quality writing that makes legal concepts understandable. As a result, the series is designed to be easy to read and is not unduly cluttered with footnotes or cites to secondary sources.

In order to facilitate student mastery of topics, the Mastering Series includes a number of pedagogical features designed to improve learning and retention. At the beginning of each chapter, you will find a "Roadmap" that tells you about the chapter and provides you with a sense of the material that you will cover. A "Checkpoint" at the end of each chapter encourages you to stop and review the key concepts, reiterating what you have learned. Throughout the book, key terms are explained and emphasized. Finally, a "Master Checklist" at the end of each book reinforces what you have learned and helps you identify any areas that need review or further study.

We hope that you will enjoy studying with, and learning from, the Mastering Series.

Russell L. Weaver
PROFESSOR OF LAW &
DISTINGUISHED UNIVERSITY SCHOLAR
UNIVERSITY OF LOUISVILLE,
LOUIS D. BRANDEIS SCHOOL OF LAW

AUTHOR FOREWORD

This book provides a readily accessible and concise discussion of land use and zoning. It is written for several audiences. First, for people studying land use and zoning in a law school or in a land planning course, or on their own. Second, for people who find themselves working in the field of land use and zoning and who have never had a course in the subject. Third, for people appointed to a zoning board and lacking in knowledge of the planning and zoning process. Fourth, for property owners seeking an understanding of the process that empowers others to impose limitations and regulations on how they use their property.

For many people, land use and zoning may seem like a subject of limited scope, but in practice, it is a subject that touches on many elements of everyday life. Land use regulation, through planning and zoning, covers a variety of topics beyond those related to heights, locations, and size of buildings. It covers what you can do on your property and with your property. In addition, it can raise issues related to the composition and definition of a family, the regulation of speech, signs, flags, art, and architecture. It also regulates religious activities, and addresses problems related to affordable housing, discrimination, homelessness, squatting, climate change, and the integration of technology into the built environment. Planning and zoning also raise multiple issues related to making our built environment safe and easy to navigate by people with disabilities and by people seeking to age in place. In short, many of our most pressing social issues are encountered in a land use and zoning practice.

This book provides a complete overview of the entire subject area. It will equip the reader with the knowledge to understand all the basic concepts and issues in land use and zoning. In this regard, it is important to remember that land use and zoning law are primarily based on state law, and consequently variations may exist. Material herein is based on the general requirements and laws that apply across the United States. In addition to providing broad knowledge of the subject matter, this book will assist readers in formulating robust questions and prompts for doing more detailed analysis including the use of AI research engines to explore specific topics more deeply.

Robin Paul Malloy, JD, LLM
E.I. WHITE CHAIR AND DISTINGUISHED PROFESSOR OF LAW
SENIOR FELLOW, BURTON BLATT INSTITUTE FOR
DISABILITY LAW AND POLICY
KAUFFMAN PROFESSOR OF ENTREPRENEURSHIP AND INNOVATION
SYRACUSE UNIVERSITY COLLEGE OF LAW
414 DINEEN HALL, 950 IRVING AVE., SYRACUSE, NY 13244
EMAIL: RPMALLOY@SYR.EDU

ACKNOWLEDGMENTS

Many of the ideas and concepts explained in this book are updated, refined, and synthesized explanations of ideas addressed in some of my other related land use and zoning publications.

R.P. Malloy, LAND USE AND ZONING LAW: PLANNING FOR ACCESSIBLE COMMUNITIES 2D EDITION (with Malagrino, Carolina Academic Press, 2022; 1st edition by Malloy 2018).

R.P. Malloy, DISABILITY LAW FOR PROPERTY, LAND USE, AND ZONING LAWYERS (ABA Press 2020).

R.P. Malloy, LAND USE LAW & DISABILITY: PLANNING AND ZONING FOR ACCESSIBLE COMMUNITIES (Cambridge University Press, 2015).

Malloy, *Network Capabilities in Land Use and Disability Law*, 74 AMERICAN UNIVERSITY LAW REVIEW 461 (2024).

Malloy, *Advancing Accessible Communities* 27 VIRGINIA JOURNAL OF SOCIAL POLICY AND THE LAW 232 (2020).

Malloy, *Accessibility as a Public Good*, included in PHILOSOPHICAL FOUNDATIONS OF DISABILITY LAW to be published by Oxford University Press (Beaudry, Herring, Robinson, eds.) (Accepted and in the editing process—print date in 2026).

Malloy, *A Primer on Disability for Land Use and Zoning Law*, 4 JOURNAL OF LAW, PROPERTY, AND SOCIETY 1 (2018).

Malloy & Spencer, *Sidewalks and the Americans with Disabilities Act*, 41 ZONING AND PLANNING REPORT (April, Issue 4, p. 1).

Malloy (with Spencer and Crane), *Land Use Law and Sidewalk Requirements Under the Americans with Disability Act*, 51 REAL PROPERTY, ESTATE, AND TRUST LAW JOURNAL 403 (2017).

Malloy, *Land Use Law and Disability* 38 ZONING AND PLANNING LAW REPORT 1 (April 2015, Vol. 38, Issue 4).

Malloy, *Inclusion by Design: Accessible Housing and the Mobility Impaired*, 60 HASTINGS LAW JOURNAL 699–748 (March 2009).

I also wish to acknowledge the work of my law student research assistants who aided me in my proof reading and footnoting. They are Zachary Cuttito, James B. Doar, Cole D. Mathews, Jenna Lawryn Mazza, Gregory R. Patrick, and Lauren Spiezia.

MASTERING LAND USE AND ZONING

CHAPTER 1

Common Law Land Regulation—Prelude to Zoning

ROADMAP

- Common Law
- Trespass
- Nuisance
- Private Regulation of Land
    - Deed Restrictions
    - Covenants Running with the Land
- Limitations of the Common Law
- Public Trust Doctrine

Land use planning and zoning are essential tools of contemporary land regulation. They influence the relationships among people and property, and they identify and coordinate the locations where particular uses can be located. Planning and zoning rules, however, also have implications that go beyond defining and coordinating land uses. These rules may impact on the definition of families, the expression of free speech, and the exercise of religion. Consequently, planning and zoning can shape and influence the very nature of community life. This book addresses a wide variety of issues that come within the practice of land planning and zoning. To begin with, we look at common law approaches to land regulation. This serves as a prelude to the later development of public land regulation pursuant to planning and zoning codes.

Contemporary land regulation includes private law, with its common law background rules, and legislatively enacted planning and zoning codes. For the most part, when we study and practice land use law and zoning, we tend to focus on public land regulation. Nonetheless, we need to be aware of private regulations and restrictions on land. Private rules can play an important role in controlling land uses. Private land regulations are typically located in deeds, and covenants and restrictions. These private regulations are in addition to common law causes of action for trespass and nuisance.

In this chapter, we explore common law land regulations and traditional private law restrictions as a prelude to contemporary planning and zoning.

a. Common Law

Under the common law, property ownership not only includes surface rights but also traditionally includes rights to the center of the earth and the height of the heavens; *cujus est solum, eius est usque ad coelum et ad inferos*. Ownership provided the property owner with four basic rights: the right to use and possession; the right to exclude others; the right to transfer the property; and the right to the profits attributed to ownership of the asset. The common law also provided that a property owner had a right to use property for any lawful purpose so long as no harm was caused to others; *sic utere tuo alienum non laedas*. Legally recognized harms caused to others were generally categorized as falling under trespass or nuisance, and these became the primary ways of limiting the use rights of property owners. If a use did not meet the specific requirements of trespass or nuisance, it was considered a permitted use.

Much of the law in this chapter is covered in detail in a first-year property law course and book. This law is important to land use and zoning because it still provides useful ways of regulating land that supplement contemporary zoning law. Traditional common law concepts also inform the background rules of state law that set the stage for takings claims under the Fifth Amendment to the United States Constitution. (For a discussion of the role of background legal rules related to takings, see *Lucas v. South Carolina Coastal Council*, 505 U.S. 1003 (1992).) It is therefore important to review some of these basic property law rules as a prelude to understanding contemporary land use and zoning law.

b. Trespass

A trespass involves the entering of another person's property without permission. It violates the property owner's right to exclude others from the use and possession of the property. A trespass can be committed by either a person or an object. For example, I might walk across your property without your permission, or I might throw rocks onto your property. In throwing the rocks, I do not personally cross your property line, but the rocks do. A trespass might also include building a house on a lot and having part of the home extend across the property line of an adjoining property owner. Even if the intrusion is unintentional and very small, it is still a trespass. In the case of the house, this trespass might ripen into adverse possession if the intrusion continues for the requisite period of time. Depending upon the circumstances and the local law, a trespass can result in civil or criminal charges against the trespasser. While the right to exclude is a strongly held right of property ownership, it is not absolute. There are, in property law, exceptions and defenses to a violation of a property owner's right to exclude under the doctrines of *necessity* and *privilege.*

The doctrines of necessity and privilege provide exceptions to a property owner's absolute right to exclude. For example, under the doctrine of necessity, a couple may be entitled to dock their boat on someone else's private property in an effort to seek shelter and safety from a suddenly arising storm. The people seeking shelter must be reasonable in their use of the property and are responsible for damage that they cause to the property. Another example of necessity is when property is landlocked. Consider an example of 'A' granting land to 'B' and the grant fails to include an access point of ingress and egress. After a conveyance, the grantor might be required to allow the grantee an easement of necessity across its land given that there is no practical way for 'B' to access the land. In addition to necessity, privilege is also an exception to the right to exclude. Privileged entry on to another person's property occurs when a person enters the land of another at a reasonable time and in a reasonable manner to retrieve property that belongs to him. The person entering the land may be liable for damage caused and generally only enjoys the privilege if permission was originally sought and for various reasons was unable to be obtained. In the absence of necessity and privilege, entries onto the property of another would be considered trespasses.

As it relates to planning and zoning law, trespass was one tool that the common law courts had for dealing with regulation of property use. Trespass caused harm to another. Under the principle of an owner having the right to make any lawful use of property so long as no harm is done to others, harm occurs if one's use imposes a trespass onto the property of another. Thus, such a use can be restricted. This might prevent a property owner 'A' from hunting while standing on 'A's own property if in doing so 'A' has to shoot an arrow or bullet across 'B's property to hit a target. By crossing the property line, the arrow and bullet would amount to a trespass of 'B's property by 'A'. Likewise, if home owner 'A' is having his house spray painted on a windy day and some paint is blown on to adjoining home owner 'B's property such that it leaves small spots of paint on 'B's house and on the car parked in 'B's driveway, this too is a trespass. The same is true of a factory that emits dust and soot from its manufacturing facility that lands on the property of another. *See generally Bove v. Donner-Hanna Coke Corp.*, 258 N.Y.S. 229 (N.Y. App. Div. 1932). In these cases, even if hunting, spray painting, and manufacturing are otherwise lawful uses on one's property, they can be regulated, restricted and prohibited under the traditional common law concept of preventing an unlawful trespass.

Less tangible intrusions on another's property are more problematic for the common law. Consider the cases of odor from a pig or cattle farm escaping across a property line, of wind turbulence from a wind farm disturbing airflow on an adjoining property, or light from flood lights crossing a property line and interfering with a neighbor's property use. While each of these situations may arguably involve some form of trespass, the cases are much easier to win when framed as nuisance rather than as a trespass. *See, e.g., Spur Industries, Inc. v. Del E. Webb Development Co.*, 494 P.2d 700 (Ariz. 1972) (involving a cattle feedlot operation); *Amphitheaters, Inc. v. Portland Meadows,* 198 P.2d 847 (Ore. 1948) (involving the intrusion of light pollution on an outdoor drive-in movie theater).

c. Nuisance

Unlike trespass, which primarily focuses on addressing the right to exclude others, nuisance law concerns itself with the use and enjoyment of property. In general, a nuisance involves the unreasonable use of property in a way that imposes a substantial interference on the use and enjoyment of others. A physical invasion of the property is not required, although it is possible that a physical invasion may be both a trespass and a nuisance. A use is generally not considered to be a nuisance if the use provides benefits to the user or public that outweigh the harm or costs imposed by the use.

There are two categories of nuisance—private and public. A public nuisance involves conducting an unreasonable use of property that substantially impacts the use and enjoyment of the public. In general, this involves showing that the use has a substantially negative impact on the health, welfare, safety, and morals of the public. This may include aesthetic matters as well (a house that does not comport with the neighborhood, storing trash in the front yard, or parking damaged automobiles on blocks in your front driveway). In contrast to a public nuisance, a private nuisance involves making an unreasonable use of your property in a way that results in substantial harm to the use and enjoyment of another's property. This might include playing loud music late at night so that neighbors cannot sleep or using your single-family home's garage as a mechanic shop for fixing other people's vehicles.

Sometimes the same conduct may be both a private and a public nuisance. The difference is really one related to the scope and nature of the negative effects of the use. If the use interferes with one or a limited number of neighbors, it can be a private nuisance; but if it interferes with the use and enjoyment of a large number of community members, it may be a public nuisance. An example of something that might be both a private and public nuisance is a small factory emitting pollutants into the ambient air. If the factory is in a rural location and only one or two homeowners are affected, it is probably a private nuisance. On the other hand, if the factory is located in a crowded urban area with many homeowners affected, then it is probably a public nuisance.

Sometimes a use of property may seem reasonable and may not substantially interfere with the use and enjoyment of a reasonable person on nearby property. At other times, however, a nearby property owner may be sensitive to an adjoining property owner's use, or may be making a use of their own property in a way that is sensitive to effects caused by the use of a nearby property user. In general, nuisance law does not account for a sensitive use or user. *Amphitheaters, Inc. v. Portland Meadows,* 198 P.2d 847 (Ore. 1948). There are, of course, exceptions. For example, if I am building a new home and I know that on the adjoining lot my neighbor has already built a home with solar panels on its roof, I may have to modify my building plans to account for the sensitive use my neighbor is already making in terms of needing access to sunlight. While I might have the legal right to place my new home anywhere on the lot, certain locations that block sunlight from getting to my neighbor's roof may be considered a private nuisance. *Prah v. Maretti,* 321 N.W.2d 182

(Wis. 1982); *Fontainebleau Hotel Corp v. Forty-Five Twenty-Five, Inc.*, 114 So. 2d 357 (Fla. Dist. Ct. App. 1959).

A nuisance involves a *spillover effect* or a *spillover externality* when one property owner's use of their property imposes a negative impact on the use, enjoyment, and rights of an adjoining neighbor or on the public. This can be particularly problematic when the spillover effect imposes uncompensated costs on others. *See generally, Bove v. Donner-Hanna Coke Corp.*, 258 N.Y.S. 229 (N.Y. App. Div. 1932) (byproducts of industrial production discharged into the ambient air); *Spur Industries, Inc. v. Del E. Webb Development Co.*, 494 P.2d 700 (Ariz. 1972) (animal smells escaping into a residential neighborhood); *Amphitheaters, Inc. v. Portland Meadows*, 198 P.2d 847 (Ore. 1948) (light from a nearby race track disturbing an outdoor drive-in theater).

Some of the issues that arise in such a situation can be readily grasped with reference to the case of *Boomer v. Atlantic Cement Co.*, 257 N.E.2d 870 (N.Y. 1970). The *Boomer* case involved a private nuisance dispute among adjoining property owners. Atlantic Cement owned property on which it operated a facility that discharged pollutants into the ambient air. These discharges affected the property of surrounding landowners and in response, they sued seeking to enjoin further operation of the cement facility. In deciding the case, the court considered the potential for development of new technology to mitigate future discharges but noted that the company was using current technology at the time. The court found that enjoining the operation of the facility would cost Atlantic Cement in excess of $45 million, whereas the negative impact of the operation on surrounding property owners was less than $1 million. In this case, the decision was made to permit Atlantic Cement to continue operating. As an alternative to closing down the facility, the surrounding property owners were compensated for the negative impact on the value of their property. One way of looking at this outcome is that awarding $1 million to correct the problem (making surrounding property owners "whole" by awarding compensation) was much cheaper than enjoining the operation of the facility at a cost to its owner of more than $45 million. In addition, because the company employed a number of people and added value to the local economy, closing the plant would have had negative economic repercussions for the entire community, beyond the $45 million cost to Atlantic Cement.

The action in this case was brought as a private nuisance, meaning that the operation of the facility was a nuisance to a limited number of people and that the operation of such a facility (a cement factory) was not a nuisance to the public in general. Under similar facts, an action might have been brought by a public official to enjoin the activity as a public nuisance if the operation of the facility posed a threat to the public health, safety, and welfare of a larger population.

Under traditional land use law, a property owner has no right to operate a nuisance on his property, and the government can enjoin the particular use under its police power to protect the public health, safety, welfare, and morals. Thus, property owners such as Atlantic Cement do not have a right to operate if their operation imposes a nuisance. Because a property owner has no right to operate a nuisance, preventing a use that amounts to a nuisance is not considered a taking under the Fifth Amendment to the U.S. Constitution. As a starting point, therefore, one must appreciate that nuisance law has long been a source of authority for government to limit the use rights of a property owner; it is a traditional background legal principle.

Modern land use law now limits many more uses than those that rise to the level of a nuisance. Let us consider the *Boomer* situation in terms of externalities and the problem of transaction costs to suggest a further basis for government regulation of land uses. In the *Boomer* case, Atlantic Cement was making a use of its property that imposed costs and burdens on adjoining properties. The discharge of pollutants into the ambient air, resulting in dirt and dust on adjoining properties, is a classic example of a spillover effect (also known as an externality). Because the spillover imposes burdens and costs on the adjoining properties, to the detriment of the owners, it is identified as a *negative* externality. In the language of property, Atlantic Cement is obtaining a free negative servitude over the adjoining properties because it is, in effect, using the adjoining property to deposit dust and dirt that it is unable to contain on its own property but that it must generate as part of its normal operations (dust and dirt are normal by-products of the production process). In other words, if Atlantic Cement wanted to avoid having a spillover effect on adjoining properties, it would need to acquire much more land to encircle its operations and "catch" all of the particles escaping from its facility. In the alternative, it would need to invest in a way to reduce and eliminate the discharge. If they are already employing the best practices and latest technology, then the law has to deal with the by-product of needed production and activity.

Determining if the negative servitude in this example is free might turn on the question of who was there first: Atlantic Cement or the adjoining property owners. If the adjoining property owners were there first, then Atlantic Cement moved in and its operations imposed costs on the adjoining property owners and diminished the value of their land. In this case, Atlantic Cement obtains the servitude for free, unless it pays the adjoining owners for the cost of the servitude—and the owners may be unwilling to sell. Conversely, if Atlantic Cement were located on its property prior to the arrival of adjoining property owners (a residential subdivision is built several years later), it could be argued that the adjoining owners moved to the nuisance and were able to acquire the property at a discounted price because of the presence of its operation next door. In the situation of moving to the nuisance, it might be held that the homeowners have already been compensated for the impact of the servitude at the time of purchase because they were indirectly compensated as a result of the discounted purchase price. In other words, the negative effects of Atlantic Cement's operations result in a lower cost of acquiring the nearby property, and this lower acquisition price reflects an up-front compensation for the discharge of dust and dirt on surrounding lands. Situations such as this raise conflicts among property owners, and the greater the number of property owners involved, the more complex and difficult an amicable resolution becomes.

In a situation such as that illustrated by the *Boomer* case, it may be difficult for private parties to coordinate land uses. The potential for difficulty increases as the number of adjoining property owners increases, and as the specificity of property rights is less clear. In complex situations with multiple parties and competing interests, the costs and benefits for each party become more difficult to appreciate. In such cases, local government can sometimes assess the problem better than the immediately affected individuals, and then be able to work out a regulatory arrangement that might be more tolerable than that which the property owners can accomplish on their own.

The difficulty of coordinating uses in a complex set of relationships is often a reason given for supporting regulation. However, this rationale is weakened in certain situations. For example, when property rights are clearly defined; the nature of the issue between property owners is well understood; the costs and benefits readily determinable; and the coordinating parties easily identifiable; a private market solution might be achievable. This is particularly true when there are simply two or a very limited number of parties involved. The fewer the number of parties, the easier it is to coordinate negotiations. The easier it is to coordinate collective action, the lower the transaction costs, meaning that it becomes more likely that individuals can coordinate land uses on their own with limited or no public regulations.

Under the right conditions, individuals might be able to bargain among themselves to resolve tension as to the best use of property. While the parties may disagree on some points, they can also bargain to see if there is a price or an exchange element that can resolve their differences. If property owner 'A' does not want property owner 'B' to place a new house on the adjoining lot in a position that blocks 'A's view of a lake or access to sunlight, 'A' can pay 'B' to place the house differently on the property. The fact that 'B' may want a high price for agreeing to such a request is simply part of how the market works. The market will respond to the party who values the view and the access most. In the alternative, the bargaining process may lead the parties to an appreciation of an outcome that positions both houses so that each may enjoy a view and receive adequate sunlight. It is possible, and sometimes desirable, to allow individuals to resolve some land use coordination problems with minimal regulation.

However, coordinating land uses involves more than consideration of costs and benefits, it frequently also involves a need to mediate deep and intense differences among people regarding how best to use property based on competing political, social, cultural, and aesthetic values. For these reasons, it may be difficult for individuals to achieve good community-wide outcomes when everyone simply seeks to pursue their own self-interest. Unlike the individual decision to purchase a home or to rent a particular apartment, the coordination of multiple and complex land uses across an entire community is more difficult. Sometimes having access to experts and a little distance from an underlying relationship or conflict, as in being a kind of impartial spectator, is beneficial. Moreover, handling every property conflict as a "one-off" particularized transaction is costly and inefficient if the basic conflict can be regulated and coordinated with a general rule applicable to multiple properties. That is, if elected and appointed officials can make a good estimation of a good result for most people, it can be easier to just regulate to achieve the land use goal. Then, individuals with specified difficulties under the general rule can be provided with a procedure for seeking a variance and an exception to the general rules as applied to their particular circumstances.

d. Private Regulation of Land

In addition to public regulation of land through such mechanisms as zoning codes, land use plans, and building codes, private parties can limit and restrict land uses via private mechanisms. Two key mechanisms for private land regulation include the use of deed restrictions and the use of covenants running with the land.

i. Deed Restrictions

One means for private regulation of property is in transferring property with specified limitations and restrictions in the instrument of conveyance, typically a deed. A grantor might limit the use of property being sold by granting the property as a fee simple determinable containing language such as, from "grantor to grantee so long as grantee never uses the property for a commercial business." In such a case, if the grantee uses the property for a commercial business, the property will automatically revert back to the grantor or the grantor's heirs and assigns. Another way to regulate land use is by including restrictive covenants in the instrument of conveyance. These covenants do not define the estate interest being conveyed but they do impose limitations on how the property can be used. These covenants typically run with the land and bind future grantees, heirs, and assigns. Typical covenants might relate to the use of the property, or to the height, bulk, and location of any structure on the property. The estate benefited by the covenants can enforce it, and this is what makes it a useful private land regulation.

It should be noted that a leasehold is an estate interest, and a leasehold conveyance can include many land use restrictions as lease terms between the parties. Lease terms can regulate use, noise levels, subletting, and other activities of the tenant. Using restrictions in a lease, a landlord can control and regulate the property.

ii. Covenants Running with the Land

In a first-year property course, one covers covenants running with the land. These covenants are sometimes referred to as *covenants, conditions, and restrictions* (CCRs). In addition to including covenants in a deed, covenants are often created using separate instruments. The purpose of covenants is to establish restrictions that limit the use of property for the benefit of others or for all of the properties collectively. Covenants bind the original parties, their assignees, and successors. This means that they can be enforced by such parties. Common law requirements include a need for horizontal and vertical privity for the benefits and burdens of the covenant to run with the land. There is also a requirement that the promises between the parties "touch and concern" the land. Some of these elements have been modified under contemporary court decisions and under the influence of the Restatements of Law, but the point is that the common law established ways to regulate land even without public zoning.

Contemporary examples of using covenants include recording them to establish rules and guidelines for subdivision developments and planned unit developments (to be discussed further in future chapters). Real covenants can be positive, requiring certain actions to be taken, or negative, requiring one to refrain from taking specified actions. For example, a positive covenant might be one that requires the maintenance of a certain structure in good repair, and a negative covenant might be one that prohibits building a structure on the land with a height of more than thirty-five feet. Typically, money damages are awarded for violation of a positive covenant, and an injunction is the remedy for violation of a negative covenant.

In subdivisions, it is common to have a Home Owners Association (H.O.A.) charged with enforcing the restrictive covenants that typically cover land use matters. Lot owners within the subdivision are members of the H.O.A., and the H.O.A. is governed by bylaws and functions with an elected board to carry out the duties of the H.O.A. While the H.O.A. can enforce the covenants governing the property, most subdivisions empower individual lot owners to bring an action to enforce the rules as well. Enforcement actions usually involve seeking an injunction against a property owner undertaking a land use or a structural improvement in violation of a restrictive covenant. This might include adding a fence or a shed when fences and sheds are prohibited. Even if a shed is permitted on a lot, the use of certain construction materials may be prohibited, and its size and height may also have to meet certain requirements.

In addition to covenants, the common law also included equitable servitudes as a means to control land use and development. Generally, equitable servitudes are found where the formalities of a covenant running with the land are not present. They can bind the original parties and the subsequent owners of the lands when the buyers of the land have actual or constructive notice of the restriction. In contemporary law, equity generally grants enforcement of both positive and negative servitudes.

e. Limitations of the Common Law

The common law tools of land regulation that relied on trespass and nuisance proved too limited in their usefulness as the country industrialized and became more densely populated. Spillover effects and externalities generated by the use of one's property became more difficult to control. Dealing with the needs of public health, safety, welfare, and morals often went beyond clear cases of trespass and nuisance. Furthermore, actions in trespass and nuisance are case-by-case and fact specific determinations. This means that every situation must be litigated individually rather than being able to manage and coordinate property uses by general regulatory rules. Zoning codes, on the other hand, permit a local government to manage and coordinate land uses for multiple land owners at once. Regulating complex societies by relying primarily on actions in trespass and nuisance was generally inefficient and ineffective.

Deed restrictions, restrictive covenants, and servitudes also presented limitations. These restrictions and covenants required cooperation and coordination at a level typically requiring a close alignment of interests among a small group of people sharing a common interest in a property. As such, they often focused on a narrow set of private interests and did not fully account for broader public health and safety concerns.

f. Public Trust Doctrine

Another common law doctrine that governs land regulation is the *public trust doctrine*. While not typically thought of as zoning, it provides an important foundation for dealing with the environment and natural resources. The doctrine is primarily a state common law matter. The doctrine identifies such things as air, water, and wildlife as resources that are held for the benefit of all people. In order to protect and manage these resources, the state holds them in trust for the benefit of the people. This is the basis for state regulation of air quality, wildlife, water resources, rivers, and lakes.

The doctrine of public trust goes back to Roman law and was incorporated into early English common law. The public trust was attributed to the sovereign; the sovereign being the emperor or the crown (king or queen as might be the case). With the formation of the United States, the individual states inherited this common law power. In *Martin v. Waddell's Lessee*, 41 U.S. 367 (1842), the U.S. Supreme Court affirmed the public trust doctrine and held that members of the public had a right to fish in navigable and tidal waters. This was because the underlying land and the water were part of the public trust, and as such they were held by the state for the benefit and use of the public. Later cases clarified and expanded the public trust to cover navigable waters, submerged lands, tidelands, and wildlife. Importantly, the public trust doctrine does not include land above the ordinary high-water mark of navigable waters. However, the state may have police powers to regulate such lands above or beyond the ordinary high-water mark of navigable waters. *See, e.g., Rock-Koshkonong Lake Dist. v. State Dep't of Natural Res.*, 833 N.W.2d 800 (Wis. 2013) (addressing efforts by the state to regulate for the protection of wetlands).

The public trust also covers the rights of people to engage in commerce such as shipping and fishing. The states are responsible for managing and protecting the public trust, and they can also establish a process for creating rights in private parties to use these public trust resources.

While the public trust is generally held by the individual states, it is also argued that the federal government also has the power of the public trust with respect to certain federal properties and resources. For example, the Federal government regulates migratory birds (Migratory Bird Treaty Act: 16 U.S.C. § 703), clean water (Clean Water Act Wetlands Protection: 33 U.S.C. § 1344; Clean Water Act: 33 U.S.C. § 1251), and clean air (Clean Air Act: 42 U.S.C. § 7401) for the public benefit. Support for federal authority of the public trust can be found in the Property Clause, Commerce Clause, and Supremacy Clause of the U.S. Constitution.

CHECKPOINTS

- **Common law.** Land regulation was possible under the common law before the development of modern planning and zoning codes.
- **Trespass.** One way to control land uses under the common law is with an action in trespass. Trespass involves a nonconsensual invasion of the property rights of another. This could involve something very tangible such as walking or building on another person's property, or something more abstract such as suing for an intrusion of dust particles, noise, and light escaping from one property and interfering with another property owner's right to exclude.

- **Nuisance.** Land uses were also regulated by the law of nuisance. Nuisance is an action based on the interference with a person's peaceful use and enjoyment of her land.
- **Private nuisance** involves a use that interferes with one or a very small number of other property owners.
- **Public nuisance** is a use that interferes with the use and enjoyment of the public at large.
- **Deed restrictions** also limited and regulated land uses. Deed restrictions were binding on the grantee and the grantee's heirs, successors, and assigns.
- **Restrictive covenants** regulated land by imposing positive and negative requirements. Restrictive covenants run with the land and are binding on the heirs, successors, and assignees of the parties to the covenants. When all of the formalities of a legal covenant are not present, the courts sometimes enforce an equitable servitude.
- **Limitations of the common law.** While the law of trespass, nuisance, deed restrictions, and restrictive covenants provide means for regulating land uses, they are generally inefficient because they are limited in their scope and applicability. They are also not well suited to coordinating and mediating the multiplicity of competing activities and interests in a modern and complex society.
- **The Public Trust Doctrine** is primarily a state common law matter, but the federal government also protects the environment and natural resources for the benefit of the public. The doctrine identifies certain resources such as air, water, and wildlife as things that are held for the benefit of all people. In order to protect and manage these resources, the state holds them in trust.

CHAPTER 2

Introduction to Modern Land Use and Zoning

ROADMAP

- Setting the Stage for Land Use and Zoning
- Planning Compared to Zoning
- Zoning Pursuant to a Plan
- Legislative and Quasi-Adjudicative Functions
- Standards of Review
    - De Novo Review
    - Rational Basis
        - Fairly Debatable
        - Rational Basis
        - Rational Basis Supported by Competent Evidence on the Record
    - Intermediate Scrutiny
    - Strict Scrutiny
- Delegation, Dillon Rule, Home Rule
- Preemption
- Unified Development Code
- Downzoning and Upzoning
- Relationship with Real Estate Development and Transactions

Planning and zoning are relatively modern concepts. While there was and continues to be some land regulation provided for under the common law, there were few legislative land regulations prior to 1900, and these regulations were limited and piecemeal. As we have seen, the common law generally relied on trespass and nuisance to control land uses along with private covenants and deed restrictions. And early approaches to land regulation were typically designed to control such things as fires by regulating the distance between buildings, and by controlling building heights so that fires might be prevented from spreading to an entire town. Such regulations responded to the limited firefighting equipment available at the time. Likewise, other early land regulations were limited and focused on clear matters of the public health, welfare, safety, and morals.

This chapter provides an introduction and overview of contemporary land regulation. Many of the topics addressed herein are expanded upon in later chapters.

a. Setting the Stage for Land Use and Zoning

Modern planning and zoning really emerged in the late 1800s and early 1900s. In the case of *Yick Wo v. Hopkins*, 118 U.S. 356 (1886), the U.S. Supreme Court upheld a restriction on laundry uses by California on the grounds that such uses raised fire risks, and their operation could be a public nuisance. And in *Hadacheck v. Sebastian*, 239 U.S. 394 (1915), the U.S. Supreme Court upheld a ban by Los Angeles on the use of private property for a brickyard. While states contemplated the rising problems associated with urban growth and rapid industrialization, New York City adopted the first comprehensive and general municipal ordinance regulating land uses in 1916.

With urban growth and rapid industrialization many urban communities became crowded, and housing conditions were unsanitary. Likewise, noise, pollution, and waste increased, and private property owners did little to mitigate or abate these problems. Uses on some properties were negatively affecting other properties, such as when steel production involved a manufacturing process that emitted large amounts of smoke and dust that imposed costs on surrounding properties. In other situations, incompatible uses were being located next to each other and posed safety risks including injury or death to people. This was the case when manufacturing and trucking facilities were located near other uses such as primary schools or playgrounds. In order to reduce the safety risks and negative consequences of incompatible uses being located in close proximity to each other, states began to regulate and restrict land uses under their inherent claim to police powers.

The police powers are inherent rights of sovereigns, and each of the fifty states of the Unites States are legally considered sovereigns. The federal government has the power to regulate as well, but its powers generally arise under the Necessary and Proper Clause and the Commerce Clause of the U.S. Constitution. In our federal system, the Supremacy Clause makes federal law, where applicable, controlling over state and local law. For the most part, however, the power to regulate land use has remained within the jurisdiction of the individual states.

The police power is held by the states and empowers the states to regulate land uses to protect the public health, safety, welfare, and morals. The states in turn can delegate police powers to regional and local governments within their jurisdiction. This delegation, made through specific enabling statutes, empowers local governments to enact and enforce land regulations to protect the public health, safety, welfare, and morals. These regulations often conflicted with common law notions that a private property owner can make any lawful use of property so long as the owner does no harm to others; and harm was generally limited to situations of trespass and nuisance. Planning, and the zoning regulations used to implement plans, went beyond preventing trespass and nuisance. Consequently, early planning and zoning regulations were challenged as unlawful and in violation of both the common law and the Constitution.

The breakthrough case on public land regulation was *Village of Euclid v. Ambler Realty*, 272 U.S. 365 (1926). In *Euclid*, the Supreme Court upheld a local zoning ordinance that divided the community into zones and separated land uses within and between these zones. The zones identified permitted uses within a zone, and regulated such things as the density, height and bulk of structures, as well as established building setback requirements from identified boundary lines. This was the first time that the Supreme Court spoke authoritatively on the subject, and it upheld the right of states and local governments to regulate private property under the exercise of their inherent police powers. Since *Euclid*, it has become accepted that local governments have the legal authority to regulate land uses beyond controlling for trespass and nuisance. Even with this acknowledgement, questions continue as to the proper balance of private and public control over land use decisions. The questions arising since *Euclid* involve the scope, extent, and nature of legally permissible public regulation of private property, and the determination of when regulation goes so far that it requires compensation under the Fifth Amendment Takings Clause. If compensation is due to a property owner, a further question concerns the amount of compensation that must be paid by the government.

b. Planning Compared to Zoning

Planning and zoning are two different functions. Most communities will, therefore, have separate departments dealing with planning and with zoning. Each of these departments will need to work collaboratively among and between departments to develop, manage, and enforce land use and development objectives. Land planning professionals may have backgrounds in urban planning, urban and landscape design, architecture, historic preservation, and environmental and administrative policy. In contrast, zoning officials are more likely to have expertise in property law and its regulation, code requirements and their enforcement, and local government and administrative law.

In larger cities, there may be both a planning department and a zoning and code enforcement department staffed by professionals. In addition, there may be an appointed board for each of these departments. These boards are usually composed of members appointed by the elected officials of the local jurisdiction, or in some cases elected, and they serve for a stated period of time. The boards typically make decisions based on the input and recommendations of their staff. In larger cities, board members may be compensated, whereas in smaller communities, these positions may be held by volunteers.

Planning and zoning are traditionally done at the local level, and planning and zoning requirements apply only within the jurisdictional boundaries of the relevant local government. At the same time, many states have developed and authorized regional planning and state-wide planning requirements. This means that local planning and zoning officials may have to work with regional and state officials on some areas of land regulation. In addition, there are federal regulations that may also impact state and local land use, such as federal regulations protecting wetlands, migratory bird habitats, and accessibility of the built environment to people with disabilities.

Importantly, there can be both private and public land planning and regulation. Private land planning and regulation is usually accomplished through the use of deed restrictions and covenants. Enforcement of private covenants and restrictions is a matter of private concern, and a dispute may require a court proceeding to resolve the rights of parties with competing claims and interpretations of the land regulations. In contrast, public land regulations are developed and enacted as legal regulations by local governments and apply to the property within the jurisdiction. The local government is responsible for the enforcement of the public land regulations. This means that private parties can file a complaint with the local planning and zoning office if they believe someone is violating the regulation, but it is up to public officials to enforce the code. Similarly, requests for exceptions to land regulations also take different routes depending upon their public or private nature. Private land restrictions will be governed by private property law and by their enforceable terms. For example, changing a covenant running with the land may require the consent of all parties benefited and burdened by the covenant. Covenants governing a subdivision may expressly provide for a method of change including a requirement of a super majority vote of homeowners in the subdivision to grant an exception for a requesting homeowner. Public land restrictions, on the other hand, are changed and modified by governmental action. Exceptions to certain land regulations in a zoning code may be applied for by appealing to the local zoning board of appeal. State and local law will govern the criteria for exceptions to the code and the issuing of permits for uses allowed under the code.

Both public and private land restrictions, in the context of land planning and zoning, are supposed to be focused on regulating land uses and not on regulating the users of the land. With respect to private restrictions, they are subject to constitutional review as in the case of making racial restrictions unenforceable. Public regulations are also subject to review, and under traditional zoning law, they cannot be directed at such things as the race or religion of the property owner, or at the way in which legal title is held. In other words, public zoning decisions should not turn on whether a land use is for a Catholic Church, a Mosque, or a Jewish Temple. The religious affiliation of the property owner should be irrelevant. Likewise, as to the form of ownership. It should make no difference if the property is owned by an individual, a partnership, a corporation, or a not-for-profit organization.

Thus, both private and public land restrictions are subject to legal limitations based on an individual's or a group's identity. Planning and zoning regulations are about the safe use of property so that the public health, safety, welfare, and morals of the community are protected. *Sunrise Check Cashing v. Town of Hempstead*, 986 N.E.2d 898 (N.Y. 2013), is an example of a case in which a zoning provision was set aside as illegal because it regulated the users and not the use. On its face, the zoning provision in question regulated the location of check cashing operations. However, the evidence behind the enactment of the zoning regulation indicated that the concern was with the type of people who used these services and not with the consequences of the activity itself. The record indicated that poor people often used these services and that this was believed to be undesirable for the community. Based on the evidence in the record, the court held that the zoning ordinance was targeted at regulating a stereotyped user and not at the actual use. Therefore, they found the ordinance to be illegal.

In addition to land planning and zoning, there are other sources of land regulations to be aware of when working in this area. There are building codes that do not regulate land use, but they do regulate building design and construction. There are also fire codes, and accessibility codes for ensuring that land uses and buildings are designed to be safe and accessible to people with disabilities. Some of these codes are administered by local officials that specialize in such codes. The codes themselves may be local or state-wide in applicability. Building codes are an example. Exceptions to a building code, for instance, would go to the building code enforcement office and not to the planning or zoning boards.

As a lawyer or other land use professional, you will likely deal with a planning board when you are assisting a client in obtaining approval for a development plan. In such a case, you will need to work with the planning office to complete plans for development layout and location of required improvements such as roads, sewer lines, and electric cables. The planning board will work with developers on the density, height, and location of structures on a parcel and deal with aesthetic issues such as landscaping and lighting. You will likely work with the zoning board to obtain required permits for a given use and to seek exceptions or variances from the strict requirements of an applicable zoning code. The planning process is done in accordance with local rules and procedures, but in general, it is more discretionary than zoning. In the planning process, a property owner works with the planning office to achieve a well-designed project whether it be a residential subdivision, an office building, shopping center, warehouse, or manufacturing facility. In some ways, planning is more about standards of design and use, whereas zoning is more about rules and enforcement of those rules.

When a property owner has a use or a design feature that violates the zoning code, they will need to deal with the zoning department. The zoning department and the zoning board of appeals implement and enforce the local zoning code. Legal activities include seeking a permit for a permitted use under the zoning code, and applying for an exception to the strict letter of the code when a property owner has difficulty complying with a regulation as applied to the property in question. If there is a difficulty or if there are special circumstances, the zoning board of appeal can grant a property owner an exception from the zoning regulations. To do this, special criteria will need to be applied. These exceptions are called *variances*, and a zoning board of appeal can grant either a *use* or an *area* variance.

A use variance is a request for permission to conduct a use on the property that is not currently permitted under the zoning code. For example, a request for a multi-family residential use on a property zoned for single-family use. An area variance is a request for a variance from rules regulating such things as density of development on the property, height restrictions of structures, and setback distances for structures in relation to various boundary lines. Setback requirements are one tool used to control the placement of structures on property. Use variances and area variances are different, and both are matters that must be addressed by a zoning board. Variances will be discussed in detail in Chapter 5.

Variance requests may arise from a property owner seeking to add a pool or deck to their home. In other situations, a developer may be negotiating with the planning board for the best layout and design for a development project, and the planning board may request that the developer undertake certain design elements that violate the zoning code. This may happen if the planning board believes that a certain project, such as a Starbucks, should be constructed closer to the road line than permitted so that more cars can stack up to enter a drive-thru window from the rear of the property. Given that the planning board does not enforce the zoning code, the developer would need to go to the zoning board to seek the variance that the planning board is requesting for approval of the developer's Starbucks project. Note that it is the developer, as owner of the property, that must seek the variance, and not the planning board. The planning board would communicate its rationale for the request to the zoning board and request that the zoning board approve it for the developer. The zoning board must consider and deliberate on the request for a variance but need not grant it simply because the planning board is requesting that it be granted to the developer. The zoning board must reach its own independent conclusion based on its required criteria. The zoning board may approve the request, or it may simply deny the request and send the developer back to the planning board to try and rework the development plan.

c. Zoning Pursuant to a Plan

All zoning must be done pursuant to a plan. This means that local land planners need to prepare a *comprehensive plan* for the development of a community. This plan includes provisions for growth, sustainability, climate change, and accessibility. By state statute, certain elements must be present in every local plan. These elements vary by state jurisdiction but usually include planning with respect to housing, transportation, health care, schools, policing, water, sewer, parks, libraries, and designated areas for commercial and industrial uses. Planning is an important step in making the exercise of the police power rational. Planners must accumulate information and data about the community and make projections as to future growth, infrastructure, housing, and other needs, as well as evaluate the impact of demographic changes in the population. Collecting this information, getting input from community stakeholders, and justifying the requirements of a plan are important steps in the process because the plan and the public land regulation adopted pursuant to the plan must be based on deliberation and data driven rationality rather than mere opinion and conjecture.

While the traditional view is that zoning must be done in accordance with a *comprehensive plan*, there are a wide range of positions on what constitutes a comprehensive plan and what it means for a zoning ordinance to be pursuant to the plan. Consequently, the status and importance of a comprehensive plan may vary widely as between different state jurisdictions. This means that it is important to determine what your state says about the legal relationship between a comprehensive plan and zoning enacted to implement the plan. Some states hold that zoning must be done in strict compliance with the plan, and other states hold that the plan is basically a guide or suggestion as to what should be done. Because most states do not have a really strict compliance requirement, imposing new limitations on land use and development on designated properties in a comprehensive plan does not generally make a claim ripe for a takings law claim. The new restrictions must be enacted and enforced before a takings claim arises.

Once a plan is agreed upon and adopted, a zoning code is prepared and enacted to implement and operationalize the plan. The zoning code is enacted by the local legislative body of the jurisdiction (e.g., the City Council, the Town Board, etc.). The code covers all the permitted land uses in the jurisdiction. One of the most important elements of the code is the definitions section. This section attempts to define different types of uses that will be mentioned in different parts of the code. Definitions are often problematic. For example, a property owner applies for a permit to open a drug rehabilitation center, but the code does not specifically address such a use. However, the code does identify places where a medical clinic can be a permitted use. The legal question is then one of determining if a drug rehabilitation center is a medical clinic. These definitions can be important when some property owners mobilize political opinion against a drug rehabilitation center, and the property owner argues that it is a permitted use as a medical clinic. Definitions are frequently matters of dispute, so it is important to pay attention to this part of the code. The body of the zoning code identifies by zone or district the permitted uses that can be made on every parcel of property in the jurisdiction. These provisions can be written in great detail. Other elements of the zoning code will set out the powers of the planning board and the zoning board of appeal, along with the procedure for an appeal.

In addition to the *comprehensive plan* and the *zoning code*, there will be a *zoning map*. The zoning map covers the entire jurisdiction. The color-coded map shows every parcel of property in the jurisdiction. For example, the color code might be that all properties shown in red are single-family residential (zone R-1), blue is for multi-family residential (zone M-1), green is for parks (zone P), and yellow is for commercial uses (C-1). Using the local zoning map, you identify the property that you are interested in and determine what zone the property is located in. If, for example, your property is located in zone R-1, you then turn to the zoning code sections on the permitted uses and regulations governing zone R-1 property. In the section of the code covering R-1 properties, there will be a list of permitted uses, and in general, these will be the only uses allowable in this zone. In addition to identifying permitted uses for R-1, there will be other related regulations such as those covering the height and bulk of permitted structures, various setback requirements as related to front, back, and side yards, and controls related to how structures can be situated on the parcel.

Diagram 2.1 A Zoning Map for a Small Town

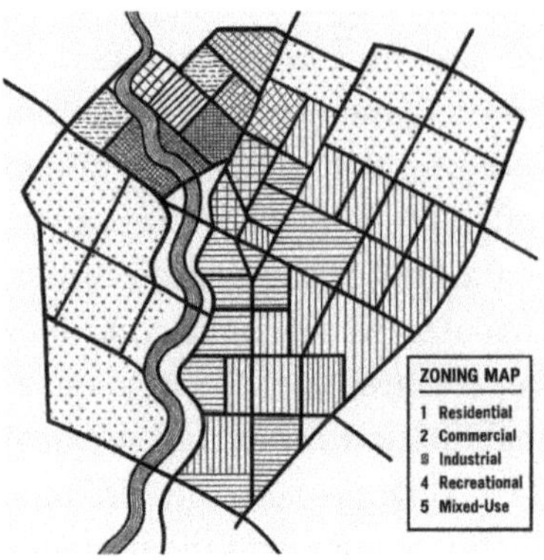

Zone Number	Zone Name	Pattern	Permitted Uses
1	Residential	Dots	Single-family homes, multi-family housing, apartments, townhouses
2	Commercial	Diagonal Stripes	Retail stores, offices, restaurants, service businesses
3	Industrial	Crosshatch	Factories, warehouses, distribution centers, light and heavy manufacturing
4	Recreational	Horizontal Lines	Parks, playgrounds, sports facilities, public open spaces
5	Mixed-Use	Vertical Lines	Combination of residential, commercial, and sometimes light industrial uses

The diagram above shows a zoning map for a small city with different zones identified for different types of permitted uses. Every lot and parcel of property within the jurisdiction will be shown on the map and coded with a guide to the permitted uses. On this map, there are five different zones, and they are identified by different graphics (dots, crosshatches, vertical lines, horizontal lines, and diagonal stripes). The different zones include; residential, commercial, industrial, recreational, and mixed-use. Once a lot is selected, one can find it on the map and then determine, based on the map key, the zoning code district that the property falls into. Once this is determined, one can then go to the zoning code to read the requirements for permitted uses on property within this zone.

d. Legislative and Quasi-Adjudicative Functions

Planning and zoning are administrative functions of local government. As such they involve both legislative and quasi-adjudicative activities. There are important legal distinctions between the legislative and quasi-adjudicative functions of local planning and zoning departments. Legislative activities involve such things as adopting a comprehensive plan and enacting a zoning code to implement the plan. Likewise, changing and amending the zoning code are legislative acts. Legislative acts are general in nature. This means that they affect property owners in a general way without specific reference to a given property or owner. In contrast, quasi-adjudicative acts address a specific property and owner. For example, designating a neighborhood as R-1 residential applies generally to all the properties in that neighborhood. On the other hand, if one property owner in that neighborhood petitions the zoning board of appeal for a variance from a requirement within the R-1 zone regulations, that is an individual and fact specific request that will require a determination specific to this property. A case specific determination is a quasi-adjudicative function and not a legislative one.

When a planning and zoning code are updated or amended, the new legislative regulations may affect a number of property owners. Changes to planning and zoning codes may impact properties differently based on location but within a given zone and classification, all properties must be treated equally. Changes need to be based on a legitimate concern for the public health, safety, welfare, and morals. When changes are made to the land use and zoning codes, residents are only entitled to a generally published notice of the change, as in a notice in the local newspaper or on the local government's official webpages. The public may be invited to public hearings when the changes are being considered. Once approved, the new regulations will apply to all covered properties within the jurisdiction.

When a specific property owner applies for a permit to develop a property, to make a change to a structure located on the property, or to obtain a variance from the strict requirements of the zoning code, the decision making process is quasi-adjudicative. This simply means that a hearing will be held that has legal consequences for a particular property. The hearing is subject to the requirements of due process. Thus, there must be individual notice, a right to be heard and to submit evidence, an opportunity to question evidence submitted by anyone appearing at the hearing to oppose the property owner's petition, and a formal record of the proceeding must be kept in the event that the property owner should seek to appeal an adverse decision. Provision may be made in the code for giving notice to adjoining property owners who may have an interest in the outcome of the petition of the property owner. Due process also requires that the decision maker and the decision process not be biased, arbitrary, or capricious, meaning that a decision must be rendered with a justifying opinion that is rational and based on competent evidence on the record.

In a typical situation, the decision maker will be a zoning board of appeal. The board is an administrative panel charged with interpreting the zoning code and with granting conditional use permits and variances. A zoning board of appeal does not enact the zoning code, nor does it adopt a comprehensive plan. A zoning board of appeal decides matters related to a specific property and property owner. It may be asked to decide if an applicant for a permit or a variance meets the requirements for the requested action. It will then decide the merits of the application and make a decision.

Most planning and zoning departments include a code enforcement officer or office. This may also be a separate office in the town or city. The code enforcement office enforces the various codes within the jurisdiction, including the zoning code. The code enforcement office responds to reports of violations or identifies violations on its own. Violations of the zoning code and decisions of a zoning board of appeal can be enforced by the code enforcement office. A failure to comply with an enforcement order can result in legal action against the property owner. To the extent that enforcement actions are brought against property owners, planning and zoning can also involve an executive function in enforcing the land use laws of the jurisdiction. The procedures for enforcement actions are set out in the zoning code and in the local laws of the jurisdiction. In an enforcement action, the code enforcement officer can file an action with the local court to compel compliance with zoning code regulations. Non-compliance can result in a fine or jail time.

e. Standards of Review

When local governments adopt comprehensive plans, enact zoning codes, and make decisions affecting the property rights of property owners, there is often litigation as to the legalities of such action. In the first instance, the litigation or disagreement will often go to an administrative decision maker. After an initial decision is rendered, the aggrieved party will have a right to appeal. One of the key questions addressed on appeal is the standard of review that the reviewing body should use when evaluating the initial decision. This is essentially a question of how much deference a reviewing body should give to the initial decision maker. As a practical matter, the standard of review applied by the appellate body is important to the initial decision maker because the initial decision maker must make certain that its decision is sufficient to withstand being overturned on appeal. Actual standards of review may vary by state jurisdiction but in general, there are some relatively clear distinctions among various standards of review. The different standards of review include the following: 1) *de novo* review; 2) *rational basis*: including fairly debatable (not arbitrary and capricious), rational basis (relative to the legislative intent), rational basis as supported by competent evidence on the record; 3) *intermediate scrutiny;* and 4) *strict scrutiny*. These standards are discussed below.

i. De Novo Review

De Novo review is generally uncommon in local zoning cases. A de novo review is one in which a reviewing court examines the law and the facts on its own. It gives little or no deference to the local administrative decision rendered by a zoning board of appeal. A court reviewing a local administrative decision (as in a decision of a zoning board of appeal) generally gives deference to the administrative decision maker. This is particularly true as to the fact finding upon which a decision is based. As to questions of law and the proper interpretation of the law, a reviewing court may do a de novo review. This is because the courts are the final arbiters of the law. Some states may have statutory requirements for certain types of issues to be dealt with under de novo review when appealed from a local administrative decision maker to the courts. Massachusetts in one such state. *See* M.G.L.A. 40A § 17.

ii. Rational Basis

Rational basis review can be somewhat confusing when reading cases and figuring out what the standard really requires. This is because there are three different levels of rational basis review encountered in zoning and land use cases. These three different levels of rational basis review include fairly debatable, rational basis, and rational basis supported by substantial competent evidence on the record.

Fairly Debatable

The fairly debatable standard is the lowest standard of review. This means that a decision maker under this standard of review will be granted the most discretion in exercising its judgment. The judgment of the decision maker will be upheld so long as the decision is at least fairly debatable. This is a standard that typically applies to review of legislative action, although it can also apply to executive actions of a city or town elected leader. In practice, a reviewing body on appeal essentially makes an inquiry as to if there is any rational justification for the decision or rule. It is not an inquiry into the mindset of the person or people making the rule or passing the regulation. It is a general inquiry as to if there is any rational justification that can be found to support the action. Consequently, legislative history and what certain people might have said in support of the regulation are not very relevant. This is because we are not bound by an individual legislator's subjective intent. We are simply asking if there is any plausibly rational justification for the regulation. In the legislative context, this standard of review provides significant discretion to the legislative branch and seeks to maintain a separation of powers as between the legislative branch and the judicial branch. The petitioner has the burden of proving that the matter is not even fairly debatable.

Rational Basis

The rational basis standard of review requires an inquiry into the intent and motivation of a decision or regulation. Under this standard, it is important to determine if a challenged rule or decision is rationally related to the justification offered for it by the person or people proposing the rule or making the decision. For example, if a regulation is passed to restrict development along the coastline so that people on a nearby highway can have a view of the ocean, giving people a right to walk across the beachfront property owner's property is not rationally related to the stated purpose of preserving a view. This was the situation in the case of *Nollan v. California Coastal Commission*, 438 U.S. 825 (1987). In *Nollan*, the Court held that there was no essential nexus between the rule, requiring a property owner to allow others to access his property, and the stated legislative purpose of preserving a view. A limitation on the height and density of buildings along the coastline might well be rational for preserving a view from a nearby highway, but eliminating a property owner's right to exclude others has little or no connection to this stated goal. Therefore, under the rational basis standard, it is important to examine legislative history and to evaluate what legislators identified as the rationale for their actions. The petitioner has the burden of demonstrating that the government's regulation or decision is not rational.

Rational Basis Supported by Competent Evidence on the Record

The rational basis supported by competent evidence on the record standard of review is applied to quasi-adjudicative decisions. This means that it is applicable to decisions of a zoning board of appeal. It could also be applied to other quasi-adjudicative decisions made by other administrative actors. This standard of review combines both the rational basis inquiry standard with an additional requirement that the decision be supported by substantial competent evidence on the record. In other words, the inquiry requires that a decision being appealed is rational in relationship to the stated purpose of the decision, and in addition, there must be substantial competent evidence on the record to support that decision. This means that unlike the review of legislative actions, it is not enough to have a rational relationship between the stated purpose and the rule or decision, there must also be a showing of evidence to support and justify the decision. Moreover, the evidence must be competent, not fraudulent or fabricated, and not simply based on the opinion of non-experts. It must also be on the record. This means it must be submitted into evidence or made a part of the official record of the proceeding. It is up to the parties to make certain to get all relevant information on the record in the initial hearing on the matter. Review of the decision will be with reference to the record, and it is therefore important to build a good record at the initial decision making stage. As with all the standards of review, if the decision maker meets the standard, their decision should be upheld even if a different decision would have been possible or preferable to the applicant or petitioner. The petitioner has the burden of demonstrating that the decision of the official is not rational and not supported by competent evidence on the record.

iii. Intermediate Scrutiny

Intermediate scrutiny is a standard of review most often encountered in cases of Constitutional Law. It is a standard higher than that of a rational basis supported by competent evidence on the record. This standard is important in land use and planning when land regulations and zoning rules raise tensions with other constitutionally protected rights. This can be the case, for example, when regulating adult entertainment outlets, commercial signs, and in some situations where zoning may treat uses differently based on gender. Gender based zoning may include zoning restrictions that limit housing opportunities for women of a certain age while not imposing a similar restriction on male occupancy. For intermediate scrutiny, the reviewing body on appeal will only uphold a decision or regulation if a three-pronged test is met. This test requires that the decision or regulation not only be rational but that it 1) advances an important or substantial government interest, 2) is narrowly tailored to further that interest, and 3) is necessary to further that interest. The government has the burden of proving that it has met this standard. If the government can carry this burden, the regulation will be upheld.

iv. Strict Scrutiny

Strict scrutiny is the highest standard of review. A common situation in which strict scrutiny review can apply in zoning is when there is a claim that particular zoning policies or practices result in racial discrimination in housing. Another common area in which this standard is applied involves zoning that restricts political speech. Under strict scrutiny, the government's interest in the rule or regulation must be compelling. This is generally interpreted as requiring 1) the rule to be necessary to achieve a compelling state interest, and 2) that the means selected for achieving the compelling state interest is the least restrictive means available. Moreover, on appeal, there is a very close look at the history, policy, practice, and impact associated with the rule or decision. The burden is on the government, not the petitioner, to show that its rule or regulation passes strict scrutiny review.

f. Delegation, Dillon Rule, and Home Rule

The police power to regulate land use is generally vested in the 50 state governments. The states in turn may delegate some of their police power to local municipalities. This is either done in the state constitution or in state statutes. One approach to delegation is illustrated by the *Dillon Rule*. The Dillon Rule is named after Justice John F. Dillon of the Iowa Supreme Court. In the 1868 case of *City of Clinton v. The Cedar Rapids & Missouri River Railroad Co.*, 24 Iowa 455, 480–82 (1868), Justice Dillon explained that as the police power is vested in the states, the subsequent delegation of state police power to local governments should be narrowly construed. In essence, the delegation should only include powers expressly delegated to the local government, powers necessarily implied by the express delegation, and those essential for the local government to carry out the goals and objectives of the delegation. The Dillon Rule was approved in a decision by the U.S. Supreme Court in *Hunter v. City of Pittsburg*, 207 U.S. 161 (1907), and has been debated in multiple cases since.

In contrast to the Dillon Rule, many states have a broader and more *permissive view* of delegation. In the permissive view, local governments are presumed to be acting within their delegated authority unless the language of the delegation limits or prohibits the local government's actions. The permissive view of delegation is often related to the concept of *Home Rule*. The idea of Home Rule is that local governments are presumed to have the authority to properly exercise the delegated police power from the state with minimal or no interference. Some states grant Home Rule power to all municipalities in the state, while others expressly limit it to designated cities of a certain size and population. Home Rule authority will usually be expressed in a state constitution or in state statutes.

g. Preemption

In a legal system such as that of the United States, there are at times questions about controlling law as to a legal question or dispute when there are inconsistencies among laws enacted by different levels of government. For example, if a state law conflicts with a local zoning ordinance, or if a federal law conflicts with a state or local ordinance. The issue is one of legal hierarchy. State law can be supreme within the jurisdiction of the state, and federal law is the supreme law of the country. When there is a conflict among these different levels of the legal hierarchy, which controls? In terms of preemption, the question to be asked is—does a law enacted by the higher legal authority control in the situation of an apparent conflict? It does if there is actual preemption by that higher authority, but not if the law in question leaves room for the other law to operate. In other words, one must determine if the higher legal authority intended to take over regulatory control of the subject matter and eliminate the prerogative of inferior law-making bodies to regulate.

For example, a state may pass legislation governing the regulation of land uses with respect to the cultivation and retail sale of marijuana. At the same time, a local municipality may have a zoning regulation prohibiting all cultivation and retail sales of marijuana within its jurisdiction. A property owner seeking to use its property for the cultivation or retail sale of marijuana may challenge the local zoning ordinance preventing this use based on the state regulation that seems to permit it. The local municipality may assert that the state regulation applies to regulate the subject matter where the activity is permitted, but the local community has the authority under its delegated police power to simply exclude the uses from its jurisdiction. The preemption question is one of determining if the state regulation occupies the field, that is, covers the entire legal domain as to these identified uses, or if it leaves room for local regulation.

A similar issue arises with respect to federal regulation. When the federal government has statutory authority to protect wetlands, clean air, and clean water, do local governments retain any authority to regulate these areas? If the field is preempted, it means that the federal government has eliminated the authority of local governments to regulate. This is sometimes the case. Often, however, the preemption will be limited. For example, the federal government may pass regulations that prohibit local communities from excluding cell towers for cell phone use, while permitting local authorities to have some input on the exact location of the towers within certain guidelines established by the federal regulations. In general, however, preemption is a legal issue arising when there are conflicts with federal or state regulation rather than when dealing exclusively with legal problems arising under local planning and zoning codes.

h. Unified Development Code

Multiple regulations can govern land development in each jurisdiction. Often this means that multiple codes must be consulted in order to accomplish a property development objective. For example, a jurisdiction might have planning and design codes, zoning codes, subdivisions codes, and water management codes. Each code addresses a specific set of land regulation matters. The idea behind a *unified development code* (sometimes referred to as a unified development ordinance) is to bring all of these codes and regulations together into one unified and comprehensive document. This is intended to make the land regulation process more efficient and to bring greater clarity and efficiency to the process of land development. The primary objective is to simplify the process of land development by locating many of the different rules in one document. When a jurisdiction moves to a unified development document, it does not necessarily mean that the substance of the rules and regulations have been changed. The procedures and the processes might be a little different because different functions have been unified under a common document, but having a unified development code does not mean that zoning rules or subdivision regulations have necessarily been changed. It is important to understand the codes that need to be consulted in the jurisdiction where the property is located.

i. Downzoning and Upzoning

Two common terms in zoning include downzoning and upzoning. When people refer to downzoning an area, they mean that the area is being zoned to a lower level of density and intensity of development. This may include reducing the number of units per acre, reducing permissible height and bulk of structures on the property, and adjusting permitted uses in the zone. Upzoning, on the other hand, refers to making changes that increase the density and intensity of uses on property. Thus, examples include increasing the number of units permitted per acre and increasing the bulk and height of structures.

j. Relationship with Real Estate Development and Transactions

In addition to understanding this material as a land use and zoning professional, it is important to appreciate the significance of this subject matter for real estate development and transactions. In most schools and in practice, land use and zoning are treated apart from real estate. However, both subjects involve overlapping considerations of property law, and they have many points at which they intersect. For example, one of the key areas of negotiation in a real estate transaction concerns land use and zoning. Confirming the permissible uses of a property, and in many cases working to adjust the permitted uses to accommodate a developer's plans, are critical parts of the deal.

Real estate transactions lawyers must be knowledgeable about land use and zoning, and about how to read and interpret a zoning code. They must also know how to get changes and adjustments of land regulations so that they can properly facilitate their client's development goals. In the drafting of a contract for purchase and sale, the status of zoning and other land regulations will be important conditions to completing a transaction. The parties will need to identify the intended use of the property with specificity and make confirmation of suitable zoning a condition to the purchase and sale. If the zoning is not suitable for the use, a contract may not be consummated, or if there is a final contract, it may have a condition that the zoning be adjusted by a zoning change or a variance prior to having to close on the transaction. With such a contract condition, failure to achieve the change or adjustment within a stated time period would typically permit a party to be excused from performance.

Land regulation is also important to title examination and to the mortgage financing of a real estate transaction. A violation of a zoning regulation is problematic from a title perspective because it may raise questions as to the marketability of the property. In general, a buyer of real property is entitled to receive *a good and marketable title*, a term with special meaning in real estate law. The term does not simply mean that it can affect the value of the property, rather it has a deeper meaning. Marketable title goes to the legal status and quality of the title to the property. Typically, a zoning violation is not technically deemed to be a title defect, but it may impact the marketability of title to the property. In many jurisdictions, marketable title means a title free of doubt about litigation; marketable title is a title that would be acceptable to a reasonably prudent buyer.

A violation of zoning may make title to a property unmarketable and permit a buyer to opt out of the deal. For example, if the zoning code requires that all structures be located at least thirty feet back from a side property line and the structure in question is only fifteen feet back, this is a zoning violation. This violation affects the marketability of the property because it raises the possibility of an enforcement lawsuit. In real estate law, the requirement of the seller to deliver marketable title is both an implied covenant and a condition of the buyer having to close on the contract. Thus, a buyer may be released from the contract if the title is not marketable. In the alternative, the buyer can review the violation and accept it, perhaps on condition that the seller pay damages for breach of the implied marketability covenant or compensate the buyer with a set-off from the contract price, and the buyer can use these funds to correct the problem. Another potential option might be to require the seller to resolve the zoning issue as a condition to going forward with the transaction. For example, in a situation with a property that has a large deck built on to the house and into the setback requirements, the seller should seek and obtain a variance to correct the problem. It is important for the seller to correct the zoning issue, because once the buyer takes title, it will be construed that the buyer takes the property subject to the defect. The issue, of course, is that a requested variance to obtain an exception to the setback requirements for the deck may be denied. If this is the case, the deck may be ordered to be taken down, and the owner will be without the value of the deck plus have the expense of taking it down.

When mortgage financing is involved, a lender will also be interested in assuring itself that the property is in compliance with zoning and other land regulations. If the property is not in compliance, the lender may be at risk of diminished value due to non-compliance or at risk with respect to the quality of title to the property that secures its loan.

CHECKPOINTS

- **Planning and zoning** became important with industrialization in the late 1800s and early 1900s. Local governments used planning and zoning to coordinate the location of incompatible uses and to avoid unsafe conditions.
- **Local governments** (cities and towns) began to regulate land uses under authority delegated to them by the state in which they were located. This authority was identified as the police power. The police power is the authority of a sovereign state to regulate private activities and property rights for the public health, safety, welfare, and morals.
- **The police power** is held and exercised by the states; the federal government generally regulates under the Necessary and Proper Clause and the Commerce Clause of the federal Constitution. The federal government has police powers in the District of Columbia and on federal lands.
- **Early planning and zoning regulations were challenged** as unlawful and in violation of both the common law and the Constitution. The breakthrough case on the legality of planning and zoning regulations was *Village of Euclid v. Ambler Realty*, 272 U.S. 365 (1926). In *Euclid*, the Supreme Court upheld a local zoning ordinance that separated uses, regulated permitted uses by districts, and controlled for such things as density, height and bulk of structures, and building setbacks from identified boundary lines.

- **Planning and zoning are two different functions.** Planning involves policy, review of property development, preparation of a comprehensive plan, and suggestions on zoning updates. A planning board functions to develop and approve plans for development projects in the community. Zoning involves regulation of land uses, and a zoning board enforces the zoning code requirements on development within the community.
- **Zoning must be rational and done pursuant to a plan.** This is an important connection between planning and zoning.
- **The planning and zoning process involves both legislative and quasi-adjudicative functions.** As an example, passing a development plan for a city or town is a legislative function, but enforcing a zoning code regulation against an individual homeowner is a quasi-adjudicative function. There are different legal considerations applicable to each of these functions.
- **Decisions made by a planning board and a zoning board are subject to judicial review.** This means that they can be appealed. When such decisions are appealed, they are subject to a legal standard of review. There are multiple standards of review that need to be considered based on the nature of the legal question involved.
    - **De novo review** is where a reviewing court examines the law and the facts on its own. It gives little or no deference to the local administrative decision rendered by a zoning board of appeal.
    - **There are three categories of rational basis review**, and they are fairly debatable (not arbitrary and capricious), rational (in relation to the legislative intent), and rational as supported by competent evidence in the record.
    - **Intermediate scrutiny** requires a higher burden of proof than rational basis, and by example, it is applicable to zoning that differentiates on the basis of gender, or that restricts commercial speech.
    - **Strict scrutiny** requires a very high burden of proof to show regulatory legality, and by example, it is applicable to zoning that differentiates on the basis of race or that restricts political speech.
- **Local planning and zoning authority relies on a proper delegation of state police power** from the state to the local government. Delegations can be read narrowly under the Dillon Rule, or broadly as when

a state designates a city or town as a place of Home Rule in planning and zoning matters.

- **There are situations in which state or federal law may *preempt* local law** on a matter related to land use. Typical examples might include state regulations on cannabis cultivation and commercial sales, or at the federal level, land protected under the federal Clean Water Act, wetlands protection, and lands protected for use by migratory birds.
- **A Unified Development Code** may be used in a local jurisdiction. It is one comprehensive and unified document that brings together what used to be covered in multiple codes. This often includes regulations related to planning and design, zoning, subdivision of land, and water management.
- **Downzoning** reduces allowable density and intensity of uses, and **upzoning** increases allowable density and intensity.
- **Land regulation and zoning are subject areas that intersect with real estate development and transactions.** Zoning is important to the real estate purchase and sale contract, title examination, and to mortgage financing.

CHAPTER 3

General Procedural and Administrative Matters

ROADMAP

- State Administrative Procedure Acts
- Related State and Federal Regulations
    - Standard State Zoning Enabling Act
    - Standard City Planning Enabling Act
- Public Hearings
- Enforcement Actions
- Zoning Board of Appeal
- Judicial Review
- Standing
    - Standing Under Disability Law
- Exhaustion
- Ripeness
- Rezoning
- Initiatives and Referendums
- § 1983 Actions
- National Zoning Atlas

Local land planning and zoning are governed by state enabling acts. These acts delegate police power authority from the state to local governments as specified in the enabling legislation. The enabling legislation is the source of local governmental authority, and the legislation, along with state court jurisprudence, will inform one of the powers granted to local government. The typical delegation provisions are often broadly written as delegating authority to local government to engage in land regulation to protect the public health, safety, welfare and morals. It then becomes a jurisprudential matter of how narrow or broadly the delegation should be read. The Dillon Rule would have us read the delegation narrowly, and the Home Rule approach would read the authority broadly. In addition to enabling legislation, there are other procedural and administrative matters that are fundamental to a local land use practice.

a. State Administrative Procedure Acts

Generally, states have state administrative procedure acts that are similar to the structure of the federal Administrative Procedure Act (APA) applicable to federal agencies (Administrative Procedures Act: 5 U.S.C.A. § Pt. I, Ch. 5, Subch. II). These state APAs outline the procedures for state agencies to propose, issue, and adjudicate regulations, including those related to various aspects of land regulation (such as environmental and natural resource regulation). They establish a process for rule making and for public participation. They also set out uniform standards for the rule making process, for formal meetings, and for adjudicatory proceedings. These standards establish uniformity and provide guidance on making state government procedures consistent with requirements for due process and equal protection. State agencies play an important role in land regulation at the state level. For example, this is the case in such areas as environmental and natural resource regulation. State regulation may overlap with local planning and zoning regulation.

As to land use and zoning, local governments are generally empowered to establish their own procedures consistent with the authority delegated to them by the state. Thus, local land use and zoning laws are not typically handled under a state APA. State environmental and natural resource regulations may come under a state APA, but local planning and zoning will require one to carefully review local procedures.

b. Related State and Federal Regulations

In a land use and zoning practice, there will be many occasions when regulations outside of local planning and zoning codes may have implications for land use decisions. For example, state environmental and conservation departments may have some authority for regulating land use in certain areas. This can include departments focused on wildlife, fisheries, wetlands, watersheds, aquifers, coastal lands, and more. It is important to determine the reach of these other state regulations when addressing land use matters under a local planning and zoning ordinance.

Generally, there are also potential federal regulations that may have implications for land use. For example, the Clean Air Act, 42 U.S.C. § 7401, and the Clean Water Act, 33 U.S.C. § 1251, may directly or indirectly place controls and limitations on land use and development. Likewise, there may be local implications for land regulation related to such things as the Migratory Bird Treaty Act and various regulations related to fish and wildlife, coastal waterways, and navigable waters. 16 U.S.C. § 703 (Migratory Bird Treaty Act); 33 U.S.C. § 401 (The River and Harbor Act of 1899); 16 U.S.C. § 661 (The Fish and Wildlife Coordination Act); Clean Water Act, § 404 (Federal Wetlands Protection). These regulations all involve the potential to limit land development and restrict land uses in order to accomplish their goals. Land uses that produce air pollution or water pollution may be restricted, and lands near waterways may be regulated to reduce negative impacts on water systems protected by federal law. Likewise, setting aside lands for migratory birds imposes limitations on local land use regulation. All of these federal acts are examples of a need to be knowledgeable about federal regulations as well as state regulations when dealing with local land planning and zoning matters. These federal regulations may limit the uses of a property in ways that differ from the language of a local zoning ordinance. Any such conflicts will need to be reconciled in order to determine exactly what uses are permitted on a property covered by multiple sources of law.

While there are multiple sources of law to be aware of in a land planning and zoning practice, the most relevant to everyday practice are likely to be the state and local planning and zoning laws that apply in the jurisdiction where the property is physically located. Understanding these regulations and their history is important. The historical foundations for local zoning and planning were established in two standardized acts that were developed in the 1920s;

the Standard State Zoning Enabling Act (1924 and revised in 1926), and the Standard City Planning Enabling Act (1928). The various states adopted planning and zoning regulations based on these standardized acts. While details have changed over time, the general structure of zoning and planning regulations still follow the outline of these two standard acts.

i. Standard State Zoning Enabling Act

The Standard State Zoning Enabling Act (SZEA) includes nine sections. The key elements of the SZEA are set out below.

1. This section grants local governments the authority to regulate land uses for the purpose of promoting the public health, safety, welfare, and morals of the community. Local governments can restrict land uses, building heights, size of structures, setbacks from property lines, size of yards, density, and open spaces.
2. Local governments can divide their jurisdiction into districts. Within these districts, they can regulate as indicated in section (1). While different regulations can control in different districts, the regulations applicable within a zoning district must be applied uniformly on all the properties within that district. Likewise, as to all districts of the same zoning category, no matter where they are located in the jurisdiction. (For example, all R-1 residential districts and all C-1 commercial districts must be treated the same no matter where an R-1 or C-1 zoning district is located.)
3. The regulations must be made in accordance with a comprehensive plan. The purpose of the plan and regulations are to lessen congestion; to secure safety from fire, panic and other dangers; to promote health and the general welfare; to provide adequate light and air; to prevent overcrowding; and to facilitate the adequate provision of transportation, water, sewerage, schools, parks, and other public requirements.
4. Provides details on the procedure for adopting and amending zoning regulations.
5. Provides for the process of making changes and amending existing land regulations.
6. Establishes a zoning authority within the local government.
7. Provides remedies for enforcing the land use and zoning regulations.

8. Provides for a zoning board of appeal or other designated body to address appeals from decisions of planning and zoning officials.
9. Provides for the resolution of conflicts between the zoning and enabling act and other local land regulations.

ii. Standard City Planning Enabling Act

The Standard City Planning Enabling Act (SCPEA) consists of four general subject areas.

1. The development of a comprehensive master plan for the jurisdiction and the organization and powers of the planning commission.
2. The control of subdivision of land.
3. Control of buildings in mapped streets, including planning for public improvements.
4. Engaging in regional planning and establishing a regional planning commission, should one be desired.

These state acts have been modified and amended over the years. Nonetheless, they still provide the general framework for planning and zoning.

c. Public Hearings

Zoning and planning decisions often require a public hearing. These hearings give the public notice of what is pending and provide opportunities for input. Local planning and zoning regulations contain the requirements for public hearings. Legislative proposals and actions usually involve hearings requiring general notice to the public.

Legislative matters can include the consideration and adoption of a new zoning code, amendments to a zoning code, and rezoning of a given area. General public notice means providing a notice of when meetings will be held and where they will be located. Typically, legislative matters do not require personal and individual notice to residents. The Chair of the public meeting can set time limits and other parameters for public participation. Typically, time limits might be set as limiting each member of the public to three minutes for comment.

For matters concerning the application of the planning and zoning regulations to a specific property, notice must also be given. These situations involve applications for building permits, variances, and approval of site development plans that go to the planning board and to the zoning board. In these situations, a notice will be posted to the public on local government web pages, a newspaper, or on a media outlet of general circulation in the community. In addition, the individuals involved in the application must be given individualized notice along with specified third parties. Typically, adjoining property owners and property owners within a stated distance of the property being considered will be identified in the regulations as third parties entitled to individual notice.

At the public hearings, the chair of the meeting may limit time for public input. The hearings may include a public component featuring discussion of the project and the issues, input from the petitioning party and local planning and zoning officials, and an opportunity for other interested parties in attendance to speak on the matter. After the public part of the hearing, there may be discussion among board members before rendering a decision.

d. Enforcement Actions

Local governments have the authority to enforce the zoning ordinance. Generally, violations of the zoning ordinance are discovered when they are reported to the planning and zoning office by a neighbor or upon inspection. Inspections may be related to checking building compliance with a recently issued building permit or may be the result of observation of properties by code enforcement officers while out in the neighborhoods. A property owner with a violation will be given notice to cease the violation and an opportunity to correct the problem. In the alternative, the property owner could seek a variance for the alleged code violation. A petition for a variance may or may not be granted after a hearing. If the property owner does not comply with an order or seek and obtain a variance, there may be a fine imposed or an enforcement action may be brought in court. Typically, a court proceeding will be stayed pending a property owner's timely seeking of a variance from the local zoning board of appeal.

e. Zoning Board of Appeal

Local jurisdictions will have a zoning board of appeal (ZBA) (sometimes called a zoning board of adjustment) as well as a planning board. A planning board typically reviews subdivision applications and provides site plan review along with other designated functions. The ZBA deals with interpreting and enforcing the zoning code. Both a planning board and a ZBA are standing committees or boards of the local jurisdiction. The local jurisdiction can decide the size of these boards subject to any state requirements. It is typical to have five to seven members, with one member designated as Chair. In most situations, these boards will have a dedicated attorney or at least have access to a general town or city attorney office.

A ZBA has several key functions. First, it has jurisdiction to interpret the zoning ordinance when the meaning of a provision is unclear. For example, questions may arise when a definition does not seem to squarely cover a requested use. This may be the case with the meaning of a commercial garage, a home occupation, a front yard, or an accessory use. Or, as in the example used in Chapter 2, it may be an issue when a proposed use is for a drug rehabilitation center and the code does not include such a term. The code may include the term medical clinic, but then it must be determined if a drug rehabilitation center is a medical clinic within the meaning of the code. Second, a ZBA can take appeals from a property owner who has been denied a permit or use by an administrative officer in the planning and zoning office. For example, a property owner may go to the planning and zoning office to request a permit to add a shed to her property and the administrative officer may deny the permit because the shed design does not comply with the requirements of the code. The property owner can appeal the denial of the permit. Third, a ZBA makes decisions concerning petitions for area and use variances. In the case of our shed example, the property owner might acknowledge that the shed design is not in compliance with the zoning regulations but may petition for an exception to the rules based on special or unique circumstances. Fourth, a ZBA is often delegated original jurisdiction over the issuance of special and conditional use permits. These are permits that require investigation before they can be issued. They may require considerations of traffic flow and parking capacity as part of the permitting process. Typically, such determinations are given to a ZBA rather than a single administrative official in the office. Uses requiring special or conditional permits are specified in the local ordinance. Fifth, a ZBA can make a determination as to a reasonable accommodation and a reasonable modification to zoning and planning regulations when an applicant has standing to request one under our disability laws. These requests are focused on adjusting the rules of the zoning code in order to render an appropriate accommodation or modification for the individual.

ZBA proceedings deal with the application of a zoning ordinance to specific people and specific properties. Consequently, the actions of a ZBA are not legislative but rather quasi-adjudicative. The ZBA functions as an administrative body rendering quasi-adjudicative decisions. Therefore, the standard of review of a ZBA is higher than for the legislative acts of a city council or a town board. A ZBA must render decisions that are rational and supported by substantial competent evidence on the record. ZBA decisions must provide rationalizations and justifications; they cannot be cursory or conclusory. The members of the ZBA are responsible for helping to build the record that will form the basis of their decision. A complete record will generally consist of petitions, testimony, surveys, photos, letters, exhibits, and development plans along with other items. A ZBA hearing will operate much like a somewhat informal court proceeding. The requirements of due process and equal protection must be adhered to in a ZBA proceeding.

Property owners will typically end up with a ZBA hearing in one of three different ways. First, they may have a petition or application for a use that requires a special or conditional use permit under the zoning ordinance. These uses are not "as of right" and require consideration of specified criteria. A typical example of such a use might be a drive-thru fast-food restaurant or bank. Such uses raise traffic and safety considerations even in zones and districts where they are permitted, so they usually require special evaluation. A ZBA generally has original jurisdiction to decide on the issuance of special and conditional use permits.

Second, a person may go to the planning and zoning office for a permit to do something that she believes is permitted by the zoning ordinance. However, the administrative official at that office may look at the permit application and interpret the zoning ordinance as not permitting the use as described in the application. Perhaps the official believes that the use is not permitted or that while the use is permitted, it violates an area restriction applicable to the property. The official therefore rejects the application. The aggrieved property owner might then appeal this decision to a ZBA by filing a petition of appeal with the ZBA. In this appeal, the property owner will be asking for an interpretation or an area or use variance as the case may require.

Diagram 3.1 Zoning Process

Typical Petition Process for a Building Permit or Zoning Variance

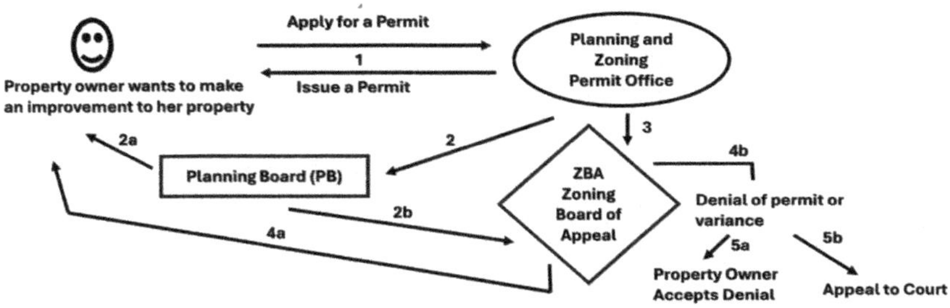

1) Owner applies for permit, and if the proposal is within the code requirements, a permit is issued.
2) If PB review is required, the application is sent to PB. They can approve (2a) or send to ZBA if a variance, an interpretation, or an accommodation is required (2b).
3) If the permit office believes the project is not within the code requirements, it denies the request, and the owner can appeal to the ZBA for a code interpretation, the granting of a variance, or a reasonable accommodation.
4) The ZBA can approve and grant a variance or an accommodation (4a), or it can deny the application (4b)
5) The owner can accept the denial by the ZBA (5a) or appeal the decision (5b).

Third, a property owner might have a project that requires planning board approval. Perhaps it is a proposal for a subdivision or for a commercial project requiring site approval. The property owner's optimal design may not be fully consistent with the current zoning ordinance; or in the process of working with the planning board, the property owner may be asked to make some design and construction changes that while good from a planning perspective, violate some provision or sections of the zoning ordinance, such as a height restriction or a property line setback. In such a case, the planning board will send the property owner to the ZBA to request a variance so that the project can be completed as the planning board hopes. The planning board will typically provide the ZBA with reasons for its design and construction requirements. The ZBA takes the planning board recommendations under advisement but must make its own independent decision and decide how best to interpret and apply the code to the situation. It might disagree with the planning board and send the property owner back to the planning department for further design and construction modifications. On the other hand, it may agree with the planning board's recommendations and approve the plans as recommended by the planning board. If the ZBA denies the application, the petitioner can appeal the ZBA decision to the appropriate review body, usually a court.

f. Judicial Review

Decisions of a ZBA can be appealed for judicial review. Usually there is a set time period, thirty or forty-five days, in which the aggrieved party can file an appeal of a decision of the ZBA. Generally, these appeals are to a state trial court, and the review of the ZBA decision is limited. In some states, such as Massachusetts, there are specialized land courts that can take appeals from a ZBA. The court reviewing the ZBA decision generally gives deference to the ZBA unless it is a jurisdiction with de novo review. In the typical situation, the reviewing court does not seek to replace the judgment of the ZBA so much as to review the record to ensure that the hearing before the ZBA was conducted fairly and in accordance with the state provided procedures. Review will focus on the record created at the ZBA and on the basis of the ZBA decision. As a quasi-adjudicative body, the ZBA's decision must be rational and supported by substantial competent evidence on the record. If the decision meets this standard, it will generally be upheld on review, even if other outcomes might have been equally valid. In a few states, judicial review is not as limited. In these jurisdictions, specified zoning decisions or all zoning decisions may be subject to *de novo review*. This means that the reviewing court does not give deference to the ZBA decision but can take in new evidence and make its own findings. As an example, Massachusetts generally provides for de novo review of ZBA decisions, M.G.L.A. 40A § 17.

In practice, it is important to confirm if your state provides limited review or de novo review of ZBA decisions. In some instances, de novo review may depend on the nature of the decision and the appeal. In rare situations, a trial court may determine that a ZBA decision is clearly erroneous, and in such cases, it may also conduct a de novo review. *See, e.g., Morris Communs. Corp. v. City of Bessemer, Zoning Bd. of Adjustment*, 712 S.E.2d 868, 365 N.C. 152 (2011) (Petitioner alleged that the zoning board made an error in its interpretation of the zoning law with respect to a sign that the petitioner sought to replace. As to an error of law, the court can do a de novo review of the issue).

In situations where a property owner has asked for an exception to the zoning ordinance based on seeking a reasonable accommodation or a reasonable modification under our disability laws, an appeal of a ZBA decision can go to state court or in the alternative immediately to federal court without exhausting state administrative or judicial remedies.

g. Standing

In order to challenge a zoning decision, a party must have legal standing. The requirement of standing limits the scope of people entitled to bring a legal challenge. To have standing, a person must have a direct injury as a result of the zoning provision or decision. The immediate property owner and those with a legal interest in the property generally satisfy this requirement. The injury must be specific as to them and not just general in the way that it might impact a number of property owners. Neighbors with adjoining property typically have legal standing if they can show that a decision imposes an injury on them. In addition, some zoning ordinances give standing to people within a certain distance of the property in question. Cities and towns also have standing and can challenge the decisions of their own planning and zoning boards. In presenting a zoning case it is important to plead facts demonstrating standing. A lack of standing will permit a court to dismiss the case.

i. Standing Under Disability Law

Given that our disability laws intersect with land planning and zoning, it is important to understand some of the basic standing issues that are relevant in these situations. This section outlines standing under the Americans with Disabilities Act (ADA), 104 Stat. 327 (codified as amended at 42 U.S.C. § 12101–12213 (2016)); the Fair housing Act (FHA), 42 U.S.C. § 3601 (2016), amending Civil Rights Act of 1968, Pub. L. No. 90-284, Title VIII, 82 Stat. 81 (codified as amended at 42 U.S.C. § 3601 (2016)); and the Rehabilitation Act (RHA), 29 U.S.C. § 794 (2016). Standing issues may arise when a person with a disability is seeking an exception to the zoning code as a reasonable accommodation or as a reasonable modification (particularly as an alternative to a variance). More particularized claims may include a person with a disability asserting that a land regulation discriminates against them, fails to make a *facility, program, service, or activity* accessible to the fullest extent possible, or renders them unable to enjoy their property in a way that is similar to other property owners who do not have disabilities.

Under the ADA, FHA, and RHA, a plaintiff must show an injury in fact that meets the following three requirements: (1) the asserted injury is concrete and particularized, or an actual and imminent injury that is not hypothetical; (2) the injury is fairly traceable to a challenged action of the defendant; and (3) the injury is likely to be redressed by a favorable decision. Furthermore, an organization representing people with disabilities may have standing to bring a suit if there is a strong nexus between the organization and the person or people with a disability. This may be the situation when you have an organization seeking to obtain a permit for a group home or a drug rehabilitation center.

h. Exhaustion

The doctrine of *exhaustion* requires that an administrative decision of an agency, such as that of a zoning permit officer, may not be appealed until the plaintiff has pursued all their administrative remedies. In other words, the plaintiff must have exhausted its administrative remedies. As an example, if a property owner goes to the planning and zoning office for a permit and the officer denies the permit request, the applicant must appeal to the ZBA before they can go to court. Appealing to the ZBA is provided for as a part of the administrative process, and the property owner, applicant, must appeal to the ZBA before being able to challenge the matter in court.

The requirement to exhaust administrative remedies has several exceptions. First, if the challenge is a facial challenge to the validity of the regulation or ordinance as opposed to an "as applied" challenge. Second, if it can be demonstrated that seeking a further proposed administrative remedy will be futile. Third, if it can be demonstrated that the available administrative remedy will be inadequate. Fourth, when a decision is made by a board authorized to consider a reasonable accommodation or modification under disability law, such as a ZBA, a denial of the petition can be appealed directly to the federal courts without proceeding with any further state or local process.

i. Ripeness

The doctrine of ripeness is focused on making certain that there is a real controversy before appealing a decision to the courts. The courts do not want to deal in hypotheticals. A typical example might include the situation of a newly adopted comprehensive plan. When the new plan is adopted, it may provide for limiting uses on certain properties. A property owner affected by the new plan would not generally be able to sue on the plan, but would have to actually apply for a use that is not permitted under the plan, and be denied, before the matter would be ripe for appeal.

j. Rezoning

There are generally two categories of rezoning. One type involves adjusting and amending the zoning map. The second type involves adjusting and amending the text of a zoning code. When rezoning a map, the focus is on changing the zoning district or districts that apply to properties within the jurisdiction. In contrast, rezoning of text involves amending the language of a given zone to include or modify the uses permitted within that zone. These adjustments and amendments are generally legislative functions. In executing these changes, a local government must develop information in support of the rationality of the changes being made. Local officials must also be careful to avoid the problem of *spot zoning* when doing rezoning. Spot zoning concerns arise when an individual parcel is singled out and treated differently from other parcels within the same zoning district. Spot zoning is addressed in more detail in Chapter 4.

k. Initiatives and Referendums

Planning and zoning may sometimes involve dealing with an initiative or a referendum. Simply stated, an *initiative* is a means for community members or local government officials to put a proposed change to the planning and zoning regulations in front of the voters. The voters can approve or reject the initiative. The *referendum* functions differently; it provides an opportunity for voters to confirm or reject legislation that has been passed. The initiative and referendum process are set out in state and local law.

l. § 1983 Actions

In the context of land use and zoning, the U.S. Code, 42 U.S.C. § 1983, protects against violations of a property owner's rights to due process, equal protection, and just compensation in the situation of a taking under the Fifth and Fourteenth Amendments to the Constitution. A federal § 1983 action is typically a supplemental remedy based on a state or local action that violates a person's constitutional rights.

In *Bower Associates v. Town of Pleasant Valley*, 814 N.E.2d 410 (N.Y. 2004), New York's highest court evaluated a § 1983 action. The case provides a good illustration of how a state court deals with a federal claim that is typically brought in a federal court. The opinion dealt with two different situations in which property owners had been denied permits under local zoning law. The denials by local zoning officials were appealed in state court, and the lower state courts held in favor of the property owners. It was determined that the zoning officials had acted in an arbitrary and capricious way and that, in at least one of the two situations, equal protection of the laws was denied. Based on victories against the local zoning officials, the plaintiffs then sought damages for violation of their federal constitutional rights under § 1983.

The court in this case acknowledged that such claims are generally brought in federal court; nonetheless, it had made prior decisions regarding § 1983. Thus, it felt comfortable deciding this case. In its opinion, the court applied federal law and set out standard rules of decision. The first rule applied to claims of a violation of due process.

> Drawing on federal precedents, we set out the two-part test for substantive due process violations. First, claimants must establish a cognizable property interest, meaning a vested property interest, or "more than a mere expectation or hope to retain the permit and continue their improvements; they must show that pursuant to State or local law, they had a legitimate claim of entitlement to continue construction." Second, claimants must show that the governmental action was wholly without legal justification.

In other words, making out a claim asserting a violation of due process requires a claimant to first show that it has a cognizable property right as defined by state law and that this right has vested. Second, the claimant must show that the decision of the zoning officials is arbitrary and capricious, wholly without legal merit. With this multipart test in mind, the court went on to indicate that only the most egregious official conduct can be held to be arbitrary and capricious in the constitutional sense. The finding under state law that a zoning action is invalid because it was rendered in an arbitrary and capricious way is not sufficient for finding a violation of federal due process. To be actionable under § 1983, the arbitrary and capricious action complained of must be accompanied by evidence of the most egregious official conduct.

The second rule set out by the court is applicable to an assertion related to a violation of equal protection.

> ... [A] violation of equal protection arises where *first*, a person (compared with others similarly situated) is selectively treated and *second*, such treatment is based on impermissible considerations such as race, religion, intent to inhibit or punish the exercise of constitutional rights, or malicious or bad faith intent to injure a person.

In this case, there was no evidence that the claimant was selectively treated based on an impermissible ground such as race or religion. Thus, the claimant had to prove malicious or bad faith intent to injure as part of the assertion of its right to equal protection being violated. It failed to demonstrate the presence of an impermissible motive, and its claim failed.

An action pursuant to § 1983 is also important in the context of takings law. In the case of *Knick v. Twp. of Scott*, 588 U.S. 180 (2019), the U.S. Supreme Court overruled earlier case law and held that a land owner was not required to pursue a claim in state court before bringing a claim under § 1983 in federal court for violation of the Fifth Amendment Takings Clause. This means that a claimant does not have to exhaust a state court remedy before pursuing a constitutional takings law claim in federal court.

m. National Zoning Atlas

The National Zoning Atlas (NZA) was initiated in Connecticut as part of a state-wide program identified as "Desegregate Connecticut." This project examined issues of lingering segregation across the state. The project involved mapping a variety of zoning rules along with demographic information for each local jurisdiction within the state. From this starting point, other people became interested in the project and wanted to do a similar project in their own states. This undertaking then grew into a nationwide project for the creation of the NZA. The goal is to map every local jurisdiction in the country. The NZA is available for free online at the following website: https://www.zoningatlas.org/atlas.

The atlas collects information on zoning districts and their permitted uses, parking requirements, minimum lot sizes, height restrictions, connectivity to transportation, maximum density requirements, percentage of land within the jurisdiction that is zoned for different types of uses, developments requiring public hearings, and a variety of other matters. The NZA can provide a reference source for determining what other communities are doing in terms of zoning, and when matched with demographic information, it can be used for comparing how certain zoning regulations correlate to race and income disparities among communities.

The maps can be used for a comparative study of zoning trends and for identifying potential discriminatory implications from certain zoning practices. In other words, the maps can be educational zoning tools, and at the same time serve as vehicles for setting a foundation for alleging discrimination based on disparate treatment or disparate impact analysis. The maps can also form a basis for seeking greater uniformity among local jurisdictions in accordance with certain broader state and federal policy goals.

CHECKPOINTS

- **State Administrative Procedure Acts** outline the procedures for state agencies and their subdivisions to propose, issue, and adjudicate regulations. These can apply to state land regulation agencies. Generally, local land use and zoning jurisdictions have their own published procedures.
- **Related State and Federal Regulations**. In a land use and zoning practice, there will be many occasions when regulations outside of the planning and zoning codes may have implications on land use decisions.
- **The Standard State Zoning Enabling Act (SZEA)** includes nine sections. They cover granting local governments the authority to regulate land uses for the purpose of promoting the public health, safety, welfare, and morals of the community; dividing the jurisdiction into districts or zones; zoning pursuant to a comprehensive plan; establishing procedures; provisions for amendments; establishing a zoning authority; enforcement; establishing a ZBA; and a method of resolving conflicts with other laws.
- **The Standard City Planning Enabling Act (SCPEA)** includes four key elements: developing a comprehensive master plan; developing regulations for control of subdivisions; building controls; and engaging in regional planning if desired.

- **Zoning and planning decisions often require a public hearing.** These hearings give the public notice of what is pending and provide opportunities for input.
- **Enforcement actions** can be brought by local governments to enforce the zoning ordinance. Generally, violations of the zoning ordinance are discovered when reported to the planning and zoning office by a neighbor or upon inspection.
- **Zoning Board of Appeal (ZBA)** deals with interpreting and enforcing the zoning ordinance. A ZBA makes quasi-adjudicative decisions. It renders interpretations, adjudicates area and use variances, and evaluates conditional and special use permits.
- **Judicial Review of ZBA** decisions is provided for under state law. Review can be limited, with deference given to the ZBA, but in some jurisdictions or some situations, review may be de novo.
- **Standing** is available to a person with a direct and specific injury as a result of a zoning provision or decision.
- **Standing under disability law.** Under the ADA, FHA, and RHA, a plaintiff must show an injury in fact that meets the following three requirements: (1) the injury is concrete and particularized or an actual and imminent injury that is not hypothetical; (2) the injury is fairly traceable to a challenged action of the defendant; and (3) the injury is likely to be redressed by a favorable decision.
- **Exhaustion.** Generally, a claimant must *exhaust* administrative remedies before appealing to the courts. There are limited exceptions.
- **Ripeness.** The courts do not like to address hypothetical questions; thus, a matter must be *ripe* before it will be adjudicated.
- **Rezoning** can be done by amending a zoning map or by amending the text of a zoning code. Rezoning is a legislative act, and it must be done in a way that avoids impressible spot zoning.
- **Initiatives and referendums** are two different ways that voters can participate in passing and amending zoning codes and maps.
- **§ 1983 actions** provide a remedy for property owners who have had their constitutional rights to due process, equal protection, and protection against improper takings violated.

- **National Zoning Atlas (NZA)** collects information on zoning districts across the country and identifies, by jurisdiction, the permitted uses and requirements of zoning districts.

CHAPTER 4

Public Regulation of Land—Zoning

ROADMAP

- Regulating Pursuant to the Police Power
- Euclidean Zoning
- Uses and Accessory Uses
- Conditional and Special Use Zoning
- Floating Zones
- Overlay Zones
- Aesthetic Zoning
- Historic Districts and Landmark Preservation
- Spot Zoning
- Subdivisions
- Planned Unit Developments (P.U.D.s)
- Site Plan Review
- Alternatives to Euclidean Zoning

The common law rules of land regulation proved difficult to administer as populations grew and density levels increased. With industrialization, there were also many competing uses operating within close proximity to one another, sometimes raising health and safety concerns. Common law concepts were cumbersome and difficult to employ due to their case-by-case application and the difficulty of coordinating land uses across diverse and rapidly growing urban communities. Public regulation emerged as a way to overcome some of these difficulties. Communities began adopting generalized public land regulations applicable to multiple properties sharing similar uses and characteristics and separating them from other uses perceived to be inconsistent. This made coordination of uses easier and more efficient than simply relying on individuals bargaining over deed restrictions, covenants, and other private land use regulations.

Public land regulation and zoning are supposed to reduce conflict among property owners. They do this by establishing regularity and consistency in land use coordination and by minimizing uncompensated and negative externalities. To the extent that this is accomplished, long-term planning and investment are enhanced.

a. Regulating Pursuant to the Police Power

Initial challenges to public land regulation and zoning centered on questioning the authority of local governments to restrict and prohibit land development in the absence of a demonstrated nuisance or trespass. State and local governments, however, have the authority to regulate land uses pursuant to the police power. The police power is an inherent authority of every sovereign to regulate and enforce regulations for the promotion of the public health, safety, welfare, and morals. In so regulating, the police power is to be exercised in accordance with due process and cannot be used to promote unlawful discrimination.

Under the Tenth Amendment to the Constitution, any powers not explicitly granted to the federal government are reserved to the states. The police power is considered an inherent power of a sovereign, and the original states were considered sovereigns invested with this authority. This is what allocates the police power authority to the states. The police power can be used to regulate land uses as well as other activities. For example, the police power also allocates authority to the states to regulate such things as hospitals and health care; emergency services; law enforcement and fire services; road, bridge, and sewer construction and operation; and the development of other infrastructure within the state.

The police power must be exercised in accordance with due process. The constitutional reference points for due process are the Fifth and Fourteenth Amendments. In contemporary jurisprudence, due process involves two different elements: *procedural due process* and *substantive due process*. Procedural due process establishes the process that the government must follow in making rules and decisions that burden individual rights. Procedural due process in government decision making typically requires such things as notice and an opportunity to be heard. The type of notice and the extent of the opportunity to be heard can vary with the nature of the government proceeding and decision making. Substantive due process involves the process of protecting fundamental rights. Traditionally, fundamental rights include the protection of private property rights and the protection of other civil and constitutional rights.

In the mid-twentieth century, the rise of the administrative state led to a rising deference to state regulatory power over the use of private property. Subsequently, property regulation was treated differently than regulation affecting fundamental civil and constitutional rights. In general, property regulations are treated in a manner similar to economic regulation and are held to be a proper exercise of the police power so long as they are rational and do not go too far. For example, a regulation that results in a violation of the Takings Clause of the Fifth Amendment to the U.S. Constitution is a regulation that goes too far. In addition to federal constitutional protections of property, state constitutions may also provide for the protection of property rights.

b. Euclidean Zoning

Euclidean zoning gets its name from the famous case of *Village of Euclid v. Ambler Realty Co.*, 272 U.S. 365 (1926). This case was the first to present the question of the constitutionality of zoning to the United States Supreme Court. The Court upheld the constitutionality of zoning ordinances (codes) as a valid exercise of the state police powers. Today, we understand the elements of the *Euclid* case as a baseline reference point for a variety of zoning techniques. While many current zoning regulations do not conform to the original Euclidean elements, they are still best understood with reference to the way in which they deviate from the elements established in the *Euclid* case.

The key elements of Euclidean zoning, as established in the *Euclid* case include:

1) A local government may establish multiple zones for differentiating and separating conflicting and competing land uses within their jurisdiction. The demarcation of these zones will be upheld so long as the zones are rational, not discriminatory, and they are established pursuant to a comprehensive plan.
2) Within these various zones, regulations may be established with respect to the specific uses prohibited and permitted.
3) Among the various zones and uses permitted, there is an established hierarchy of uses. For example, the typical Euclidean zoning code identifies single-family residential uses as the highest and most protected use of land. Then might come multi-family residential, retail, and commercial, all the way down to industrial.
4) This hierarchy is important because traditional Euclidean zoning is *cumulative*. This means that a higher ranking use can be permitted within a zone designated for a lower ranking use, but a lower ranking use cannot be conducted in a zone established for a higher ranking use. Thus, single-family housing can be built in a retail zone, but a retail store cannot be built in a single-family residential zone.
5) Uses permitted in a zone are "as of right." This means that they are not conditional or discretionary. If a property owner proposes to develop and use land for a use permitted by the zoning code, the property owner is entitled to have a permit issued to allow the use.

The *Euclid* case involved a *facial challenge* to a village zoning code. A facial challenge means that the regulations are challenged as invalid on their face. In the zoning context, it usually means that the local government is challenged for exceeding its authority to regulate. At the time of the *Euclid* litigation, property rights were strongly protected and most people believed that they had the right to use their property for any lawful purpose "so long as they did no harm to others." Harm to others was typically defined as causing a nuisance or committing some form of a trespass. As such, property owners believed that they should be free to develop single-family housing, retail, commercial, and industrial uses wherever they wished, unless it could be established that the use and its location imposed a nuisance or involved a trespass.

Nuisance and trespass actions are fact specific, and each case is evaluated on its own merits. The fact specific nature of an inquiry means that context is important. In *Euclid*, the Court explained that, "[a] nuisance may be merely a right thing in the wrong place, like a pig in the parlor instead of the barnyard." *Euclid,* 272 U.S. at 388. This means that a nuisance may involve a lawful use, but if that use is contextually in the wrong place, it may be considered a nuisance. The idea behind developing zoning codes is that a community can establish general rules regulating uses and their proper location rather than deciding every issue related to every property on a case-by-case basis. A zoning code permits the coordination of land uses by zone and the separation of incompatible uses by general rules. Where these general rules impose a *practical difficulty* or *unnecessary hardship* on an individual property owner, that owner is provided with a process for requesting an exception, known as a variance.

As a result of the U.S. Supreme Court's opinion in *Euclid,* local governments are able to regulate and coordinate land uses even in the absence of a cause of action for nuisance or trespass. Moreover, the Court recognized these local zoning ordinances and codes as legitimate legislative acts passed by local governments pursuant to their exercise of the police power in furtherance of protecting the public health, safety, welfare, and morals. Because they are legislative acts, they are entitled to deference by the courts. This reasoning is consistent with the concept of separation of powers.

In reviewing challenges to the legal authority of local governments to pass regulations limiting land uses, the standard of judicial review of these regulations is that of "fairly debatable." *Euclid,* 272 U.S. at 388. The fairly debatable standard of judicial review means that the legislation will be upheld as long as it is not arbitrary or capricious. The important element here is that the courts do not investigate the legislative intent or look to what particular legislators said when the regulation was discussed and passed. Instead, the question is one of identifying any rational explanation that supports the regulation as a valid exercise of the police power. Consequently, rational explanations might be identified after the fact.

Under the facts of *Euclid,* local governments are affirmed in their ability to make rules and regulations controlling land uses. They also have the authority to interpret and adjust the general rules and regulations to accommodate specific cases of *practical difficulties* and *undue* and *unique hardships*. These adjustments are exceptions to the rules and regulations and are referred to as *area variances* (based on practical difficulties) and *use variances* (based on undue and unique hardships). Individual property owners are required to persuade local officials of the reasonableness of granting a variance. When a variance is granted, the variance runs with the land, meaning that the benefit of the variance is enjoyed by future owners and assignees of the property.

The Court in its *Euclid* decision recognized the changing context of American life. It was a time of rapid industrialization, urbanization, and innovation in urban development. Cities were becoming more crowded, factories were putting out smoke and ash, and the automobile was reshaping the landscape. Thus, when the zoning regulations of the Village of Euclid were challenged as being in violation of the Constitution, the Court responded by saying:

> Building zone laws are of modern origin. They began in this country about 25 years ago. Until recent years, urban life was comparatively simple; but, with the great increase and concentration of population, problems have developed, and constantly are developing, which require, and will continue to require, additional restrictions in respect of the use and occupation of private lands in urban communities. Regulations, the wisdom, necessity, and validity of which, as applied to existing conditions, are so apparent that they are now uniformly sustained, a century ago, or even half a century ago, probably would have been rejected as arbitrary and oppressive. Such regulations are sustained, under the complex conditions of our day, for reasons analogous to those which justify traffic regulations, which, before the advent of automobiles and rapid transit street railways, would have been condemned as fatally arbitrary and unreasonable. And in this there is no inconsistency, for, while the meaning of constitutional guaranties never varies, the scope of their application must expand or contract to meet the new and different conditions which are constantly coming within the field of their operation. In a changing world it is impossible that it should be otherwise. But although a degree of elasticity is thus imparted, not to the meaning, but to the application of constitutional principles, statutes and ordinances, which, after giving due weight to the new conditions, are found clearly not to conform to the Constitution, of course, must fall.
>
> The ordinance now under review, and all similar laws and regulations, must find their justification in some aspect of the police power, asserted for the public welfare. The line which in this field separates the legitimate from the illegitimate assumption of power is not capable of precise delimitation. It varies with circumstances and conditions. A regulatory zoning ordinance, which would be clearly valid as applied to the great cities, might be clearly invalid as applied to rural communities.

Id. at 386–87.

With the *Euclid* decision, the Court established the constitutional legitimacy of zoning. It recognized that local communities could regulate land uses in accordance with a zoning code passed and implemented as an exercise of the police power as delegated to the local government by the state.

In addition to regulating land uses, *Euclid* affirmed local regulation of building height and bulk, lot coverage, and setback requirements from roads and adjoining lot lines. By regulating these elements, the zoning code could control density, and create space between buildings and structures, while limiting height and bulk to permit sunlight and air circulation. For setback requirements, measurements can be clearly stated such as, "no structure shall be placed closer than 25 feet from a side yard boundary line." Likewise, height restrictions are easily stated by identifying the maximum height of a permitted structure in terms of feet, meters, or other common formulations. Regulating lot coverage and bulk are also covered by modern zoning codes.

Below is a diagram showing a house on a lot with zoning code setback requirements. The requirements include a front yard setback of 30 feet from the sidewalk; a side yard setback of 20 feet from the property line; and a rear yard setback of 15 feet from the property line. This means no structures can be placed within these setbacks. The term "structure" is typically a term specifically defined in the local zoning code. The zoning code will also include a height restriction, such as limiting the height of any structure to no more than 37 feet.

Diagram 4.1 Zoning Setbacks

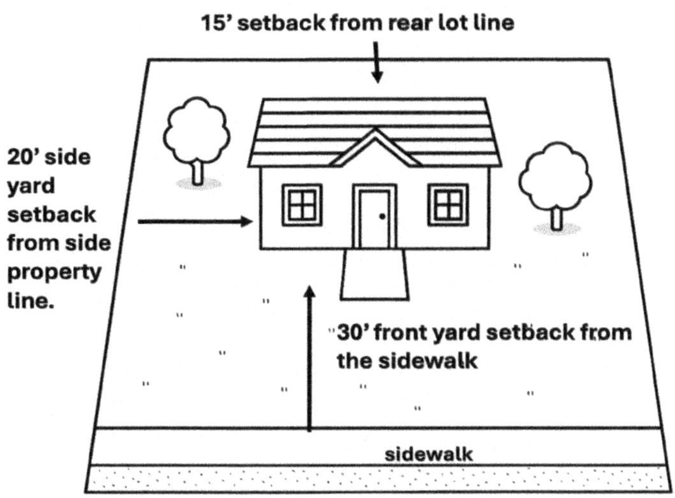

Zoning Setback Requirements for Location of Improvements

Diagram 4.2 Floor Area Ratio

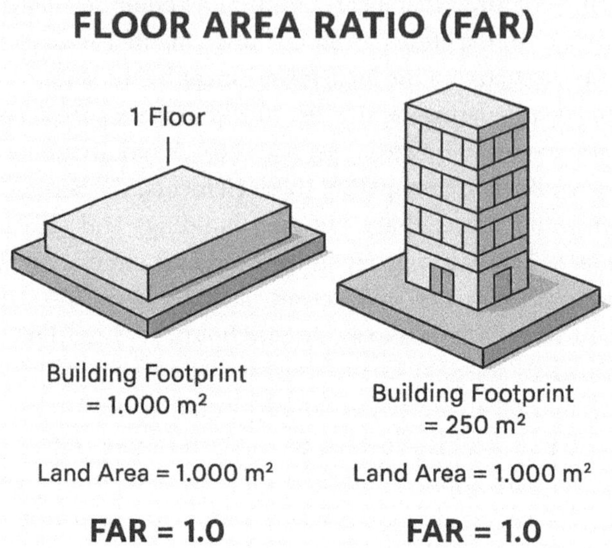

Another way to address lot coverage is in terms of the *floor area ratio (FAR).* Lot coverage is usually restricted in terms of the percentage of a lot that can be covered by a structure or by nonpermeable surfaces, including concrete patios and walkways. One way that some codes address lot coverage is by providing a FAR. The floor area ratio is helpful in situations where a structure will be multi-story and perhaps have some interesting design features.

A FAR is calculated by taking the sum of square feet per floor of all the floors in a building and dividing it by the total area of the property in square feet. The FAR does not control for height; it focuses on lot coverage. It might be regulated in simple terms by restricting such coverage to no more than 25% of a given lot. On the other hand, it might be regulated using a stated *floor area ratio* (FAR) of some amount such as .5. A FAR of .5 would mean that a structure placed on a lot can cover no more than 50% of the lot based on a single-story structure. If the property owner decides to build a two-story structure on the lot, the structure can only cover 25% at ground level so that each of the two floors would add up to .5 (.25 + .25). If the property owner wished to build a ten-story building in a zone with a .5 FAR, then the building footprint could only cover 10% of the lot. When applying a FAR to a property, it is important to determine how the local zoning code measures space in the structure. For example, some FAR regulations do not count stairwell or elevator shaft spaces in the determination of square feet per floor. Of course, a FAR restriction would also need to be applied in combination with other height, bulk, and setback requirements.

The image above illustrates a FAR. On a lot, the FAR is 1.0. If the builder constructs a one-story building on the lot, the building can cover the entire lot, less the required setbacks. If the building is four stories, then the structure can cover one-quarter of the lot. In each case, the FAR is one ($1 \times 1 = 1$; $4 \times .25 = 1$).

Euclid was further clarified in a later case. In *Nectow v. City of Cambridge*, 277 U.S. 183 (1928), the Court addressed an "as applied" challenge to a zoning regulation. *Nectow* held that even when a zoning regulation is legally permitted under the fairly debatable standard, the actual establishment of zones and uses is still subject to review. The plaintiff in *Nectow* did not challenge the local government's power to regulate but rather it challenged the setting of zoning district lines and the limitations on uses within these zones. The plaintiff asserted that the zoning regulation actually adopted was not rational as applied to his property. That is, the regulations did not accomplish the purpose they were supposed to accomplish as applied to his property, and the Court agreed. By its decision, the Supreme Court established the standard of review for setting zoning district lines and criteria for permitted uses within these districts. The standard established was that of rational basis review. This standard is higher than the fairly debatable standard applied to evaluate the question of local authority to regulate land uses pursuant to the police power. In contrast to the fairly debatable standard, the rational basis standard requires an examination of the intent and purpose behind the rules and regulations. The actual application of the rules and regulations must be rational in terms of their intended purpose and not simply with reference to any rational purpose that might be offered. This means that an examination of legislative history is appropriate in order to establish the purpose behind the regulation.

An additional element of traditional Euclidean zoning is that land use regulations must be for the protection of *the public* health, safety, welfare, and morals and not used to simply provide a benefit to an individual. This was made clear in *Pennsylvania Coal Co. v. Mahon*, 260 U.S. 393 (1922). This case involved a state regulation restricting coal mining underneath a populated area. In framing the opinion of the Court, Justice Holmes identified the matter as a "case of a single private home." *Id.* at 413. In so doing, the case was positioned as a matter not affecting the public but rather just one individual.

Framing the case in this way allowed the Court to question the regulation in terms of the apparent absence of an intent to protect the public more broadly.

The *Pennsylvania Coal* case also addressed issues of land regulation under the Due Process and Takings Clauses of the Constitution. In this regard, property regulation is limited by requirements for due process of law and by Fifth Amendment protections against unlawful takings of property by the government. In addressing limitations to property regulation, the Court acknowledged that not all regulations were prohibited.

> Government hardly could go on if to some extent values incident to property could not be diminished without paying for every such change in the general law. As long recognized some values are enjoyed under an implied limitation and must yield to the police power. But obviously the implied limitation must have its limits or the contract and due process clauses are gone. One fact for consideration in determining such limits is the extent of the diminution. When it reaches a certain magnitude, in most if not in all cases there must be an exercise of eminent domain and compensation to sustain the act. So the question depends upon the particular facts. The greatest weight is given to the judgment of the legislature but it always is open to interested parties to contend that the legislature has gone beyond its constitutional power.... The general rule at least is that while property may be regulated to a certain extent, if regulation goes too far it will be recognized as a taking.... [A] strong public desire to improve the public condition is not enough to warrant achieving the desire by a shorter cut than the constitutional way of paying for the change. As we already have said this is a question of degree—and therefore cannot be disposed of by general propositions.

260 U.S. at 413, 415–16.

The above quoted elements of the case opinion tell us that state and local governments have the authority to regulate land uses and to restrict property rights as a proper exercise of their inherent police power, but regulation has its limits, and *it must not go too far*. The determination of what it means "to go too far" is contextual and fact specific. Thus, there is a need for a case-by-case determination of a takings claim. Moreover, at the same time, the desire to protect the public should not be cause to forget the constitutional protections that we have for private property. The regulation must be accomplished in a constitutional way.

The question of *when regulation goes too far* also carries over to the tension between land regulation and other fundamental rights beyond those of property. In each type of case, a fundamental question involves determining if the regulation goes too far. For instance, zoning codes often regulate signs and the location of adult entertainment venues. *See, e.g., City of Renton v. Playtime Theaters, Inc.*, 475 U.S. 41 (1986) (holding that the city of Renton's zoning regulation prohibiting adult theaters within 1,000 feet of a residential zone was a content neutral time, place, and manner regulation that is acceptable under the First Amendment to the Constitution). Likewise, they regulate the location of places of worship (e.g., churches, mosques, temples). These regulations may involve a tension with First Amendment rights to free speech, expression, and religious exercise. Similarly, the use of zoning to regulate single-family residential housing may intrude on the definition and composition of families. *See, e.g., Village of Belle Terre v. Boraas*, 416 U.S. 1 (1974). This raises tension with the rights of privacy and free association. In all of these situations, the question arises as to when local land regulation "goes too far."

In these and other situations, land use and zoning regulations are in tension with other constitutionally protected fundamental rights. When tension arises between zoning and other fundamental rights, judicial review may be elevated to intermediate or strict scrutiny. This means that less deference is given to local planning and zoning officials, and these officials must have stronger justifications for their regulations as compared to a case evaluated under a rational basis review. Not only must the justifications be better developed and articulated, but the regulations will also typically need to be written more narrowly and with greater specificity. *See, e.g., Reed v. Town of Gilbert*, 576 U.S. 155 (2015) (holding that the Town of Reed's ordinance regulating signage was content based, subject to strict scrutiny review, and that the ordinance was not narrowly tailored enough to serve the town's compelling interests in aesthetics and traffic safety).

The *Euclid, Nectow, and Pennsylvania Coal* cases provide a basic framework for understanding traditional Euclidean zoning. Together with limitations on regulation imposed by the protection of other fundamental rights under the Constitution, they provide a baseline for understanding, by reference, much of the land use and zoning law that developed post-*Euclid*.

An overview of the legal tools that a property owner might raise in a challenge to a zoning regulation are outlined below. Having these tools in mind will equip one to better understand Justice Holmes' admonishment that regulation is permissible so long as it doesn't "go too far." Property owners may challenge the interpretation and application of code provisions, and they may employ the following basic legal "tools" in challenging a land use and zoning regulation that limits their rights to use and develop their property. (These tools are explored more fully elsewhere in the book; in particular in Chapters 6 and 7.)

- The rule or regulation exceeds the delegated authority of the local government (Dillon Rule vs Home Rule).
- The rule or regulation is directed at benefiting an individual rather than the public.
- The rule or regulation violates traditional protections of property under the Due Process Clause.
- The rule or regulation violates equal protection.
- The rule or regulation violates the Takings Clause of the Fifth Amendment to the Constitution.
- The rule or regulation conflicts with other fundamental rights protected by the Constitution, such as rights to speech, expression, and the exercise of religion.
- The rule or regulation is limited by background legal rules of the common law, including nuisance and trespass.

c. Uses and Accessory Uses

Traditional Euclidean zoning regulated uses on property as outlined above. In addition, permitted uses on a property often include the right to *accessory uses*. In general, accessory uses are uses that are *customary and incidental* to the primary use that is permitted under the land use regulations. *See, e.g., Mortimer v. New Britain Township Zoning Hearing Board*, 93 A.3d 936 (Pa. Commw. Ct. 2014). Like other uses permitted under Euclidean zoning, accessory uses were permitted as of right. Today, accessory uses are generally permitted but in many zoning codes they are treated apart from the primary use.

A classic example of an accessory use is a car garage located with a residential use. A car garage is customarily located with a home. It is customary because it is a normal and not an unexpected use in relationship to a residential home. The garage is also considered an incidental use to the primary use because it is a subsidiary use. The primary use of the property is for living in the home on the lot while the garage is simply a common feature of a home, and its purpose is subsidiary to the primary purpose.

A garage may be both an *accessory use* and an *accessory structure*. A garage attached to a house is an accessory use. A garage that is detached from the house (a stand-alone structure) is an accessory use and it is also an accessory structure. An accessory structure is a structure located on the same lot as a primary use, that is used for an ancillary purpose that is customary and incidental to the primary use.

Accessory uses must be located on the same lot as the primary use. For example, assume a person owns two small adjoining lots in an area zoned exclusively for single-family residential homes. On one lot she has a single-family residential home without a garage, and the adjoining lot is vacant. She now wishes to add a garage. The lot with the home on it is too small to locate a garage on it given zoning code setback and lot coverage requirements. Therefore, she seeks to place a detached garage on the adjoining lot. She claims that this garage will be a permitted accessory use to her single-family residential use. The problem is that these are two separate lots, and the properties are located in a zoning district designated exclusively for single-family residential uses. While a garage is typically an accessory use in relation to a single-family residential home, it must be located on the same lot as the primary use. Thus, even though she owns two adjacent lots, she cannot put a garage on the adjoining lot. The garage cannot be a primary use on a lot in a single-family residential zone.

In addition to being customary, an accessory use must be incidental to the primary use. Another common example beyond that of a garage is when people have an office in their home. Perhaps they sell insurance, practice law or accounting, or do clothing alterations using a part of their home to engage in such activities. Traditionally, a home office has been considered an accessory use unless prohibited. Again, the particular use must be both customary and incidental.

Other examples might include a gas station that also provides a convenience store (or a convenience store that also sells gasoline); an auto mechanic garage that also sells a few cars on the side; and a grocery store that operates a café or provides sit-down food service inside. In each of these cases, one must determine the primary use and then the accessory use. If a zoning code permits a gas station or auto shop in a given location, can the property owner also operate a convenience store or an automobile sales operation on the same property even if convenience stores and automobile sales are not otherwise permitted within that same zoning district? Perhaps, if they are accessory uses to a lawfully permitted primary use. What about our third example? If a grocery store is permitted to operate in a zone that prohibits cafes and restaurants, can it open a café or a restaurant inside its grocery store?

In each of the three examples set out above, if we are to argue that the seemingly unpermitted use is permitted as an accessory use, we must ask if the proposed use is a customary and incidental use related to and incidental to the primary use. Looking more closely at the grocery store example, we must explore the nature of a grocery store. This has changed over time. In the past, baked goods, candies, alcohol, kitchen supplies, and seasonal gifts were not found in grocery stores. Now it is common and customary that we find all of these things within the permitted use of a grocery store. If so, then such activities might be permitted in a grocery store even when not otherwise permitted as a use in the zone. Assuming we determine that it is customary, we must then determine if it is incidental. This is something that might be assessed in several different ways. First, one might look at the square feet dedicated inside the store to dining and food service relative to the number of square feet for other more traditional grocery uses. If the square feet for in-store dining are small relative to the size of the entire store, then it might be determined to be incidental. Another way to look at this might be based on net revenue. Even if in-store dining occupied a lot of space, we might conclude that it is incidental if sales or profits from this activity were small relative to the other activities within the store. A third way to look at this might be based on budget. If the budget, as opposed to revenue, for in-store dining activities is small relative to the budget for the entire store, it might be incidental.

Another situation to consider is when a property owner attempts to have an additional use on her property while asserting it is simply part of the primary use. For example, a property owner with a home located in a single-family zone has an attached garage and she decides to finish off the area over the garage and make it into a livable apartment space. If the garage apartment space is a fully integrated part of the house, it might be considered a part of the primary use. If, on the other hand, the garage apartment has its own electric and water meters and is not used by the primary owners of the property, it may well be seen as an unpermitted use because it transforms the property into a multi-family dwelling when only single-family dwellings are permitted. *See Mortimer v. New Britain Township Zoning Hearing Board*, 93 A.3d 936 (Pa. Commw. Ct. 2014) (court ruled that the addition on Mortimer's home was an unpermitted accessory use to his home and not a part of the primary use).

d. Conditional and Special Use Zoning

As noted, Euclidean zoning has certain characteristics, one of which is that permitted uses are "as of right." This means that if the zoning code lists a drive-through dining facility as a permitted use, a property owner can seek to obtain a permit for that use as of right. The property owner must still comply with lot regulations such as setbacks and lot coverage requirements. This contrasts with conditional and special uses. *See, e.g., Town of Rhine v. Bizzell*, 751 N.W.2d 780 (Wis. 2008) (court strikes down a zoning ordinance making all uses conditional within a zone with no uses as of right); *Rise, Inc. v. Malheur County*, No. 10-cv-00686, 2012 U.S. Dist. LEXIS 44994 (U.S. Dist. Ore. Feb. 13, 2012) (dealing with a conditional use permit for a group home).

A conditional use, or what is sometimes referred to as a special use, is a use permitted in a zone provided that certain conditions are met. Conditional use permits are issued upon review and approval by planning and zoning officials. A drive-through dining facility and a drive-through bank are prime examples of uses requiring conditional use permits to operate in a zone. Typically, a zoning code will expressly identify particular uses as conditional uses within a zone that also has uses permitted as of right. The conditional or special use is permitted in a zone but must meet special criteria before obtaining approval. For example, a bank or a fast food business may be an appropriate use in a zone but may pose special safety issues based on how it is developed on its lot. Businesses operating a drive-through window typically have special requirements for ingress and egress to the property, and requirements that there be enough room on the property to stack automobiles while people wait in their cars to be served. Stacking room is important so that waiting vehicles are not sticking out into ongoing traffic on the street.

Obtaining a conditional use permit typically requires a demonstration to a zoning board of appeal that the conditions can be met. The property owner will have to appear in front of the board for a public hearing and will have an opportunity to present evidence demonstrating that its proposed project meets the zoning code requirements including the required conditions. In our drive-through example, this might include demonstrating evidence as to the size of the lot, its location with respect to nearby intersections, easy and safe plans for ingress and egress, and traffic studies supporting the appropriate space for stacking on the lot. The public will have an opportunity to address the proposal and challenge or present evidence as well.

The zoning board of appeal will make a decision with respect to the request for the issuing of the conditional use permit. The zoning board's decision must include an explanation of its rationale for the decision. The property owner, if unsatisfied with the board's decision, can appeal that decision. Usually, the appeal is to a court in the jurisdiction. The standard of review applied to the zoning board determination is that of a rational basis supported by substantial competent evidence (sometimes courts do not include the word "substantial" and simply say a rational basis supported by competent evidence). Note that the phrase substantial competent evidence establishes a burden that is less than that of a preponderance of the evidence. In a challenge to a board decision, the property owner has the burden of demonstrating that the decision is not rational and not supported by competent evidence. *See Wisconsin Community Services, Inc. v. City of Milwaukee*, 465 F.3d 737 (7th Cir. 2006) (on appeal, court ruled that the ADA required the City of Milwaukee to approve Plaintiff's special use permit because Plaintiff made a showing that the decision of the zoning board of appeal was not rationally supported by competent evidence on the record).

e. Floating Zones

The floating zone is inconsistent with traditional Euclidean zoning. Euclidean zoning permits a local jurisdiction to establish zones for specific types of uses. These zones are identified on a zoning map and then rules applicable to uses in each zone are spelled out in the zoning code. In contrast, a *floating zone* starts out as a zone that is not fixed on a zoning map. Instead, it is a zone approved by legislative act that establishes certain criteria for a land use. At the outset, it exists in written form only and has no physical location. A floating zone is typically approved for a land use desired for the community, such as senior housing, multi-family housing, industrial development or something else. The zone establishes criteria such as the size of the total acreage required for a proposed development project, let us assume 10 acres. And then provides other criteria for a permitted or conditional use. Once a floating zone is defined and enacted, it metaphorically "floats" over the local jurisdiction until it gets "anchored" to a specific location at a later date. Once approved and anchored to the zoning map, the zone is no longer floating. Sometimes a floating zone may include a date certain by which it must become anchored or it will expire; an expiration date is referred to as a "sunset" provision. *See e.g.*,

Beyer v. Burns, 567 N.Y.S.2d 599 (N.Y. Sup. Ct. 1991) (court held that floating provisions are permissible when established according to the town's comprehensive plan and that such zones may be limited by a sunset provision).

The floating zone is designed to encourage developers of certain desirable projects to think about coming forward with a project and identifying a suitable location for developing the use. When a developer comes forward with a plan to develop a specific parcel of land in a way that meets the floating zone requirements, he applies for the anchoring of the zone at his planned location and seeks plan approval, usually involving site plan review with the planning office, and a permit from the zoning office. The anchoring process differs from the initial process of enacting a floating zone. The anchoring process is not legislative but adjudicative. The anchoring of the zone on the zoning map at a specific location is a quasi-adjudicative act, meaning that there is a different standard of review for each step, the legislative and the quasi-adjudicative.

The image below provides an illustration of a zoning map for a small urban community. The community has adopted a floating zone illustrated by the cloud floating over the city. The zone establishes criteria for Multi-Family Senior Housing uses, including a requirement that the zone must be established on a contiguous parcel of land of size seven acres or more. Until a developer presents a project consistent with the zone requirements and the city approves it, the zone exists on paper but is not anchored to any specific location on the zoning map. Once a project is accepted and approved, the zone will no longer be floating over the city but will be anchored and shown at a specific location on the zoning map.

A floating zone must be consistent with the local comprehensive plan and must be carefully crafted to serve the public interest after due deliberation. Consistency with the comprehensive plan and careful deliberation are important in establishing a floating zone in order to defend against a challenge to the zone by property owners who might object to its eventual anchoring near their property. Such a challenge could be based on a claim that the newly anchored zone amounts to impermissible *spot zoning*. Spot zoning is potentially illegal because it may violate equal protection and due process by treating one parcel of land within an established zone differently than surrounding parcels. This results from anchoring the floating zone on a map that already has all of the zones identified. The very fact of placing it in this new location means that it is zoned differently than the surrounding properties. It may be asserted that this is spot zoning, but spot zoning may be permitted if it serves an important public interest.

Diagram 4.3 Floating Zone

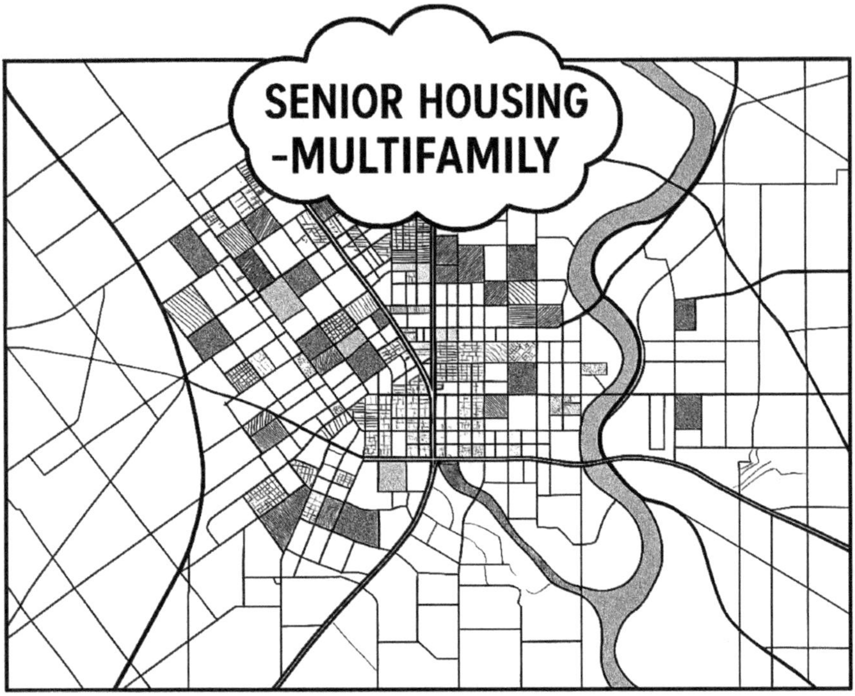

f. Overlay Zones

Overlay zones are different from floating zones. Overlay zones are anchored to specific lands within a jurisdiction. In essence, they establish multiple zoning districts over the same land. For example, we may have a zoning map and code designating an area of a city as single-family residential. This area may include a neighborhood near a small lake. The land around the lake is a wetland that the city wishes to protect for environmental reasons. To do this, the city enacts an overlay zone identifying wetland areas within the single-family zone where no structures can be built. We can think of this by imagining a zoning map identifying all of the zones in the city, including the single-family residential zone near the lake. Given this map, imagine another map, perhaps set out on transparent see-through plastic, that we can set down over the first map. The second map is the overlay map because we lay it over the top of the first map and then we can see what properties are within our wetland protection zone. Land within the protection zone boundaries must comply with both sets of zoning regulations (the single-family zone regulations and the wetlands protection regulations). A result might be that the owner of a one-acre lot in the single-family residential neighborhood by the lake can build a single-family home on her lot, but a quarter of her lot falls within the boundaries of the protected wetland, meaning that even if she can build a house on the lot, she will not be able to construct a structure within the boundaries of the wetlands protection zone.

Overlay zones are often used for environmental purposes. They may also be used to protect historic districts or landmark buildings located in various places and zones within a city. There are also other uses for an overlay zone. For example, in *Ani Creation, Inc. v. City of Myrtle Beach*, 440 S.C. 266 (2023), the city created an overlay zone to regulate the location of smoke shops and tobacco stores, in the city's downtown area. Regulating and restricting the locations was done to make the downtown area more family friendly. Nine stores in the downtown area sued alleging illegal spot zoning based on singling out their smoke and tobacco retail operations for different zoning treatment compared to other types of shops and retail stores in the area. On review of the regulations, the South Carolina Supreme Court did not find spot zoning and instead confirmed the legality of the overlay zone.

The map below provides an example of an overlay zone. Here, the zoning code covers all of the residential lots depicted on the map. Under the code, all of the lots can be used for a single-family residential home together with accessory structures such as sheds, patios, and pools. The River Protection Overlay zone is a map placed over the underlying zoning map, and it indicates locations where no structures or uses can be built or located. The River Protection Overlay zone limits the uses permitted on the underlying zoning map. In order to protect the river, no structures or uses can be placed within the protection zone. This means that owners of lots within the River Protection Zone will not be able to make use of their full acreage in the same way as other lot owners in the same zone.

In the diagram below, the gray shading on either side of the river represents the overlay zone. The overlay only affects activity on that portion of a lot within the overlay. In the diagram, all of the lots abutting the river have lot lines that extend to the riverbank. To the extent that the gray shaded area covers a part of a lot, this portion of the lot is subject to the overlay zoning regulations in addition to the regular single-family residential zoning.

Diagram 4.4 Overlay Zone for River Protection Area

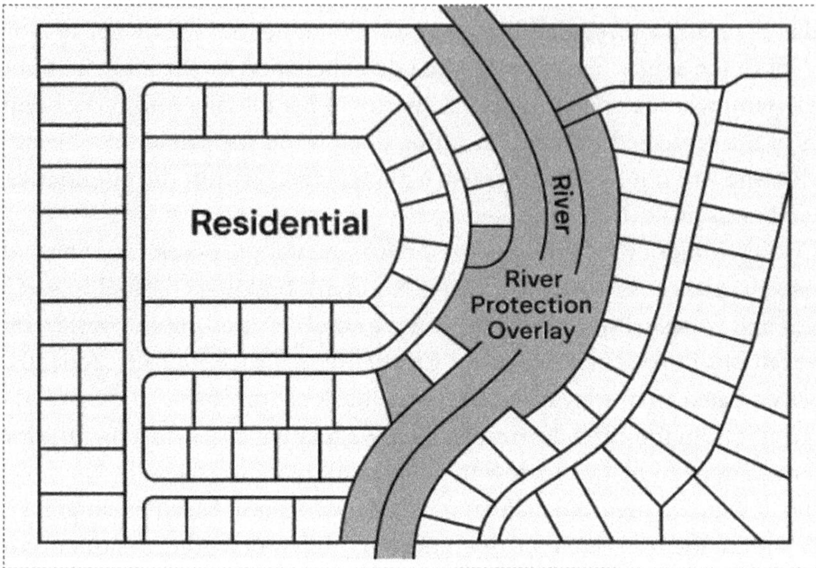

g. Aesthetic Zoning

Aesthetic zoning is used to control the design, feel, and character of a neighborhood. This can include restrictions on the types of structures that can be built, the way that structures can be situated on a lot, the architecture of the structures, materials that can be used in construction, the types of things that can be placed on a lawn area, and landscaping. Aesthetic zoning ordinances typically include provisions for an appointed or elected architectural review board, or something equivalent, to review and approve design and build plans. The board will consist of several members charged with evaluating any proposed building or modifications to ensure that the work will comply with the aesthetic standards established by the local ordinance. Usually, best practices would include having an architect and a landscaping expert as members of such a board. A concern with this type of zoning is that aesthetics reflect personal preferences and are therefore subjective, but courts have held that such regulation may still be validated as serving the public interest as long as criteria for evaluation are provided for board decision making.

> The concept of the public welfare is broad and inclusive.... The values it represents are spiritual as well as physical, aesthetic as well as monetary.

> It is within the power of the legislature to determine that the community should be beautiful as well as healthy, spacious as well as clean, well-balanced as well as carefully patrolled.

Berman v. Parker, 348 U.S. 26 (1954).

While aesthetics are often grounded in subjective and personal preferences, such zoning cannot be arbitrary and capricious. Decisions as to approval or denial cannot be purely subjective, they must be based on established criteria set out with a reasonable degree of specificity so that property owners know what is expected of them. One court explained it this way:

> Clearly, ... aesthetic standards are an appropriate component of land use governance. Whenever a community adopts such standards they can and must be drafted to give clear guidance to all parties concerned. Applicants must have an understandable statement of what is expected from new construction. Design professionals need to know in advance what standards will be acceptable in a given community. It is unreasonable to expect applicants to pay for repetitive revisions of plans in an effort to comply with the unarticulated, unpublished ... [requirements]. It is equally unreasonable, and a deprivation of due process, to expect or allow a design review board ... to create standards on an ad hoc basis, during the design review process.

Anderson v. City of Issaquah, 851 P.2d 744, 755 (Wash. Ct. App. 1993).

Aesthetic requirements and architectural review boards are also used in many private common interest communities with an H.O.A.

h. Historic Districts and Landmark Preservation

Historic districts and landmark preservation acts are forms of aesthetic zoning that protect the public welfare. The power to zone for aesthetics includes the authority to protect and preserve important historical and cultural places, uses, and structures. With clearly identified criteria, these regulations can be focused on a geographic area or on single properties. Often the protection is directed at an aspect of architecture and design. While some property owners object to zoning that regulates the designs they wish to use in new construction, or regulations that prevent the taking down of old structures on their property, contemporary courts have upheld aesthetic zoning and zoning for historic preservation. Such zoning can focus on an individual property such as protecting the Penn Central train terminal in New York City, or on a neighborhood, as in preserving an historic district like the French Quarter in New Orleans. Several courts have spoken on how aesthetics and historic preservation are part of protecting the public welfare. As such, it is within the traditional scope of the exercise of the police power. In *Figarsky v. Historic Dist. Comm'n*, 368 A.2d. 163 (Conn. 1976), the court said:

> In a number of recent cases, it has been held that the preservation of a historical area or landmark as it was in the past falls within the meaning of general welfare and, consequently, the police power.... We cannot deny that the preservation of an area or cluster of buildings with exceptional historical and architectural significance may serve the public welfare.

A key consideration in these situations is one of determining what is historical and worthy of protection. Generally, something is not historical for zoning purposes simply because it is old. There is usually a requirement for a finding that a place or structure has historical, cultural, or architectural value in a way worth preserving. Such determinations generally require evaluation by a panel of informed experts. Such experts might include a review board comprised of historians, architects, builders, and others. Many towns and cities have historic districts. A few well-known examples include the French Quarter in New Orleans, Williamsburg, Virgina, parts of old Charleston, South Carolina, and parts of historic Savannah, Georgia. Property within an historic district will be subject to special zoning regulations. In addition, many historic districts have strict building requirements for any updates or restoration work. There may also be tax benefits for property owners within these districts.

Related to historic districts are historic buildings and landmarks. These are not districts but generally individual structures that possess special historical, cultural, or architectural value. They may be located in a variety of zoning districts within a community. When there are multiple such buildings and landmarks in a community, it is typical that an overlay map will be developed to use with an underlying zoning map to identify the location of these protected structures.

In *Penn Central Transportation Co. v. City of New York*, 438 U.S. 104 (1978), a landmark preservation ordinance was challenged. It was determined that the landmark preservation act in the city of New York was constitutional and not a taking under the Fifth Amendment to the Constitution. The case involved the owner of Penn Central station in New York and its plans to construct a high-rise addition on top of the iconic rail station. Under the landmark preservation act adopted by the city, the property owner's plans were not approved. This prevented the owner from further developing the building according to plans that were otherwise in compliance with the requirements of the zoning code. As a consequence, the owner was unable to add additional square footage to the property that would have generated millions of dollars in new revenue. The property owner asserted that the landmark regulation was not a proper exercise of the zoning power because it did not regulate an identifiable zone but rather it regulated individual landmarks located in various zones across the city. In addition, the property owner argued that the regulations amounted to a taking in violation of the Fifth Amendment. The Court held that the landmark zoning ordinance was a valid exercise of the police power, even though the lack of an identifiable zone was inconsistent with strict Euclidean zoning, and it determined that the regulations did not amount to a taking.

In its opinion, the Court said the following:

> Over the past 50 years, all 50 States and over 500 municipalities have enacted laws to encourage or require the preservation of buildings and areas with historic or aesthetic importance. These nationwide legislative efforts have been precipitated by two concerns. The first is recognition that, in recent years, large numbers of historic structures, landmarks, and areas have been destroyed without adequate consideration of either the values represented therein or the possibility of preserving the destroyed properties for use in economically productive ways. The second is a widely shared belief that structures with special historic, cultural, or architectural significance enhance the quality of life for all. Not only do these buildings and their workmanship represent the lessons of the past and embody precious features of our heritage, they serve as examples of quality for today. "[H]istoric conservation is but one aspect of the much larger problem, basically an environmental one, of enhancing—or perhaps developing for the first time—the quality of life for people."...
>
> The New York City law is typical of many urban landmark laws in that its primary method of achieving its goals is not by acquisitions of historic properties, but rather by involving public entities in land-use decisions affecting these properties and providing services, standards, controls, and incentives that will encourage preservation by private owners and users. While the law does place special restrictions on land-

> mark properties as a necessary feature to the attainment of its larger objectives, the major theme of the law is to ensure the owners of any such properties both a "reasonable return" on their investments and maximum latitude to use their parcels for purposes not inconsistent with the preservation goals.

438 U.S. at 107–10.

Penn Central is an important case not only because it validated the landmark preservation ordinance, but because it also established an important set of criteria for determining if a taking has occurred. This aspect of the case is explored in more detail in Chapter 6.

Another consideration when regulating historic properties involves coordinating the preservation of the past with compliance under contemporary accessibility requirements provided for in our disability laws. When dealing with the Americans with Disabilities Act (ADA), 42 U.S.C. §§ 12101 *et seq.*, the Rehabilitation Act (RHA), 29 U.S.C. § 794 (2016), and the Fair housing Act (FHA): 42 U.S.C. § 3601, 51, 124; Fair Housing Amendments Act of 1988, Pub. L. No. 100-430, 102 Stat. 1619 (codified as amended at 42 U.S.C. § 3601 (2016), 167 (covering historic housing), it is important to keep in mind that historic preservation must also include provisions for making these places accessible to people with disabilities. A tension arises in some situations when the architectural features of a building or of an historic district include barriers to accessibility. In such cases, the requirements for accessibility are balanced against the elements that make the location worthy of protection in the first instance. Modifications and barrier removal should not undermine the historical, cultural, and architectural values being preserved, but at the same time, modification may be required in order to make the location accessible to people with disabilities.

In *Molski v. Foley Estates Vineyard and Winery, LLC*, 531 F.3d 1043 (9th Cir. 2008), the court addressed a claim raised by a paraplegic who visited a winery tasting room and encountered barriers and access difficulties. The winery tasting room was officially recognized as an historic property. Under disability law, the property was still required to be accessible to the maximum extent feasible. The winery built an accessory structure adjacent to the historic tasting room and made that facility fully accessible to people with disabilities. The new structure served as an additional tasting room. The winery demonstrated that wheelchair access to the historic tasting room was not possible without doing new construction that would undermine the elements of the building that were part of the reason for it having protection. The new tasting room was designed and built to meet the needs of people with certain disabilities so that they might have a similar opportunity to enjoy wine tastings. The court did not think that the alternative tasting facility satisfied the requirements for accessibility. The court determined that even though the accessory structure was an alternative way of providing access for people with disabilities, the interior of the historic building needed to be accessible to the maximum extent possible notwithstanding an inability to add an appropriate wheelchair ramping system for safe access to it. This determination recognized that even if some people with disabilities might not be able to enter the structure without a ramp, other people with different disabilities might be able to enter. For these people, the interior of the historic structure had to be made as accessible as possible. Thus, interior barriers needed to be removed and such things as pathways, bathrooms, doorways, and doorknobs would still need to be adjusted to meet accessibility standards.

i. Spot Zoning

Spot zoning is generally not permitted. Spot zoning happens when one or a few properties are singled out for zoning changes that are not applied to surrounding properties. Spot zoning raises concerns because it generally does not occur in the context of a broad review of the comprehensive plan for a community. Instead, spot zoning generally represents a piecemeal adjustment to zoning that is not necessarily pursuant to a comprehensive plan. Spot zoning also raises questions of due process and equal protection.

As an example of spot zoning, let us consider a neighborhood zoned exclusively for single-family residential housing. Within the zoning district, all properties are to be treated similarly. Different zoning districts may have different requirements, but within a given zone, all properties are to be treated equally. Now assume that one property owner with a two-acre lot seeks to put a coffee shop (a retail use) on his property because that use will make the property much more valuable. On making a petition to the local legislative body, the property owner gets a change in the zoning from single-family residential to retail use so that he can operate a coffee shop serving the neighborhood. All of the surrounding properties within the neighborhood and zoning district remain as they were. No one else gets a retail use. This zoning change has focused on one lot and treated it differently than the surrounding properties. This singling out of the one property for different treatment, without a comprehensive consideration of the area, is what gives rise to an assertable claim of impermissible spot zoning.

Generally, spot zoning is associated with a legislative change in the zoning for one or a few parcels of land located within a given zone, and not with changes pursuant to an area or use variance. Use variances change the permitted use on an individual property. There are specific criteria under state and local zoning law for a use variance, and a zoning board must follow the criteria. Since use variances are provided for, it is difficult to classify them in the same way as zoning code changes that may be reviewed as potentially spot zoning. On the other hand, one should be cautious. The variance process should not be used to achieve a neighborhood rezoning by piecemeal granting of multiple variances in an effort to avoid an unfavorable climate for proper legislative rezoning. If the use variance process looks like a form of implied spot zoning designed to assist an individual property owner in a situation where changes in the area might more properly call for a legislative review of a neighborhood, then there might be a problem. In other words, if the petitions for multiple use variances hinge on significant changes to the neighborhood where the property is located, it may be more appropriate to have a legislative review to evaluate and update the zoning for the entire neighborhood rather than to work piecemeal by granting a series of use variances to individual property owners.

Reverse spot zoning is also problematic. Reverse spot zoning is when a zoning change is made in a zoning district that changes the regulation on all of the properties in the zone but leaves one property out. The property left out is then surrounded by neighboring properties that have had their uses changed, let us say from residential to commercial, for example.

How does one know when spot zoning is impermissible?

> First, spot zoning may occur whether a small parcel of property is subject to *more or less restrictive* zoning than the surrounding properties. Second, to determine whether *impermissible* spot zoning has occurred, a court is required to conduct a two-part analysis. After determining that spot zoning has actually occurred, the court must determine whether the record shows the spot zoning is in the public interest.

Foothill Communities Coalition v. County of Orange, 166 Cal. Rptr. 3d 627 (Cal. Ct. App. 2014).

This means that one must first identify a fact pattern that corresponds to spot zoning. If one has a situation that looks like spot zoning, the task is not complete until a second look is taken. In this second look, one must consider if the spot zoning observed is consistent with the comprehensive plan, and if local zoning officials gave due consideration to the public interest in proceeding to change the zoning in a way that resulted in spot zoning. If the local planning and zoning authorities determined that the spot zoning protected and promoted the public health, safety, welfare, and morals, then it may be permissible.

j. Subdivisions

Below is a subdivision map as recorded in the public records of Hendricks County, Indiana. The map is also known as a *plat*. The plat identifies all of the lots within the subdivision by number, indicating the size of each lot, and the location of roads and utilities. Prior to platting, this property would have been one large land parcel. Once the local government accepts the new subdivision, the plat can be recorded in the public records, and the developer can then sell lots to individual homeowners. The new legal description for any given lot will make reference to the lot number of the property as shown on the recorded plat of the subdivision in the public records.

The subdividing of land is controlled by state and local government. Subdivision controls are usually distinct from the zoning code but relate to the overall plan for community development and land regulation. Subdivision regulations have to do with subdividing land parcels and not with the regulation of land uses. The regulations can address the size and shape of lots and the infrastructure requirements for servicing the newly subdivided lots. *See generally*, *State ex rel. Anderson v. Town of Newbold*, 954 N.W.2d 323 (Wis. 2021) (landowner can be prohibited from subdividing property because the resulting lots would not meet a town's applicable minimum lot standard). In *Town of Hollywood v. Floyd*, 744 S.E.2d 161 (S.C. 2013), the court ruled in favor of the Town's stop work order against a developer of a proposed subdivision because the developer did not conduct a traffic study as required by the Town and failed to demonstrate that the subdivision traffic would not add to safety concerns on the abutting roadway. This was a case of subdivision controls being used to address the availability of proper infrastructure. Like zoning, regulation of the subdivision of land is an exercise of the state police power. Thus, local authority over the subdivision of land must be delegated from the state. Typically, subdivision regulations are separate from the zoning code.

Diagram 4.5 Subdivision Plat (Map)

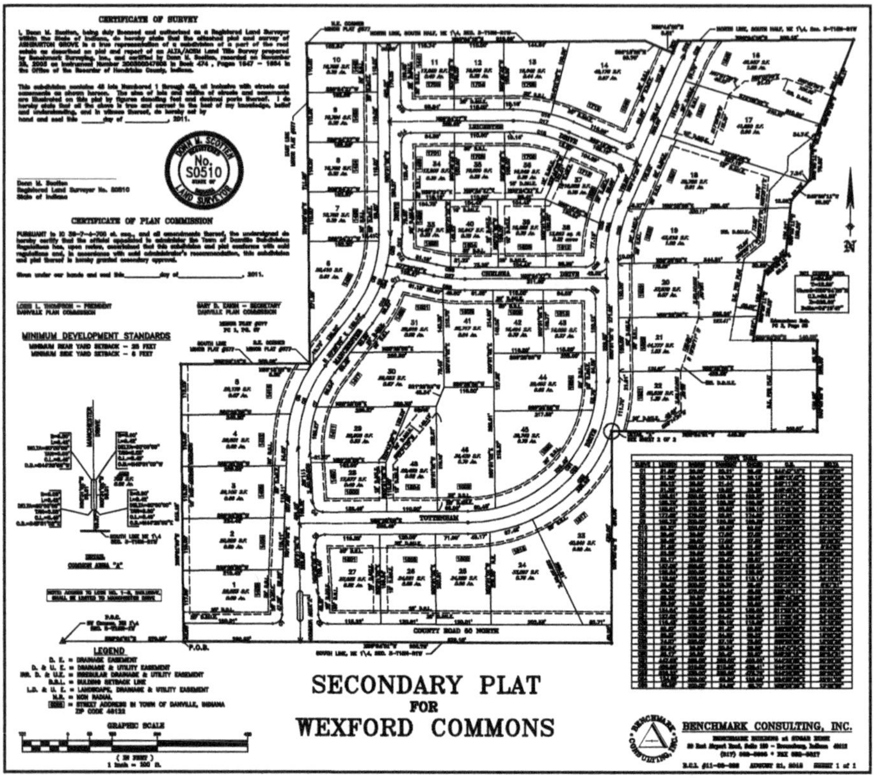

Subdivision controls apply to the sale, lease, and development of land. A subdivision is literally the division of a parcel of land into multiple parcels or lots. Subdivision controls provide local planning authorities with an ability to control land development activities and to keep track of individual land parcels for tax and other purposes. Usually, subdivision controls appear in their own section of a local government code. They are not administered by zoning boards and more often are reviewed and approved by planning boards or some other designated office within local government. In some jurisdictions, subdivision regulations are combined with zoning and construction codes and collectively referred to as *unified development codes*. This allows for a more unified approach to reviewing and regulating land development.

In subdividing land, a property owner usually prepares a plat or map of the proposed subdivision. The requirements for these plats are spelled out in the subdivision regulations. Typically, in addition to showing lot lines for the subdivided parcels, the plat must show where roads, utilities, water run-off, and other supporting infrastructure are to be located. In working toward plat approval, there may also be negotiation over the location of these property improvements and over such things as *buffers* between lots within the subdivision and as between the subdivision and neighboring properties.

Buffers may include tree and shrub plantings, fencing, and berms. All of these options mitigate the visual, noise, and light impacts of a developing property on surrounding properties. The cost of mitigating buffers is one way of internalizing the perceived externalities generated by the development of a specific property. Therefore, the buffers should be located on the developing property and not the neighboring properties. *See Hoffman v. Mayor and City Council of Baltimore*, 79 A.2d 367 (Md. 1951) (indicating that buffers must be located on the property being developed and neighboring property should not be used as a buffer in the absence of evidence that some form of buffering on adjoining property is in the public interest).

Subdivision development should be done in accordance with or consistent with the comprehensive plan. Ideally, subdivision approval is coordinated with planning and zoning. Once a subdivision plat is approved and accepted by the local government, it is recorded in the public land records of the county in which it is located. Legal descriptions of the lots within the subdivision will then refer to the legal description of the property with reference to the recorded plat of the subdivision.

Many contemporary subdivisions have shared or common elements such as greenspace, club houses, and playgrounds. Consequently, there are often a number of private rules and restrictions on shared use and obligations among property owners. These would be set out in covenants and restrictions applicable to the subdivision. In order to coordinate and enforce these various negative and affirmative obligations, it is typical that a not-for-profit entity will be put in place. This entity will typically be identified as a home owners association or H.O.A. Property owners within the subdivision will be members of the H.O.A. by virtue of their ownership, and they will vote to elect a board to administer the various rules and regulations.

Subdivisions are sometimes dealt with in a similar way to Planned Unit Developments (P.U.D.s) (discussed below). Both can be used to develop new communities.

k. Planned Unit Developments (P.U.D.s)

A Planned Unit Development (P.U.D.) is provided for in the general laws of a local jurisdiction and may be part of a comprehensive plan. The P.U.D. is not a typical zone but is generally provided for within local zoning regulations. The P.U.D. provides a mechanism for flexibility and doing mixed-use development. Recall that Euclidean zoning permits only certain categories of use in any given zoning district. So, this means we might find a single-family zone and a separate multi-family zone designated for a community. These would be distinct zones and uses. In a P.U.D., one typically finds a mix of multi-family and single-family homes along with shared amenities and green spaces. There may also be inclusion of professional, retail, and commercial uses. The P.U.D. has an approval process that includes a significant level of negotiation among developers and planning officials. Many traditional Euclidean constraints do not apply to a P.U.D., and uses within the P.U.D. develop from intensive bargaining. The P.U.D. creates a type of zone in which an area of land is set out to be governed by the requirements agreed to for the P.U.D. rather than by other applicable zoning regulations in the zoning code. In this sense, a P.U.D. functions like its own unique zone. There are, of course, requirements and criteria that govern the points of negotiation in establishing a permitted P.U.D. In other words, just because negotiation is involved does not mean that this is a purely discretionary process.

In addition to flexibility and mixed-use development opportunities, the P.U.D. provides an opportunity to negotiate for *higher density*—building more housing units per acre than the typical zoning permits. With or without higher density, a P.U.D. offers a mechanism for the *clustering* of structures and preservation of open space. For example, assume a developer has a ten-acre parcel of land. The developer might subdivide the property into ten lots of one-acre each. Assume this complies with a zoning code requirement that all single-family homes built in this neighborhood must be on lots of a one-acre minimum. The lots would have a house and a surrounding yard. This results in nice yards around each house but no large open spaces. In a P.U.D., the developer could be approved to build houses on smaller lots of one third of an acre, and to cluster the housing by placing all the units in one corner of the ten-acre project property. This arrangement could be negotiated and applied to property in a neighborhood that otherwise requires building on one-acre lots. By clustering the housing on one portion of the ten-acre parcel, the developer could subdivide that portion of the property into ten lots of one third of an acre each. This would result in each lot having a house and a much smaller yard compared to that of a one-acre lot. At the same time, the P.U.D. would also have 6 and 2/3 acres remaining in the ten-acre project. Part of the P.U.D. negotiation process would involve deciding on what could be in this open space. The collective open space could be used by all owners and occupiers of lots in the P.U.D. for such things as a park, playground, club house, pool, and walking trails. Another alternative is that the open space could be left as a nature preserve. The significance of the P.U.D. is that it can be used to create more flexibility in land use. It permits mixed-use development, and depending on how it is designed, it can provide more or less density as well as useful common space. Referencing the above example, clustering results in the same overall housing density as that of developing the ten one-acre size lots into one-acre parcels—one house per acre as computed against the total ten-acres.

In negotiating a P.U.D., there will often be a *mixed-use* element. For instance, in our above example, perhaps the planning officials will require that the ten-acre parcel include ten lots of one-third of an acre with three lots for single-family homes, three lots for two-family townhouses, and the remaining lots for four-unit quadraplex housing units. Thus, within the P.U.D., you would have both single-family and various multi-family uses. Such an arrangement is not consistent with traditional Euclidean zoning.

Within a P.U.D. there are often shared or common elements. Consequently, while the P.U.D. is a public land planning device, it often requires a number of private rules and restrictions on shared use and obligations among properties owners. These would be set out in covenants and restrictions applicable to the approved P.U.D. and recorded in the public land records. It also typically requires a variety of easements. In order to coordinate and enforce these various negative and affirmative obligations, it is typical that a not-for-profit entity will be put in place. This entity will typically be identified as a home owners association or H.O.A. Property owners within the P.U.D. will be members of the H.O.A. by virtue of their ownership, and they will vote to elect a board to administer the various rules and regulations.

In all of these situations, it is important to understand that a P.U.D. must be specifically provided for in the local land use regulations. Thus, you must locate the provisions for P.U.D.s within the authority delegated to the local jurisdiction.

1. Site Plan Review

Site plan review is a process that includes a review of development and construction plans for a project to make sure that the project meets local land planning and zoning regulations. It applies to new construction as well as new additions. Generally, site plan review will involve people from various local offices such as planning, zoning, and building code enforcement. Much of the work of site plan review is carried out through the planning department. The planning department will ensure that the project is consistent with the comprehensive plan and will work with the developer in negotiating the placement of buildings, infrastructure, ingress and egress, and buffers on the site. There is typically discretion in negotiating some of these points, so it is important for a property owner to work cooperatively with the planning department.

The process of site plan review begins with an application by the owner of the property. The application will have to meet various requirements for drawings, surveys, and detailed development plans. These plans will be reviewed by the planning board and other interested departments, and also be shared with the public at one or more public meetings.

When the planning board approves a site plan, it may be a plan that includes some conflicts with the zoning code. For example, given the shape of the lot and the goals of the planning department, there may be a planning department requirement to place a building closer to the street than the zoning setback requirements allow. A planning board may make these recommendations for site development but typically lacks the authority to change the zoning applicable to the property. In such a case, the planning board requires the property owner to petition the zoning board of appeal for a change or exception in the rules (termed a "variance"). The planning board will make a recommendation to its local zoning board of appeal asking them to provide the variance (exception) to the zoning code in order to accomplish the plan. A zoning board of appeal usually has the authority to grant variances and to interpret the zoning code. It will hold a hearing to decide if, under local and state law, a variance should be granted. The zoning board of appeal will deliberate on the planning board requirement but must make its own independent decision. It can agree with or deny the planning board request. If the zoning board agrees, then a permit for development can be issued. If the zoning board disagrees, then the property owner must go back to the planning board to determine if there is another feasible way to accomplish the development goal. It is not unusual for developers to go through multiple versions of a site plan before receiving final approval. From the point of view of a property owner/developer, each review can be costly in terms of time, professional fees, and reworking of plans to meet new requirements.

m. Alternatives to Euclidean Zoning

A baseline for understanding planning and zoning is our traditional reference to Euclidean zoning. Most importantly, this method of planning and zoning is based on dividing a jurisdiction into zones. These zones identify permitted and prohibited uses. The goal is to separate and manage uses so as to advance the public health, safety, welfare, and morals. Over the years, people have complained that strict Euclidean zoning lacks flexibility and, as a result, modifications have been introduced in many zoning codes.

In addition to changes in zoning codes over time, there have been changes in the way land planners approach their work. As zoning lawyers, we focus on the language and requirements of the zoning code no matter what approach is taken by our local planning office. Nonetheless, different approaches to planning may influence what we do in zoning. Therefore, it is helpful to have some familiarity with a few newer zoning terms and the basics of a few contemporary planning alternatives.

- *Concurrency.* This concept requires development of land uses to match the ability of local governments to provide services for the approved uses. Thus, development of single-family residential subdivisions should occur at a rate that is consistent with development of expanding roads, water and sewer lines, schools, and other public services such as police and fire protection. Concurrency is a way to manage growth. Local governments, however, may not prevent development by simply refusing to approve needed and related infrastructure. Local governments may slow down the rate of growth so that infrastructure can be built, but they must continue to make plans for developing and financing the infrastructure that is needed.
- *Form-Based Zoning.* Instead of focusing on uses, as in Euclidean zoning, form-based zoning centers on the importance of buildings and streetscapes in determining the character and livability of a community. Thus, planning considers the public facades of buildings, the bulk, mass and placement of buildings in connection to other build-

ings, the streetscape, and open space among and between buildings. In general, controlling the style, features, and placements of structures and spaces becomes more important than regulating the particular uses within these structures.

- *Incentive Zoning.* Sometimes local governments want to encourage certain types of development such as affordable housing, community playgrounds, parks, and open space. One way to encourage private parties to develop these uses is by providing incentives for them to undertake such projects. To do this, a community might use incentive zoning. This involves establishing guidelines and criteria for granting an approved list of incentives to builders to encourage them to provide the desired amenity or benefit. This might come in the form of granting a developer a density bonus permitting a building to be taller than the zoning restrictions allow, or permitting a developer to have a density bonus in order to build more units per acre than the zoning code otherwise permits. Another typical form of incentive involves providing an expedited review and approval process to a developer. This can save on project costs. These incentives and the conditions attached to them must be carefully crafted to avoid problems with the potential for being challenged as unconstitutional conditions.
- *Mixed-Use Zoning.* Mixed-use zoning permits different land uses within a given zone or within a given structure within a zone. An example might be a zone that permits commercial and retail uses at street level, and residential or office uses on upper floors of the same building. When a structure is located in a given zone, such as a commercial zone, it would be permitted to have only one use under Euclidean zoning. Permitting multiple uses in the same building, commercial and residential, is possible because of the a mixed-use zone in the zoning code.
- *Network Zoning.* Network zoning focuses on functional elements of the built environment and has been suggested as a way to think about making the built environment more accessible to people with disabilities, as well as for uses that are infrastructure heavy such as data centers. This approach favors land regulations that facilitate the safe and easy connections between and among uses. By aligning zoning with connective infrastructure, communities are better positioned for economic growth and for greater accessibility. This approach moves

away from thinking only in terms of strict zones for different uses and instead promotes organizing land use in terms of infrastructure needed to safely connect a variety of uses within and across local jurisdictions. We can think of this in terms similar to nodes, hubs, clusters, and networks; much like a computer network. In this approach, *nodes* are individualized uses that need to be connected to hubs, and clusters (a group of hubs), and ultimately to broader networks. These larger scale networks include uses that depend on such things as larger economies of scale and more integrated and secure infrastructure. Many of these connections will employ and require the coordination of smart technologies and enhanced modes of transport. These connections form networks, and these networks are focused on building complete communities at multiple scales.

- *New Urbanism.* In general, new urbanism focuses on promoting walkable communities with mixed uses including housing and retail, transportation alternatives to the automobile, increased density, green spaces, and the bringing of structures closer to the streetscape while placing parking lots behind buildings to create a greater sense of a neighborhood.
- *Performance Zoning.* This type of zoning focuses on specifically defined performance standards as a more flexible way of regulating uses. For example, instead of describing the various types of uses that can be made in a given industrial zone, the code might describe the permitted noise levels of operation, intensity of use, impact of lighting on nearby properties, and requirements for containment of water run-off in the zone. Uses that meet the performance standards would be allowed in the zone. Thus, instead of developing a list of specific permitted uses, the code would develop a list of performance standards for uses in a zone. Uses typically must also be consistent with the character of the neighborhood and surrounding properties.
- *Transect Zoning.* This is generally used with form-based zoning. Basically, it involves looking at the jurisdictional landscape of a community and dividing it into transitional zones where a form-based zoning approach can be used to create a hierarchy of uses going from the most natural or rural uses to the more dense and intense uses of an urban center. Transect zones might include zones identified in a hierarchical form ranging from natural habitat, rural, suburban, gen-

eral urban, urban center, to urban core. In each transect zone, form-based zoning would address the intensity and density of structures, and shape a landscape designed to facilitate a sense of community, neighborhood, and connectivity.

In practice, a given jurisdiction may have elements of several approaches to planning, and these may all be reflected in elements of their zoning code.

CHECKPOINTS

- **Under the Tenth Amendment to the Constitution**, any powers not explicitly granted to the federal government are reserved to the states. This is consistent with the police power authority of the states. The police power is an inherent aspect of state sovereignty. The police power can be used to regulate more than land use.
- **The police power** must be exercised in accordance with due process. In contemporary jurisprudence, due process involves two different elements: procedural due process and substantive due process.
- **Euclidean zoning** gets its name from the famous case of *Village of Euclid v. Ambler Realty Co.*, 272 U.S. 365 (1926). This case was the first to present the question of the constitutionality of zoning to the United States Supreme Court. The Court upheld the constitutionality of zoning ordinances (codes) as a valid exercise of the state police powers.
- **The key elements of Euclidean zoning**, as established in the case include: the demarcation of zoning districts that authorize a local government to manage and coordinate land use; a hierarchy among the permitted uses; cumulative zoning based on this hierarchy; and uses permitted in a zone are "as of right."
- **The power to zone** is exercised in accordance with the police power and pursuant to a comprehensive plan. When a zoning regulation is passed by a local legislature, it must be rational using a fairly debatable standard of review.
- **Rational as applied.** When zoning regulations are applied to a particular property, they must be rational as applied. And the drawing of district lines, the categories of uses, and other elements in the zoning code must be evaluated on a rational basis standard.

- **Accessory uses** are uses that are *customary and incidental* to the primary use that is permitted under the land use regulations.
- **A conditional use**, or what is sometimes referred to as a special use, is a use permitted in a zone provided that certain conditions are met. A drive-through dining facility and a drive-through bank are prime examples of uses requiring conditional use permits to operate in a zone.
- **The floating zone** starts out as a zone that is not fixed on a zoning map. Instead, it is a zone approved by legislative act that establishes certain criteria for a land use. Its location is fixed at a later date.
- **Overlay zones** are anchored to specific lands within a jurisdiction. In essence, they establish multiple zoning districts over the same land.
- **Aesthetic zoning** is permissive to protect the public welfare, but it must be based on clear criteria and be applied in a way that is not arbitrary or capricious.
- **Historic districts** and landmark preservation acts are forms of aesthetic zoning. State and local governments may regulate land uses for aesthetic reasons under their police power authority.
- **Spot zoning** is generally not permitted. Spot zoning happens when one or a few properties are singled out for zoning changes that are not applied to surrounding properties.
- **Subdivision controls** are usually distinct from the zoning code but relate to the overall plan for community development and land regulation.
- **The Planned Unit Development (P.U.D.)** provides a mechanism for flexibility and doing mixed-use development.
- **Site Plan Review** is a process that includes a review of development and construction plans for a project to make sure that the project meets local land planning and zoning regulations.
- **Alternatives to Euclidean zoning.** A baseline for understanding planning and zoning is our traditional reference to Euclidean zoning. There are, however, newer forms of zoning to be aware of and they include: zoning concurrency, form-based zoning, incentive zoning, mixed use zoning, network zoning, new urbanism, performance zoning, and transect zoning.

CHAPTER 5

Variances and Other Standard Zoning Concepts

ROADMAP

- Area Variances
- Use Variances
- Public Utility Variances
- Non-Conforming Uses
- Vesting
- Contract Zoning
- Development Agreements

Planning and zoning involve the regulation and control of land uses. As we have discussed, these land regulations must be applied uniformly to properties within a given zoning district. In other words, the rules and requirements applicable to single-family residential properties should be applied uniformly to all such properties within a given designated zoning district. Variations can be established as between zones, such as between a Residential-1 zone and a Residential-2 zone, but within each zone, there should be uniformity and consistency with respect to the delineated rules and regulations. Seeking an exception to the required regulations is referred to as a variance. There are two primary categories of variances; area variances and use variances.

In addition, land regulations may change over time to reflect changing circumstances and new concerns about public health, safety, welfare, and morals.

The need for change raises related questions with respect to the problem of current legal uses becoming non-conforming, and the determination of when development rights under a given version of the regulations become vested. Two methods that have been used to try and address the uncertainty of potential regulatory changes during a long-term development project are *contract zoning* (generally, not permitted) and the use of *development agreements* (generally permitted). In this chapter, we discuss these and related concepts.

a. Area Variances

As a matter of good practice and due process, zoning and planning codes generally provide a basis for seeking relief from a regulation or requirement if a particular property or property owner experiences *practical difficulty* or an *undue and unique hardship* in complying with the requirements of the code due to certain circumstances typically not of the property owner's own making. The seeking of relief from a code requirement involves a petition for a variance. Relief based on a practical difficulty in complying with a land regulation is referred to as an *area variance*. An area variance involves a request for an exception from regulations covering such things as the setback distance between a structure and a road or a property line, the amount of lot coverage occupied by a structure, and the height of a structure. *See Mastandrea v. North*, 760 A.2d 677 (Md. 2000) (court upheld an area variance granted by the town for a wheelchair accessible path on Mastandrea's property because the decision was rational and supported by competent evidence on the record). Traditionally, an area variance, once granted, runs with the land. This means that the variance is not personal to the current property owner and that it continues to the benefit of future owners and assignees of the property.

In contemporary legal practice, many states have attempted to add more clarity and objectivity to the process of requesting and evaluating an area variance. They have done this by specifying criteria to be considered in addressing the traditional requirement for finding practical difficulty. As one example, consider New York. The New York criteria are similar to those used in other states.

In granting a petition for an *area variance* under New York law, the applicant must address five criteria (identified below). The applicant should present evidence in support of the petition for a *variance*. This evidence should include photos of the property and surrounding neighborhood, letters from neighbors, land surveys, and whatever other evidence might be appropriate in terms of addressing each of the criteria. In granting an area variance, a zoning board of appeal must determine that, "on balance," the benefits to the applicant outweigh the detriments to the community. The five criteria for an *area variance* are:

1) Whether an undesirable change will be produced in the character of the neighborhood or a detriment to nearby properties will be created by granting the area variance;
2) Whether the benefits sought by the applicant can be achieved by some method feasible for the applicant to pursue, other than the area variance;
3) Whether the requested variance is substantial;
4) Whether the proposed variance will have an adverse effect or impact on the physical or environmental conditions in the neighborhood or district; and,
5) Whether the alleged difficulty was self-created, which consideration shall be relevant to the decision of the board of appeals, but shall not necessarily preclude the granting of the area variance.

While each of the criteria must be addressed, the area variance involves a balancing test, and no single criteria is determinative. A rational decision based on the record must support the granting of an area variance. The burden of establishing the evidence as to each of the criteria is on the property owner seeking the variance.

The first element regarding an undesirable change in the neighborhood typically requires input from neighbors, architects, and realtors as to how a change might impact the look of the neighborhood and the value of the properties. The second element requires the applicant to explore options to the requested variance and to explain why alternative ways of achieving their goals are undesirable or impracticable. The third element is often problematic. What does it mean to be "substantial"? Explanations must be offered as to why the requested variance should not be considered substantial. The fourth element relates to an adverse impact on neighboring properties or the environment. An example might be a situation where a party wants to add an addition to a home, and if the proposed addition is constructed, the home will direct water drainage onto a neighboring property in a detrimental way. The fifth element is one that is typically answered in the affirmative. Typically, the property owner is voluntarily taking on a proposed change to the property (like adding a room, a deck or a pool). Difficulties in executing these desired improvements are self-created. No one is forcing them to do it. On the other hand, if the shape of the lot is odd and difficult to build on in compliance with the code, or if the lot has a difficult natural topography requiring some adjustment to the application of the code to the given lot, then these would be examples of difficulties that are not self-created.

Importantly, it is up to the applicant to provide the supporting evidence and to carry the burden in seeking to obtain an area variance. This means that the property owner/applicant must make sure to get good quality and sufficient evidence on the record in support of their petition for a variance. Failing to do this can lead to a denial of the petition for a variance. If a denial is appealed to court, a court will give deference to the findings of the zoning board of appeal.

In *Bonadonna v. Board of Zoning Appeals of Upper Brookville*, 198 N.Y.S.3d 368 (N.Y. App. Div. 2023), the court decided in favor of the zoning board in its denial of a property owner's petition for an area variance. The case involved a property owner seeking to install fencing on the property at a height exceeding the limits set out in the zoning ordinance. The property owner pointed out that other nearby properties had fencing exceeding the height restrictions of the code and explained the need for the fencing on his property. The zoning board of appeal considered the petition and applied the factors for an area variance. Based on balancing the factors, the zoning board denied the petition for the area variance, and the property owner appealed the determination to the trial court, and ultimately to the appellate division. On appeal, the decision of the zoning board was upheld. The court said that the decisions of a zoning board should be given deference so long as there is no clear error, the decision is not arbitrary or capricious, and it has support in the record. Here they found no reason to upset the decision of the zoning board. The court indicated that the property owner submitted no evidence as to when the fences on neighboring properties were constructed. For example, the neighboring fences could have been constructed prior to the current zoning code and before the current code height restrictions. In essence, the property owner did not carry the burden of establishing the justification for the variance being sought. Put another way, the court concluded that the relevant factors had been considered, and that the zoning board issued a written decision that was rational and supported by evidence in the record. Therefore, there was no reason for the court to set aside the decision of the zoning board. Deference was given to the decision of the zoning board in its decision to deny the variance. The decision of the zoning board of appeal was upheld.

b. Use Variances

A use variance involves a petition to allow *a use* that is otherwise not permitted by the zoning code. A use variance is more difficult to obtain than an area variance. A use variance might involve a petition to change the designated use of a property to multi-family residential when it is located within a single-family zone. Or it might concern a petition for making a residential property available for commercial use even though it is currently situated within a residential zone. As with area variances, use variances, if granted, run with the land. Traditionally, a *use variance* requires a property owner to demonstrate an undue and unique hardship resulting from the application of the current code to her property.

In contemporary legal practice, many states have attempted to add more clarity and objectivity to the process of requesting and evaluating a use variance. They have done this by specifying criteria to be considered in addressing the traditional requirement for finding an undue and unique hardship. As one example, consider New York. A *use variance* generally requires that a property owner demonstrate that the permitted uses under the zoning code impose an undue and unique hardship with respect to her property. The New York criteria are similar to the criteria used in other states. In New York, there are four established criteria used to evaluate a petition for a use variance. In order to obtain a use variance under New York law, a zoning board of appeal must find in favor of the property owner on each and every one of the four identified criteria. This is not a balancing test as used for an area variance. The criteria for a *use variance* in New York are:

1) The applicant cannot realize a reasonable return [considering every permitted use of the property], provided that lack of return is substantial as demonstrated by competent financial evidence;
2) The alleged hardship relating to the property in question is unique and does not apply to a substantial portion of the district or neighborhood;
3) The required use variance, if granted will not alter the essential character of the neighborhood; and

4) The alleged hardship has not been self-created.

Only if a favorable determination is made for the property owner as to each and every one of the four criteria can a use variance be granted. Thus, the use variance does not involve a balancing test. As with an area variance, the burden is on the property owner seeking the variance, and a decision either supporting or denying the request must be rational and supported by evidence on the record.

For a use variance, the property owner must demonstrate a unique hardship. This means demonstrating that other properties do not experience the same or a similar identified hardship. It must also be shown that the granting of a requested use variance will not change the essential character of the neighborhood. Furthermore, a use variance cannot be granted if the hardship complained of is self-created. For instance, if the property owner does not have to undertake the project that she has in mind and can nonetheless make a reasonable use of the property, then her hardship is self-created. This is often a key stumbling block to obtaining a use variance. A second major hurdle to overcome involves the requirement that the applicant demonstrate that it cannot realize a reasonable return for any of the permitted uses of the property—not just the most desirable use of the property. In this context, a reasonable return might be low compared to other options, perhaps as low as 20% of what might be earned by an ability to change the use on the property. Reasonableness is contextual, just as it is in takings law cases, where diminution of value can be quite high and still not be a taking because the property owner still has a viable use that provides a reasonable return.

In *Village Board of Fayetteville v. Jarrold*, 53 N.Y.2d 254, 423 N.E.2d 385 (N.Y. Ct. App. 1981), New York's highest court held that proof of inability to realize a reasonable return must be shown by *dollars and cents proof*. The case involved a petition for a use variance to permit a commercial activity on a property zoned for residential use. The petitioner presented the opinion of an architect and a real estate broker who each testified that the permitted residential use was not a good use of the property and that using the property for a residential use would entail certain special costs that would make it unfeasible. The court, however, found this to be insufficient. The court wanted dollars and cents proof that none of the permitted uses in this zone could provide a reasonable return. Dollars and cents proof includes presenting information on actual costs, market evaluations, appraisals, and financials. It is not enough to offer general and conclusory opinions as to the value.

c. Public Utility Variance

In some jurisdictions, public utilities can apply for area and use variances under a lesser standard than normally applies to other petitioners. For a public utility, the limitations imposed by local regulations are generally more flexible. The first step is to determine if the application for the variance is for a public utility.

Characteristics to evaluate for determining if an entity is a public utility include (1) the essential nature of the services offered to the public, (2) the necessity of providing the services, and (3) the presence of public regulation to ensure the reliability, accessibility, and affordability of the service. Common examples of public utilities can include cell towers, gas pipelines, wind farms, solar farms, and water and sewer infrastructure. When a public utility can show that a requested variance is a public necessity for it to render safe and adequate service, and that there are compelling reasons to support the variance, it should be granted. *See, e.g., Cellular Tel. Co. v. Rosenberg*, 82 N.Y.2d 364, 624 N.E.2d 990 (1993); *In re Freepoint Solar LLC v. Town of Athens Zoning Bd. of Appeals*, 224 N.Y.S.3d 219 (App. Div. 2024). In such situations, the public utility typically has the burden in its request for a variance, and it must demonstrate a significant hardship or difficulty in complying with the code requirements.

Some jurisdictions may simply exempt public utilities from local zoning regulation and leave regulation up to the state. Consequently, it is important to determine if a petitioner for a variance is a public utility and to confirm treatment of public utilities under state and local planning and zoning regulations.

d. Non-Conforming Uses

A *non-conforming use* is a use that is not in compliance with permitted zoning regulations. Generally, nonconforming uses are not permitted. The fact that a use is non-conforming, however, does not necessarily make it an illegal use. Many non-conforming uses are legal. These are sometimes referred to as legal non-conforming uses. A non-conforming use may arise in several ways. First, a property owner might just start making a use of her property that is not permitted by the zoning code. This would be an illegal non-conforming use. Second, there could be a change in the zoning code that makes a current use non-conforming under the new regulations. Third, non-conformity may be granted under a variance. And fourth, non-conformity may be granted as a reasonable accommodation or modification to a person with a disability under our applicable disability laws.

With the exception of the situation of a property owner just making an impermissible use of the property without approval, non-conforming uses are uses that are legal at the outset but then become inconsistent with updated land regulations and by the granting of exceptions. The updates and revisions to land regulation may reflect changes in surrounding uses and properties or plans for new uses to be developed in the future. Granting of exceptions (variances and accommodations) result, in certain properties being non-conforming with respect to other properties within the same zone, but when done properly, they actually modify the zoning on that property.

When a non-conforming use exists, the question arises as to how long it can continue. Generally, the continuation of a non-conforming use is disfavored, and the ultimate goal is to eventually discontinue such uses and have everything up to code. At the same time, property owners have property rights and expectations with respect to those rights and their property-based investments. If zoning and land use regulations change too dramatically, they might result in the claim of a taking under the Fifth Amendment to the U.S. Constitution. This would be the case if a zoning change eliminated all viable uses of the property and left the property owner with only nominal value. Generally, this is not the case. Zoning code revisions might more typically change the setbacks applicable to a lot or amend some of the uses permitted within a given zone.

As an example, consider a neighborhood with homes that were all originally built with a required twenty-foot setback requirement from the road. As the neighborhood and surrounding area changed, the local government determined that a thirty-foot setback is safer and better. With a change in the zoning code to thirty feet, all of the previously built homes are rendered non-conforming if they are closer than thirty feet to the road, even though they were all conforming prior to the code change. Naturally, it is difficult or impossible to move all of these houses further back from the road, thus they will all be non-conforming.

In order to prevent hardship and avoid a potential takings claim, these non-conforming uses are typically protected under a "*grandfather*" provision. A grandfather provision applies to a use that was conforming prior to the zoning change. It permits the use to continue under a theory of the property owner having a *vested right* to continue the use. The use is said to be "grandfathered in." Moreover, the sale or lease of the property to another who continues the same use generally does not extinguish the legal non-conforming use.

This does not necessarily mean that the non-conforming use will be permitted to continue indefinitely. A number of local jurisdictions include provisions in their planning and zoning regulations for a non-conforming use to be extinguished in the event that the non-conforming use is *abandoned*. There are two general approaches to abandonment. The first involves a factual determination that the property owner intends to relinquish a permitted non-conforming use coupled with an overt act in furtherance of such an intent. In an effort to make the determination more clear cut, some jurisdictions provide a statutory definition of abandonment. This might be defined as discontinuance of the non-conforming use for a stated period of time, without a need to demonstrate intent to abandon. So, for example, assume in time period one, a property owner lawfully operates a small retail shop on the ground level of his building and lives on the second floor. Under the code, it is a conforming use. Several years later, the neighborhood is changing, and the city adopts a new code eliminating retail uses in properties that are also used as residential homes. This change makes the prior use a non-conforming use, but it may continue under a grandfather provision. Assume that the city also has a provision that says that non-use of a non-conforming use for a period of 90 days shall be considered abandonment of the use. If the property owner shuts down her retail shop for four months while trying to sell the property and a new buyer purchases the property, the non-conforming retail use is eliminated, because it is a non-conforming use that was abandoned. Thus, the new owner cannot now operate a retail shop on the ground level. Of course, the new owner/buyer could petition for a use variance to get a retail use permitted, but such a variance is unlikely to be granted because non-conforming uses are supposed to be extinguished over time. This is a fundamental proposition, given that the land regulations have been changed in order to protect the public health, safety, welfare, and morals. It would be contradictory to then reinstate an extinguished use in the face of new regulations that have essentially declared the prior use to be incompatible with the public health, safety, welfare, and morals.

A second method for extinguishing non-conforming uses is through *amortization*. An amortization provision in a code creates a period of time in which an owner of a non-conforming use may continue operation of the non-conforming use but sets a limit on the time period. One way to think of it is as a grace period for continuing operation of the use. The legal basis of amortization is the protection of a property owner's reasonable investment-backed expectations. This is a factor in considering the question of a regulatory taking under the Fifth Amendment. Basically, an amortization period attempts to provide a reasonable period of time for the property owners to recover a reasonable amount on their investment. These amortization periods may be three years, five years, or more. The specific enabling legislation will provide a time limit and criteria for its application. Amortization establishes a clock, so to speak, for knowing when a particular non-conforming use will be extinguished.

A non-conforming use may also arise from the granting of a variance or a reasonable accommodation or modification to a person with a disability under our disability laws. A variance runs with the land and makes a non-conformity legal when granted. A reasonable accommodation or modification is personal and is determined on a case-by-case basis. As an example, a reasonable accommodation may permit a ramp to extend into a front yard setback in violation of the zoning code in order to accommodate a wheelchair user. An accommodation is not a variance. A variance runs with the land. A reasonable accommodation is personal, and it does not run with the land. A non-conforming use resulting from the granting of a reasonable accommodation should remain in effect only so long as the person entitled to the accommodation resides on the property and continues to need the accommodation.

While non-conforming uses may generally continue, there are limitations with respect to such uses. In general, one cannot expand a non-conforming use. So, in our earlier example of the property owner with a retail space on the ground floor and a dwelling unit on the second floor, he cannot expand the size, density or capacity of the non-conforming retail space after the zoning has changed to prohibit that use. Likewise, the intensity of that use cannot be increased. The ability to do upgrades and improvements of the use are also limited. While some basic safety enhancements are probably going to be permitted, the entire point of limiting upgrades and improvements is to eventually have the non-conforming use eliminated at that location. Some examples of upgrade issues might include; bringing in new and expanded refrigeration units for drinks sold in a non-conforming retail space, or paving over what has traditionally been a dirt and gravel parking lot. An issue may also arise if one was originally serving sliced pizza at the counter for takeout and after this became a non-conforming use, the owner decided to add some indoor or outdoor seating for customers.

Illustrative cases dealing with nonconforming uses include *Cigarrhilha v. City of Providence*, 64 A.3d 1208 (R.I. 2013) (zoning changed from permitting three-family to two-family homes in the zone), *Edelhertz v. City of Middletown*, 943 F. Supp. 2d 388 (S.D.N.Y. 2012) (zoning change restricted the number of units in non-owner occupied buildings and included a five-year amortization provision that was upheld), and *Giurleo v. McCusker*, 06 MISC 326990, 2010 Mass. LCR LEXIS 44 (Mass. Land Ct. Apr. 9, 2010) (a special permit was properly issued under the zoning ordinance in question to reconstruct and extend a non-conforming structure).

Another area of concern with non-conforming uses involves partial destruction of the premises. For example, if a person has a non-conforming retail space and there is a fire that causes damage to 10% of the property, can they rebuild it? What if the damage is 25% or 50%? And when rebuilding, can rebuilding include updates and renovations to the property that might otherwise not be permitted? In the absence of regulatory criteria on these questions, one will find various answers to the questions in looking at the decisions of different jurisdictions.

e. Vesting

When a property right becomes fixed, it is said to be *vested*. Vested property rights are protected by the Fifth Amendment's Takings Clause. A significant issue in a planning and zoning context concerns determining when a property interest becomes vested with respect to planning and zoning regulations. The development of land often takes a considerable amount of time and money, especially in the case of larger scale real estate developments. Many resources must be invested in property development over extended time periods. The question and risk that arises is one of figuring out how best to deal with the possibility of changes in the zoning and planning code during the development process.

The problem is that an owner of property is subject to zoning regulations established pursuant to the exercise of the police power. *See Village of Euclid v. Ambler Realty Co.*, 272 U.S. 365 (1926). And these regulations can change. Thus, the question arises as to the point in the planning and development process when a property owner can have certainty as to the rules applicable to her investment. If the rules change after a project is commenced, it might be stopped by local authorities before it is completed because it will no longer be in compliance with the newest rules. If the project is completed under the prior rules, it is a non-conforming use and will be subject to limitations applicable to non-conforming uses.

The general rule is that in the absence of a legislative rule to the contrary, a change in the zoning regulations occurring before a project is complete has retroactive application to the start of the project. Thus, the property owner has the risk of a change in the rules during the development process. This risk adds uncertainty and raises the cost of completing the project (a greater return on investment will be required to account for the risk of uncertainty). The longer the timeline for a development project, the greater the risk. One rationale for this rule is that zoning and zoning changes are done pursuant to the police power in order to protect the public health, safety, welfare, and morals. This being the case, changes in the zoning rules reflect legislative decisions about the public interest relative to the private interests of individuals. Consequently, it is proper to acknowledge the legislative determination and impose the updated zoning rules even though it may impose an inconvenience and cost on the property owner.

This rule has not been without some controversy. The counter rule is that the property owner should be able to rely on the rules as they were at the time of an application for a subdivision approval or a building permit, so long as the application complies with all of the requirements in force at the time of application. Exceptions to this counter rule are when a property owner is aware of pending changes at the time of submitting an application, and when the local jurisdictional government can show a compelling reason for exercising the police power retroactively to the date of application. *See Western Land Equities, Inc. v. City of Logan*, 617 P.2d 388 (Utah, 1980).

When applying the counter rule in support of a property owner, courts often rely on some form of *zoning estoppel*.

Quoting from the decision in *Western Equities*:

> The focus of zoning estoppel is primarily upon the conduct and interests of the property owner. The main inquiry is whether there has been substantial reliance by the owner on governmental actions related to the superseded zoning that permitted the proposed use. The concern underlying this approach is the economic hardship that would be imposed on a property owner whose development plans are thwarted. Some courts hold that before a permit is issued no action of the owner is sufficient reliance to bar application of changes in zoning ordinances because

there has been no governmental act sufficient to support an estoppel. Accordingly, a landowner is held to have no vested right in existing or anticipated zoning....

Generally, "substantial reliance" is determined by various tests employed by the courts—for example, the set quantum test, the proportionate test, and a balancing test. The *set quantum test* [italics added], used by the majority of courts, determines that an owner is entitled to relief from new, prohibitory zoning if he has changed his position beyond a certain point, measured quantitatively. A related test is the *proportionate test* [italics added], which determines the percentage of money spent or obligations incurred before the zoning change as compared with the total cost. The problem with both of these tests is that there is no predictable point short of adjudication which separates reliance that is less than "substantial" from the reliance sufficient to result in a vested right or to support an estoppel.

The *balancing test* [italics added], although likely to produce a more fair outcome in a particular case, also results in little predictability. The test weighs the owner's interest in developing his property and the reasonableness of his proposed use against the interests of public health, safety, morals, or general welfare. If the gain to the public is small when compared to the hardship that would accrue to the property owner, the actions of the owner in preparation for development according to a formerly permitted use may be seen as sufficiently substantial to justify the issuance of a permit or continuation of development despite an amendment to the zoning ordinances.

An additional requirement generally considered in zoning estoppel cases is that of the existence of some physical construction as an element of substantial reliance. Preconstruction activities such as the execution of architectural drawings or the clearing of land and widening of roads are not sufficient to create a vested right, nor generally are activities that are not exclusively related to the proposed project.

Western Land Equities, Inc. v. City of Logan, 617 P.2d 388, 392–93 (Utah 1980).

In addition to the various tests for vesting discussed in this case, many planning and zoning professionals will speak in terms of an *early vesting* jurisdiction or a *late vesting* jurisdiction. An early vesting jurisdiction might be one that has a rule that vesting occurs when a proper application is filed. A late vesting jurisdiction might be one that holds that vesting does not occur until the final certificate of occupancy is issued. There are different events along the timeline of a real estate development project that can be identified and used as a "time certain" event at which vesting occurs. The value of a fixed date for vesting (either early or late) is that it is easier to work with than a balancing test that often results in litigation.

A jurisdiction that picks a specific event, such as filing of an application, an event that comes early in the process, is a jurisdiction with early vesting. A jurisdiction that picks an event that comes late in the process, such as issuing a final certificate of occupancy, is a late vesting jurisdiction. The earlier vesting takes place, the lower the risk of change to the real estate developer. A clear vesting rule facilities planning and predictability. This enables property owners and communities to use their economic resources more wisely by avoiding unnecessary risks and cost in property development.

f. Contract Zoning

Sometimes property owners undertake long-term projects that may be subject to zoning changes and amendments during the time needed to complete development. When zoning requirements change during the development process, it can disrupt plans and destroy investment expectations. The possibility of zoning changes during development involves risk, and risk is a cost. Consequently, property owners will try to reduce the risk of zoning changes and amendments. One idea is to contract with local government authorities in order to obtain a promise that the local government will not make changes to the zoning requirements after a date certain. Usually, property owners desire the date certain to be the date that final plans in compliance with the code are submitted. Sometimes local governments agree to such contractual arrangements. The question that arises is one of the legalities of such contracts.

In general, courts have not favored contract zoning. It is typically viewed as an effort to forgo the legitimate exercise of the police power in order to benefit an individual property owner. The parties entering into these contracts cannot curtail the exercise of the police power by standards of contract law. The police power is part of our constitutional framework and of our legal tradition; private contract law cannot displace this function of state and local government. A case that makes this point clear is that of *Carlino v. Whitpain Investors*, 453 A.2d 1385 (Pa. 1982).

In *Carlino*, the court wrote:

> The concept of contractually conditioned zoning advanced by appellants lacks precedent in this Commonwealth, and authorities elsewhere differ with respect to whether to accord the concept validity. The proposition has long been recognized in this Commonwealth that individuals cannot, by contract, abridge police powers which protect the general welfare and public interest. "Where the rights of individuals under a contract which would otherwise be perfectly valid are in conflict with the 'general well-being of the State,' the rights of the individuals must give way to the general welfare." The police power of municipalities cannot be subjected to agreements which restrict or condition zoning district classifications as to particular properties....
>
> Zoning is an exercise of the police power to serve the common good and general welfare. It is elementary that the legislative function may not be surrendered or curtailed by bargain or its exercise controlled by the considerations which enter into the law of contracts....

Id. at 1387–88 (citations omitted).

g. Development Agreements

While similar in many ways to contract zoning, development agreements are not considered to be contracts and are not governed by contract law. They do, however, seek to accomplish a similar objective. The objective is to stabilize the planning and zoning requirements for a development project so that it will be more predictable. It does this by "locking-in" a reasonable expectation that zoning will not change during the course of development unless there is a clear need for it to change in order to protect the public health, safety, welfare, and morals. Should the government have reason to change the applicable zoning, the government cannot be sued under contract law for violating a "contract" agreement because a development agreement is not a contract. Legal actions and remedies provided for under contract law are not directly applicable.

Development agreements can include terms for freezing zoning requirements for a limited period of time when the local government determines that it is in the public interest to do so. Development agreements should be supported by a recitation of facts and circumstances that support the freeze as being in the public interest. The development agreements must also retain an ability for the local government to change the zoning if there is a determination that a change is needed to protect the public. If properly drafted, they are distinguishable from contract zoning and are legal. *See Santa Margarita Area Residents Together v. San Luis Obispo County*, 100 Cal. Rptr. 2d 740 (Cal. Ct. App. 2000).

Frequently, development agreements cover matters that go beyond freezing the planning and zoning requirements. Often, development agreements will cover a range of issues important to the property developer and the community. The agreement may include commitments for building or improving greenspace and establishing job training and employment opportunities for community members in doing work on the project. These additional provisions establish the public interest in negotiating for more stability and predictability for the developer by temporarily freezing the applicable planning and zoning regulations.

CHECKPOINTS

- **Area Variance.** Relief based on a practical difficulty in complying with a land regulation is referred to as an area variance. An area variance involves a request for an exception from regulations covering such things as the setback distance between a structure and a road or a property line, the amount of lot coverage occupied by a structure, and the height of a structure.
- **Use Variance.** A use variance involves a petition to allow *a use* that is otherwise not permitted by the zoning code. Traditionally, a use variance requires a demonstration by the property owner of an undue and unique hardship resulting from the application of the current code to her property.
- **Public Utility Variance.** Public utilities are often either exempted or subject to different standards for variances.
- **Run with the land.** Variances (both area and use) when granted, run with the land and benefit future owners and assignees.
- **Reasonable accommodations and modifications** under our disability laws are personal. As such they do not run with the land.
- **Non-Conforming Use.** A non-conforming use is a use that is not in compliance with permitted zoning regulations. Generally, non-conforming uses are not permitted. The fact that a use is non-

conforming, however, does not necessarily make it an illegal use. A non-conforming use may continue under a "grandfather" provision but will have limitations on its extent and scope. These limitations may include an inability to expand the non-conforming use or to increase the intensity of the use. It may also limit remodeling and rebuilding in the event of a need to repair.

- **Origin of non-conforming uses.** A change in a zoning code may make previous permitted uses non-conforming. A property that has been granted a zoning variance or an exception under disability law may be non-conforming based on the exception granted.
- **Amortization.** A zoning code may establish a rule or a set time at which a non-conforming use expires and must be terminated. The non-conforming use is permitted to continue for a period of time and this time is supposed to provide the property owner with some reasonable return on their property investment such that a taking does not occur.
- **Vesting.** Vested property rights are protected by the Fifth Amendment to the Constitution. Developers are concerned that projects that take an extended period of time to build might have the zoning and planning regulations change in the middle of a project. This can result in the need for costly changes to a project and time delays. These potential problems add to costs and undermine the profitability of the original project plan. Consequently, property owners seek to have clarity and certainty as to when their property rights are fixed (vested) under the applicable set of rules and regulations.
- **Early Vesting and Late Vesting.** Local governments have developed different rules for determining when a property owner's rights are vested. Generally, early vesting jurisdictions have rules that vest the property owner's development rights in the regulations in place at the time a full application and set of plans are officially submitted to the planning and zoning office showing a project in compliance with the current code. Late vesting jurisdictions generally fix the point of vesting much later. This might be after a building permit is issued or after a certificate of occupancy is issued.
- **Contract Zoning.** Contract zoning is when a developer tries to enter into a binding contract with a local government wherein the local government agrees not to change the zoning once the project

is approved. In general, courts have not favored contract zoning. It is typically viewed as an effort to forgo the legitimate exercise of the police power in order to benefit an individual property owner.

- **Development Agreements.** While similar in many ways to contract zoning, development agreements are not considered to be contracts and are not governed by contract law. They do, however, seek to accomplish a similar objective. They "freeze" land regulation as of a certain date but also reserve the power of the local government to change the regulation on a finding of a need to protect the public health, safety, welfare, and morals. Development agreements frequently cover subject matter beyond the freezing of land regulation.

CHAPTER 6

Limits on Zoning Regulation—Regulations that "Go Too Far"

ROADMAP

- Limiting the Police Power
- Due Process
- Equal Protection
- Discrimination
    - Disparate Treatment
    - Disparate Impact
    - Denial of a Reasonable Accommodation or Modification
- Takings

The power of government to regulate is not unlimited. In our constitutional structure there are limits on the exercise of the police power. This chapter addresses limitations on the police power such as those provided by the requirements of due process, equal protection, and the Takings Clause.

a. Limiting the Police Power

Public land regulation finds justification in the lawful exercise of the police power. This requires that the police power be asserted to protect the public health, safety, welfare, and morals. This means that the police power cannot be exercised to benefit a single individual. There must be a public element to proper police power regulation. Notably, the line between the legitimate and illegitimate exercise of the police power is not clearly defined and may vary with the circumstances. *See Village of Euclid v. Ambler Realty Co.*, 272 U.S. 365 (1926). Thus, some regulations that might be proper in an urban environment may not be proper in a rural setting, and vice versa.

While the Due Process Clause and the Takings Clause protect an individual's property rights, the meaning of these property rights is subject to change over time. As explained in *Euclid*,

> ... with the great increase and concentration of population, problems have developed, and constantly are developing, which require, and will continue to require, additional restrictions in respect of the use and occupation of private lands in urban communities. Regulations, the wisdom, necessity, and validity of which, as applied to existing conditions, are so apparent that they are now uniformly sustained, a century ago, or even half a century ago, probably would have been rejected as arbitrary and oppressive. Such regulations are sustained, under the complex conditions of our day, for reasons analogous to those which justify traffic regulations, which, before the advent of automobiles and rapid transit street railways, would have been condemned as fatally arbitrary and unreasonable. And in this there is no inconsistency, for, while the meaning of constitutional guaranties never varies, the scope of their application must expand or contract to meet the new and different conditions which are constantly coming within the field of their operation. In a changing world it is impossible that it should be otherwise. But although a degree of elasticity is thus imparted, not to the meaning, but to the application of constitutional principles, statutes and ordinances, which, after giving due weight to the new conditions, are found clearly not to conform to the Constitution, of course, must fall.

272 U.S. at 386–87.

This is a complicated statement because it offers no simple rule. Our fundamental rights in property are guaranteed and never vary, but the meaning of these rights is subject to modification and adjustment. So, we have constitutional protection of property rights but the meaning, scope, and extent of defining what property is, may be changed over time to account for new conditions, circumstances, and cultural understandings. Holding this idea in mind, it is important to remember that property rights are generally defined by state law, and federal constitutional law protects those rights from unlawful government interference and unreasonable diminution in value. Thus, the Fifth Amendment protection of property from a taking remains constant, but the underlying property right of an individual is subject to change over time. A point to consider here is that of vested rights. Property development and ownership are often very expensive, and people make major investments in property based on certain expectations. Given the nature of investment and of social and psychological attachment that accompanies property, changes in the law should not generally come as a surprise or be such as to undermine reasonable investment-backed expectations. In other words, a property owner should have some legitimate expectations as to the stability and predictability of their property rights. This facilitates investment and promotes commitment to civil government.

b. Due Process

Traditionally, property rights are protected under due process. The due process protection of property is consistent with common law tradition and is embedded within the Constitution. Due process is provided for in common law, and in the Fifth and Fourteenth Amendments to the Constitution (the Fourteenth Amendment makes due process applicable to the states). *See Pennsylvania Coal Co. v. Mahon*, 260 U.S. 393 (1922); *Penn Central Transportation Co. v. City of New York*, 438 U.S. 104 (1978); *Murr v. Wisconsin*, 582 U.S. 383 (2017).

There are two parts to due process—substantive and procedural. Substantive due process protects one's right to property, whereas procedural due process addresses the requirements for regulating property rights. Under substantive due process, a property owner has the right to use property for any lawful use so long as no harm is done to others. *See generally Pennsylvania Coal*. This is traditionally a rule that limits private land uses to those uses that do not impose uncompensated externalities and spillover effects on surrounding properties. The legal ground for regulating impermissible uses traditionally arose out of actions in trespass and nuisance. Both such actions proceed on a fact specific and case-by-case basis.

Zoning law extended the basis for regulation such that the police power can be used to protect the public health, safety, welfare, and morals even when a nuisance or trespass is not present. Due process protection arguments continue to be robust but must be framed in terms of the permissibility of regulation so long as the regulation does not "go too far." This question of "going too far" has been continuously litigated since the *Euclid* case. We see issues arise most notably in due process cases but also in regulatory takings law cases. In these regulatory cases, we specifically focus on the extent that regulation interferes with established property rights. In particular, we look at the extent and nature of the interference, the diminution in value precipitated by the regulatory interference, and the public purpose served by the regulation. While property rights can be limited and constrained by land use and zoning regulations, the extent of the regulation is subject to limitations under the Due Process Clause. This requires us to continually strike a balance in our analysis of property rights relative to changing social, political, economic, and cultural norms so that we might persuasively argue that in a given case a regulation does or does not "go too far."

Procedural due process addresses the way the government regulates and implements land use and zoning regulation pursuant to its police power. *See City of Monterey v. Del Monte Dunes*, 526 U.S. 687 (1999) (a situation in which extensive and repeated procedural delays coupled with costly regulatory limits on the property owner resulted in a taking). Traditional due process requires notice and an opportunity to be heard. In practice, this means that proposals for new land regulation generally must be noticed in some general outlet of communication to the community. This is to provide the community with notice of a potential or pending change in planning and zoning regulations. This notice is generally followed by public hearings on the new proposal before a local legislative body adopts the new regulation. As to new regulatory legislation, personal and individual notice is not required.

However, when a land regulation is to be applied to a particular piece of property or when an individual property owner seeks relief from a specific regulation, due process will require individual and personal notice to the property owner. It will also require a forum for the property owner to be heard on the matter. This hearing must not be biased against the parties. In other words, the decision maker must be neutral and objective. If a decision maker has an interest in the outcome or a conflict of interest in the matter, this could give rise to a violation of due process.

At such a meeting, the property owner has an opportunity to be heard by the governmental decision makers; the property owner may also submit supporting documents and information; and call witnesses on his behalf. Others with an interest in the issue may also be entitled to notice—typically surrounding neighbors. They too will be invited to speak on the matter and may submit evidence. Due process requires that a record of the proceeding be kept so that the property owner has access to it in the event that he wishes to appeal the decision rendered. The decision itself must not be arbitrary or capricious. This typically requires that justification for a decision be offered. A decision cannot simply be conclusory. In addition, due process limits or prohibits ex parte communications on the matter, so that the important information and evidence in the matter is available to the party whose interest is at issue.

c. Equal Protection

Equal protection guarantees emanate from both the Fifth and Fourteenth Amendments to the United States Constitution. While the Fifth Amendment does not include express language as to equal protection, this requirement has been read into the language of the Amendment as a function of due process. The rights addressed in the Fifth Amendment must be applied equally without regard to such identifying characteristics as race, ethnicity, and religion. While the primary focus of equal protection under the Fifth Amendment involves criminal proceedings, the Fifth Amendment requirement of due process traditionally includes a protection for property rights. Because due process requires rationality in government regulation, arbitrary or irrational discrimination is a violation of due process. In this way, due process and equal protection intersect.

Moreover, whereas due process focuses on the rationality of the limitations placed on the exercise of property rights, equal protection focuses on the classification of property and people under land regulations and zoning codes. Land regulations and zoning must not discriminate against people or property in terms of definitions, use classifications, and categories.

The Fourteenth Amendment expressly addresses the right to equal protection and applies to actions by the states, including local governments exercising delegated police powers. This requires that land regulation and zoning be rational and that similarly situated properties and people be treated in a similar way. This means that distinctions among cases must be made and identified when rendering potentially conflicting decisions. Decisions must be clear in identifying facts about a property that will make it either similar or dissimilar to other decisions that have been issued.

Equal protection also requires that all properties within the same zoning district or zone must be subject to the same regulatory requirements. For example, all properties within a R-1 residential zone must be subject to the same regulatory requirements. There can be regulatory differences as between different zones, just not within the same zone. Equal protection is also behind the prohibition of *spot zoning*. Spot zoning may violate equal protection because it singles out a single property within a zone for different regulatory treatment. In *Foothills Communities Coalition v. County of Orange*, 166 Cal. Rptr. 3d 267 (Cal Ct. App. 2014), a community group challenged the location of a senior housing zone on the grounds that the property designated for this zone was singled out and treated differently from other surrounding properties. The court held that spot zoning involved a two-part test. First, identifying a property that is singled out for different treatment from surrounding property, and second, determining if there is a strong public interest in treating this parcel differently. If there is a strong public interest in treating a property differently, it may be permissible.

Equal protection also applies to zoning and land regulations that have a negative impact on the exercise of religion, free speech, and on outcomes for people of a protected class. Thus, equal protection prevents intentional discrimination and disparate treatment as well as disparate impact based on such things as race, ethnicity, religion, and disability. In bringing a claim for a violation of equal protection, a property owner must make an initial showing that she has been treated differently than other similarly situated property owners. Upon carrying this initial burden, the local government must then provide a rational justification for the difference in treatment that is grounded in serving a legitimate public interest. This means that the decision must be rational in relationship to the justification or purpose of the government rule or policy. The standard of review in these cases will turn on the nature of the decision or the protected status of the claimant.

For facial challenges to legislation, the fairly debatable standard of review applies. This involves asserting that the local government has no authority for its action. In situations of quasi-adjudicative decision-making, wherein local planning and zoning professionals render a decision addressing a specific property, the standard is that of a rational basis supported by substantial competent evidence on the record. If the claimant is a person falling within a protected category, the standard of review may be higher, such as the intermediate or strict scrutiny standard of review applicable to gender or race. The standard is also higher if the land regulation discriminates on the basis of race or interferes with another protected fundamental right, such as freedom of religion and freedom of speech and expression.

d. Discrimination

Discrimination is a violation of equal protection. In the land regulation and zoning context, discrimination can be demonstrated by three different methods: *disparate treatment*, *disparate impact*, and *failure to provide a reasonable accommodation or modification* to a person protected by our disability laws.

i. Disparate Treatment

First, discrimination can arise from disparate treatment. This includes intentional discrimination, which may be expressed or inferred. Express discrimination might be evidenced by direct comments or actions that are discriminatory to the person. Inferred discrimination might arise from a failure of government officials to disassociate themselves from the discriminatory comments of others raised at a public hearing. Factors to consider in making a case of intentional discrimination include: 1) the discriminatory impact of the governmental decision; 2) the decision's historical background; 3) the specific sequence of events leading up to the challenged decision; 4) departures from the normal procedural sequences; and 5) departures from normal substantive criteria. *See, e.g.*, *Candlehouse, Inc. v. Town of Vestal*, 2013 WL 1867114, 2013 U.S. Dist. LEXIS 63353 (N.D.N.Y. May 3, 2013). Evidence of intentional discrimination can be gathered from legislative history, as well as from records of planning and zoning board meetings.

It is important to follow the standard procedure and the normal process of conducting business. Planning and zoning officials must be careful in how they proceed with their work and in how they interact with the public at public hearings. It must be clear from the record that planning and zoning officials have not allowed discriminatory comments or the discriminatory actions of others to influence their decision making.

ii. Disparate Impact

A second method of demonstrating discrimination in violation of the Equal Protection Clause is disparate impact. This method does not require a showing of an intent to discriminate. Quoting from the opinion in *Candlehouse* (cited above):

> To establish a prima facie case under this theory, the plaintiff must show: (1) the occurrence of certain outwardly neutral practices, and (2) a significantly adverse or disproportionate impact on persons of a particular type produced by the defendant's facially neutral acts or practices.... A plaintiff need not show the defendant's action was based on any discriminatory intent.... To prove that a neutral practice has a significantly adverse or disproportionate impact ... on a protected group, a plaintiff must prove the practice actually or predictably results in discrimination.... In addition, a plaintiff must prove "a causal connection between the facially neutral policy and the alleged discriminatory effect." Once a plaintiff establishes its prima facie case, "the burden shifts to the defendant to prove that its actions furthered, in theory and in practice, a legitimate, bona fide governmental interest and that no alternative would serve that interest with less discriminatory effect."

Candlehouse at *41.

This test was later clarified and applied by the Supreme Court in the case of *Texas Department of Housing and Community Affairs v. Inclusive Communities Project, Inc.*, 576 U.S. 519 (2015). In the *Inclusive Communities* case, the issue involved the location of affordable housing. Specifically, whether the Texas Department of Housing's policy of using tax credits to facilitate construction of affordable housing maintained a system of racial segregation by allocating too many tax credits for housing to be built in predominantly black inner-city neighborhoods and not enough for construction in suburban areas. The case grappled with the difficulty of demonstrating intentional discrimination and whether or not the existing law permitted a finding of discrimination in the absence of animus or discriminatory intent. Prior to this question reaching the Supreme Court, various circuit court decisions had validated a demonstration of discrimination in housing based on disparate impact without a showing of discriminatory intent. In *Inclusive Communities*, the Court upheld the view that discrimination can be demonstrated by examining outcomes and presenting proof of disparate impact.

Disparate impact analysis requires a comparison of groups by using statistical and social science evidence that indicates that the disparate outcome between the groups has a causal connection to a facially neutral land use or housing policy. The causal connection must be more than casual, and the evidence must be statistically significant.

As stated in the *Inclusive Communities* opinion:

> ... [A] disparate-impact claim that relies on a statistical disparity must fail if the plaintiff cannot point to a defendant's policy or policies causing the disparity. A robust causality requirement ensures that "[r]acial imbalance ... does not, without more, establish a prima facie case of disparate impact" and thus protects defendants from being held liable for racial disparities they did not create.

576 U.S. at 521.

Disparate impact analysis is designed to address zoning laws and housing practices that result in the exclusion of minorities from certain neighborhoods without sufficient constitutional justification. The Court opined that in defending against a disparate impact claim, local officials and developers have leeway to provide explanations for policies and practices. Appropriate explanations and justifications might make the policies and practices acceptable, even if there is a statistical difference in outcome between identifiable comparison groups.

The Court cautioned that identification of practices and policies is a more rigorous process than one might think. For example, a "one-off" decision, such as granting a variance, is not a policy. An actual policy must be at issue in making the case for an illegal disparate impact. One decision or a fact specific determination does not equal a policy. A policy might be one that requires all low-income housing to be clustered into a single neighborhood, or a zoning regulation that requires all single-family homes to be on two-acre lots with houses of 8,000 square feet or more. Such a large lot and house size makes housing very expensive and prices many people out of the market. This could produce discriminatory outcomes because, in many communities, income correlates to race, and to other factors which may indicate discrimination.

iii. Denial of a Reasonable Accommodation or Modification

A third method of demonstrating discrimination involves people protected by our disability laws. People with disabilities are a protected class under three major Acts: Americans with Disabilities Act (ADA), Pub. L. No. 101-336, 104 Stat. 327 (codified as amended at 42 U.S.C. § 12101–12213 (2016)); Fair Housing Act (FHA), Pub. L. No. 100-430, 102 Stat. 1619 (codified as amended at 42 U.S.C. § 3601 (2016), amending Civil Rights Act of 1968, Pub. L. No. 90-284, Title VIII, 82 Stat. 81 (codified as amended at 42 U.S.C. § 3601 (2016)); and the Rehabilitation Act (RHA), 29 U.S.C. § 794 (2016). People with disabilities are protected from discrimination in obtaining access to housing, and from discrimination in *programs, services, and activities* of state and local governments. There are a number of specific provisions in these various Acts that inform land use and zoning law. Some of them set specific requirements that must be met, and in other cases, a provision is made for exceptions to land use and zoning regulations when *a reasonable accommodation or a reasonable modification* is in order. There are specific criteria for determining how to evaluate requests for a reasonable accommodation or modification. *See Rise, Inc. v. Malheur County*, No. 10-cv-00686, 2012 U.S. Dist. LEXIS 44994 (U.S. Dist. Ore. Feb. 13, 2012) (addressing an accommodation for a group home); *Virginia ex. Rel. Fair Housing Board v. Windsor Plaza Condo Ass'n*, 768 S.E.2d 79 (Va. 2014) (applying criteria in a dispute with respect to limited common element parking spaces in a private condominium); *Anderson v. City of Blue Ash*, 798 F.3d 338 (6th Cir. 2015) (addressing criteria as applied to a disability where the property owner sought to maintain a miniature pony on her residential property located in a zone prohibiting farm animals). Planning and zoning officials must comply with the requirements of our disability laws, and they commit discrimination when they fail to provide appropriate accommodations or modifications when requested and appropriate. The requirements of compliance with disability law are examined in more detail in Chapter 7.

e. Takings

The Fifth Amendment to the U.S. Constitution protects private property from government confiscation or from what we more commonly refer to as a "taking." The wording of the Amendment is as follows:

> No person shall ... be deprived of life, liberty, or property, without due process of law; nor shall private property be taken for public use, without just compensation.

The Amendment identifies due process and the protection of private property from seizure as its subject matter. This is a reason that property owners commonly raise both causes of action when asserting that their property rights have been unlawfully taken in violation of the Constitution. The Fifth Amendment protects private property under the Constitution but the definition of what qualifies as property is generally determined under state law. The individual states define the meaning of property rights (the things that qualify as "property") and generally classify property into different recognizable categories. These categories may include real, personal, intangible, intellectual, and cultural property, along with fixtures. This includes establishing different forms of ownership and different estate interests in land. State law also typically defines when property rights vest in a property owner. Vested rights are protected against unlawful takings by the government.

Note that a takings claim is directed at the unlawful taking of private property by the government. This involves an action by the property owner against the government for the unlawful taking of the property without providing just compensation. These cases are sometimes referred to as *inverse condemnation* cases. When the government affirmatively elects to take private property for a public use, it does so under its power of *eminent domain* (the power to take private property for a public use) and provides compensation through a process known as *condemnation*. In a condemnation proceeding, the government acknowledges that it is taking the property and it must demonstrate that it is for a public use. In addition, the government must provide just compensation. The main issue in question in a typical condemnation proceeding is one of determining *just compensation*. This requires evidence of the fair market value of the property.

By way of comparison, when a private party takes the property of another, it generally raises a claim in trespass. And as we know from basic property law, a trespass or occupation of another's land may ripen into ownership under principles of adverse possession. If the possession does not extend for the full period established under state law of adverse possession, an adverse possessor may be legally removed from the property and may have to pay damages to the true property owner.

The Fourteenth Amendment makes the Fifth Amendment applicable to the states. It also has its own protections against government violations of private property rights. In relevant part it provides as follows:

> No State shall make or enforce any law which shall abridge the privileges or immunities of citizens of the United States; nor shall any State deprive any person of life, liberty, or property, without due process of law; nor deny to any person within its jurisdiction the equal protection of the laws.

Due process has both procedural and substantive protections for the protection of a person's life, liberty, and property.

Under the laws of the United States, the question of determining if a taking has occurred is situated within the judicial branch. In many countries in the world, property is also protected by a constitutional provision against certain forms of confiscation, but often the determination of what amounts to a taking is placed with the legislative branch. This differs from the United States, where the courts make the substantive determination as to a taking.

In addition to determining if a taking has occurred in violation of the Fifth Amendment, a determination must be made with respect to the "just compensation" to be paid to a property owner for a taking. In the United States, just compensation typically means the "full and fair market value" of the property. In other countries, the compensation for a taking might be "reasonable compensation," which may or may not mean the full and fair market value of the property.

When the government takes private property without just compensation it is a violation of the Fifth and Fourteenth Amendments. One way in which a taking may occur is when the government makes a physical invasion of a private property or confiscates private property without just compensation. The physical invasion need not be extensive. A permanent physical occupation can be a taking even if it is an extremely minor one. The degree of the invasion will affect the determination of just compensation, but an invasion, no matter how slight, is nonetheless an impermissible taking. *See Loretto v. Teleprompter Manhattan CATV Corp.*, 458 U.S. 419 (1982).

In contrast to a physical invasion, regulations may also rise to the level of a taking; known as a regulatory taking. Modern *regulatory takings* law jurisprudence often starts with a discussion of *Pennsylvania Coal v. Mahon*, 260 U.S. 393 (1922). In this case, the state of Pennsylvania passed legislation restricting the mining of coal. The legislation required that a certain percentage of coal be left in the ground in order to support ground surface activities and structures. While the case can be read to turn on a violation of due process, it is frequently cited for the extended discussion by Justice Holmes regarding the idea of regulations that go so far in limiting and restricting a property owner's use that they can amount to a taking without actually involving a physical invasion or occupation.

According to the opinion in *Pennsylvania Coal:*

> Government hardly could go on if, to some extent, values incident to property could not be diminished without paying for every such change in the general law. As long recognized, some values are enjoyed under an implied limitation, and must yield to the police power. But obviously the implied limitation must have its limits, or the contract and due process clauses are gone. One fact for consideration in determining such limits is the extent of the diminution. When it reaches a certain magnitude, in most if not in all cases, there must be an exercise of eminent domain and compensation to sustain the act. So the question depends upon the particular facts. The greatest weight is given to the judgment of the legislature, but it always is open to interested parties to contend that the legislature has gone beyond its constitutional power.

Id. at 413.

> The general rule, at least, is that, while property may be regulated to a certain extent, if regulation goes too far, it will be recognized as a taking.

Id. at 415.

Pennsylvania Coal resulted in two paths to finding a government taking of private property, one by confiscation (physical invasion or occupation) and the other by means of regulation that "goes too far." This distinction was clarified in subsequent cases.

In *Penn Central Transp. Co. v. City of New York*, 438 U.S. 104 (1978), the Supreme Court set out a number of factors to consider when seeking to determine if a regulation goes too far. The factors to consider in each factual situation are:

- *The character of the government action*—regulation vs confiscation (that is, regulation vs physical invasion and occupation). A physical taking or occupation of private property by the government is easier to determine than the extent to which a regulation might "go too far" under the *Pennsylvania Coal* case. Once a fact situation indicates that the takings claim is based on regulation, then the analysis shifts to the factors below. If it is not regulatory in nature but rather a physical occupation, then these factors do not come into play.

- *The economic impact of the regulation*—diminution in value of the property. The evaluation on this point is to compare the value of the property before the regulation and after. This would require an appraisal, and market information. The greater the diminution in value from the regulation, the greater the potential for finding a taking.
- *The extent of the interference with particular reasonable investment-backed expectations*—this is different than diminution in value. Here, we look at the property from an investment perspective and attempt to determine the reasonableness of particularized investment-backed expectations that a property owner has in the rights of ownership and development. In relation to these expectations, we ask how these expectations have been diminished or defeated by the regulation.
- *The average reciprocity of advantage*—this factor asks us to look at a kind of quid-pro-quo between the burden, or cost, imposed by the regulation and the benefits. For example, the government may need to take a strip of property across the front of everyone's yard along a given street so that a sidewalk along the roadway can be constructed for safe and easy pedestrian navigation. This imposes a cost on the affected owners of property abutting the roadway. We then ask if these same property owners benefit to a similar extent from the presence of the sidewalk. By comparing what the cost and benefits are, on average, we evaluate the extent to which the costs and benefits are reciprocal, and if they, in a sense, cancel themselves out.
- *The harm vs benefit test*—a test that was later dismissed by Justice Scalia as meaningless in the case of *Lucas v. South Carolina Coastal Council*, 505 U.S. 1003 (1992). The test would ask if the regulation is designed to prevent a harm or if it is designed to create a benefit. If designed to prevent harm, it is more likely a proper exercise of the police power. If it is to generate benefits, it is less likely to be a proper exercise of the police power and therefore an indicator of a regulation that goes too far. Justice Scalia opined that any law student can easily manipulate a burden into a benefit and a benefit into a burden,

thus the test was not very useful. For example (using our sidewalk example), is the sidewalk designed to prevent harm to pedestrians by separating them from road traffic, or is it meant to benefit property owners by providing a safe space for them and others to connect with each other? Even given Scalia's negative opinion on the matter, the harm vs. benefits test still comes up in some discussions of takings.

- *The whole parcel test*—the evaluation of these factors is to be measured against the "whole parcel." The whole parcel test requires us to evaluate these various factors against the whole parcel rather than fragmenting the property into different "pieces." This idea is best understood when we consider the common law concept of property as a bundle of sticks. In property law, we learn that each stick in the bundle can represent a particular aspect of property ownership. The whole parcel test informs us that we need to consider the impact of a regulation against the whole bundle of sticks that a person owns in a property and not just one stick. If the whole parcel still has substantial value and permits some useful enjoyment, then the regulation of one stick may not rise to the level of a taking.

The whole parcel test can be illustrated with a few examples. First, consider a zoning code that in time period one places no limits on the height of buildings. This means that the owner of the property has the right to add height and floors to the building. In essence, the air above the current building is part of the property, and these air rights can be developed. The property owner currently has a ten-story building and plans to add ten additional floors. In time period two, a new zoning rule is enacted and limits building heights to ten stories. When the property owner seeks to expand its building and applies for a permit to go to twenty stories, the permit is denied. The property owner objects and asserts that his right to develop his building to twenty-stories has been taken by the regulation. What used to be developable air rights are no longer developable. The owner argues that his right to add ten additional stories has been completely taken because none of the additional ten stories he wishes to construct are permitted even though they were available before the new regulation was enacted. Looking at the air rights (the right to build higher) in isolation, these proposed additional ten stories appear to be totally taken away by the change in the regulation. The court, however, will look at the whole property, this includes the land with the current ten-story building already located on it. The property owner still has these rights. The new regulation impacts a small portion of the owner's property rights. The property owner still owns considerable property, and this property still has considerable economic value. By evaluating the whole parcel, the extent of the negative impact of the new regulation is reduced. This means that relative to the whole parcel, the diminution in value is less and the reasonable investment-backed expectations are different than if the focus was solely on the inability to add an additional ten stories to the original building. The determination of what counts as a single and whole parcel is not always easy. Sometimes one may need to examine the history of a property to determine if what now appears to be two parcels of land should actually be treated as one whole parcel. *See Murr v Wisconsin*, 582 U.S. 383 (2017).

In *Murr*, two waterfront parcels of land in Wisconsin were purchased by a couple and they put one lot in one ownership name and the other lot in another ownership name. They built a cabin on one of the two lots. A few years later, the State of Wisconsin, seeking to protect the waterfront from over development, passed a regulation limiting development based on a defined approach to qualification as a developable lot. The legislation also contained a provision providing that contiguous lots owned by the same party shall be merged and treated as one for purposes of the regulation. A number of years after this regulation was passed, the couple transferred the two lots to their children, placing them in common ownership. In placing the two lots in common ownership, the Wisconsin regulation was made applicable to the properties. The two lots were considered one parcel, and thus, only one lot could be developed. When the children tried to sell one of the two lots to a buyer seeking to develop it separately, they were denied. Local officials said that the two lots had merged into one and that only one lot could be developed. The lot owners sued for an uncompensated taking of their property. When the case reached the U.S. Supreme Court, it determined that the two legally distinct, but commonly owned and contiguous parcels of land should be treated as one parcel for purposes of a regulatory takings analysis under the *Penn Central* balancing test. In its reasoning, the Court held that in addition to meeting the whole parcel test, the parties lacked a reasonable expectation that the result would be otherwise because the Wisconsin regulation was in place before the transfer to the children. Consequently, the Court held that there was no taking because the whole parcel test permitted the two lots to be considered as one, and that one lot was still able to be developed. The ability to use and enjoy the merged parcel provided sufficient value for the property owner.

The Court rejected the idea that the property subject to a takings claim must be defined exclusively by reference to lot lines. It indicated that a number of factors should be considered.

> These include the treatment of the land under state and local law; the physical characteristics of the land; and the prospective value of the regulated land. The endeavor should determine whether reasonable expectations about property ownership would lead a landowner to anticipate that his holdings would be treated as one parcel, or, instead, as separate tracts. The inquiry is objective, and the reasonable expectations at issue derive from background customs and the whole of our legal tradition.

Murr at 397. It went on to say:

> First, courts should give substantial weight to the treatment of the land, in particular how it is bounded or divided, under state and local law. Second, courts must look to the physical characteristics of the landowner's property. These include the physical relationship of any distinguishable tracts, the parcel's topography, and the surrounding human and ecological environment. In particular, it may be relevant that the property is located in an area that is subject to, or likely to become subject to, environmental or other regulation. Third, courts should assess the value of the property under the challenged regulation, with special attention to the effect of burdened land on the value of other holdings. Though a use restriction may decrease the market value of the property, the effect may be tempered if the regulated land adds value to the remaining property, such as by increasing privacy, expanding recreational space, or preserving surrounding natural beauty.

Murr at 397–99.

All of the factors mentioned in *Murr* are relevant to applying the whole parcel test established in the *Penn Central* case. To better understand how the whole parcel test might apply in other types of settings, it is helpful to consider a simplified example. Assume that a property owner, RPM, Inc., owns a 100-acre parcel of land that contains a contiguous 10-acre section of protected wetlands at one corner of the parcel. RPM, Inc. seeks to develop the property, but it knows that the protected wetlands cannot be developed. In an effort to enhance the overall profitability of the property, RPM, Inc. decides to transfer the 10 acres of wetlands to a different but related legal entity, MPR, Inc. As a result, RPM, Inc. no longer owns that 10 acres and is left owning only 90 acres of the original 100 acres. RPM, Inc. gets a permit to develop the 90-acres. The related entity, MPR, Inc., that now owns the 10 acres of wetlands, seeks a permit for development of its property and is denied because the wetlands are protected by government regulation. MPR, Inc. brings a claim against the government for taking 100% of its property. In such a situation, a court may look at the history of the property and the relationship between RPM, Inc. and MPR, Inc. and determine that for a takings analysis under *Penn Central*, the two parcels should be treated as one. Applying the factors identified in *Murr*, such a determination might be reasonable. It might even be concluded that RPM, Inc. purposefully structured the 10-acre sale to MPR, Inc. in order to seek a future takings claim for the diminution in value of those acres. If the court determines that the two parcels should be treated as one, it may conclude that no compensation is required because the ability to develop the 90 acres provides a sufficient return to the owner. This is a simplified example, but it is still instructive, and there are, of course, other considerations to account for if this were an actual case.

In the context of the *Penn Central* decision, the Court also addressed another important issue. It had to evaluate a regulatory provision providing the property owner with *transferable development rights (TDRs)*. In *Penn Central*, the property owner was restricted in its ability to change and expand its building. At the same time, the regulation provided for awarding the property owner with TDRs that could be used on other property. In essence, the property owner's loss of development rights at the location of the property were made up for by a right to have additional development rights at other approved property locations. The property owner could use these development rights himself, or he could sell them to another party. For example, if in our above example where the building height limitations were imposed, a TDR might be used to provide a property owner with a right to build five extra stories onto a building in another location. Perhaps the TDR could be used to add five additional stories to a five-story building in a zone only permitting buildings up to 5 stories. This would permit a ten-story building to be built in a five-story zone. This could be valuable to the person with the TDR or that person could sell it to some other party that might be willing to pay for the rights.

Importantly, a TDR cannot be applied wherever an owner desires; certain locations are preapproved in the land ordinance to receive TDRs. The key to creating valuable TDRs is that there must be a well-developed market for using and selling these rights so that they are actually meaningful. From a community's perspective, TDRs can be used to control density by spreading out development and by incentivizing development in certain locations. In the takings law context, TDRs may also come into play because they provide some valuable compensation for the lost rights on the original subject property and because they demonstrate that not all of the economic value of that property was lost as a result of the regulation limiting development. In essence, the diminution in value at the original location has been partially offset or transferred via the TDR to a new location. In this way, TDRs are elements to consider when applying the balancing test for a regulatory taking under *Penn Central.*

The distinction between a physical taking and a regulatory taking was further clarified in the case of *Lucas v South Carolina Coastal Council*, 505 U.S. 1003 (1992). In *Lucas*, the Court set out two categorical bright lines for takings law. In an opinion written by Justice Scalia, the Court identified two clear examples of a taking. First, if there is a physical invasion of the property, no matter how slight. Second, if in the regulatory context, the value of the property has been reduced to zero dollars, as was the case in *Lucas*. The difficult question in a regulatory taking is just how much loss of value is permissible before a regulation can be said to "go too far." In *Penn Central*, the property owner lost millions of dollars in potential revenues. Likewise, in *Keystone Bituminous Coal Assoc. v. DeBenendictis*, 480 U.S. 470 (1987), a coal company was required to leave 50% of its coal deposits in the ground under a regulation focused on preserving subsurface support for the surface users. Other cases, even if not directly adjudicated under the Takings Clause, also illustrate the problem of determining the extent to which property can decline in value due to a regulation and yet not be a violation of due process or amount to a taking. For example, the Court did not find that the regulations went too far in *Village of Euclid v. Ambler Realty Co.*, 272 U.S. 365 (1926), when the diminution of property value was 75%, and likewise in *Hadacheck v. Sebastian*, 239 U.S. 394 (1915), when the diminution was 87.5%. The situation of regulation that reduces the value of a property to zero dollars is extremely rare and establishes a clear case of a regulation that "goes too far" (referring back to the admonishment in *Pennsylvania Coal*). These two categorical taking situations are intended to map out the easy cases. Everything else is subject to deeper analysis and evaluation using several factors, such as the *Penn Central* balancing test for a regulatory taking.

Lucas also instructed that in determining a taking, one must look at the background legal rules operating in a jurisdiction. These background rules include the state law with respect to the definition of property, and the state law with respect to nuisances. Only property rights defined by state law, or in some situations federal law, can be the subject of a taking. Thus, the background law as to what qualifies as property is important. Additionally, recall that a property owner has no right to conduct a nuisance on her property. Since there is no right to conduct a nuisance on one's property, a regulation that prevents such a use is not a taking. Therefore, background rules on nuisance are important.

A further qualifier on takings law is that the government taking must be for a *public use*. This has traditionally meant that the government cannot take private property from one property owner and simply transfer it to another private owner. This is the case even if the potential new owner might make a better, as measured in terms of economic value, use of the property, and even if just compensation were to be paid for the taking. Traditionally, public use required that the use of the property be by the public. Examples include, taking property for a new public school, a park, or a highway.

In *Kelo v. City of New London*, 545 U.S. 469 (2005), the U.S. Supreme Court had an opportunity to review the requirement of a public use. In *Kelo*, the City of New London was seeking to revitalize a part of the community with a major economic redevelopment project. The city of New London had been identified as a "distressed municipality," and the state was backing a revitalization plan that required the assembly of 90 acres of land consisting of 115 private properties already existing on the land and 32 acres from a former naval facility. The development project would include park space, a waterfront conference center and hotel, an urban village, a riverwalk, shops, restaurants, a new Coast Guard Museum, and a research and development office park. The main occupant of the research and office park was to be Pfizer, a major pharmaceutical company. The redevelopment plan was projected to create numerous jobs and generate millions of dollars in economic activity. Public officials viewed the redevelopment project as vital to the economic health of New London.

Susette Kelo, a private property owner, was one of the people who would have her property taken for the project. She objected on the grounds that much of the project would be used by Pfizer and that the project therefore took private property for the benefit of another private party. Kelo argued that even if Pfizer could make better economic use of her property, the Constitution ought not to allow this taking because it was not for a public use. The nature of the claim required the Court to examine the history of its interpretation of the term *public use*.

A key focus of inquiry in the *Kelo* case was one of determining if taking private property for economic development is a public use. In evaluating this point of inquiry, the Court revisited its decision in *Berman v. Parker*, 348 U.S. 26 (1954), wherein it upheld a redevelopment project in Washington, D.C. In *Berman*, the redevelopment involved taking private property from within an area identified as "blighted" and committing it to a redevelopment and economic revitalization plan. Even though Berman's specific property was not itself blighted, it was within the identified blighted zone and was taken for the revitalization project. In *Berman*, the Court determined that the revitalization of a blighted area was for a *public purpose* and that this satisfied the public use provision of the Fifth Amendment. In *Kelo*, *Berman* was distinguished because the New London city project did not involve a blighted area. Blighted areas often qualify as the reasonable equivalent to a nuisance based on legislative criteria for declaring an area blighted. The situation in New London was one of economic distress but not blighted. In fact, Kelo's property was in a working middle class neighborhood.

In its examination of the history of the term "public use," the Court concluded that time and precedent had revised the original understanding of the term to include *public purpose*. Thus, the proper inquiry is one not necessarily limited to public use but also one of including an analysis of public purpose. If the taking of private property is for a public purpose, it will meet the public use requirement. Applying this to the facts of *Kelo*, the Court determined that New London's economic development and revitalization project satisfied the public purpose (public use) requirement. The opinion included the following:

> The City has carefully formulated an economic development plan that it believes will provide appreciable benefits to the community, including—but by no means limited to—new jobs and increased tax revenue. As with other exercises in urban planning and development, the City is endeavoring to coordinate a variety of commercial, residential, and recreational uses of land, with the hope that they will form a whole greater than the sum of its parts. To effectuate this plan, the City has invoked a state statute that specifically authorizes the use of eminent domain to promote economic development. Given the comprehensive character of the plan, the thorough deliberation that preceded its adoption, and the limited scope of our review, it is appropriate for us, as it was in *Berman*, to resolve the challenges of the individual owners, not on a piecemeal basis, but rather in light of the entire plan. Because that plan unques-

> tionably serves a public purpose, the takings challenged here satisfy the public use requirement of the Fifth Amendment.

Kelo at 483–84.

> ... Promoting economic development is a traditional and long-accepted function of government.

Id. at 484.

> Just as we decline to second-guess the City's considered judgments about the efficacy of its development plan, we also decline to second-guess the City's determinations as to what lands it needs to acquire in order to effectuate the project. "It is not for the courts to oversee the choice of the boundary line nor to sit in review on the size of a particular project area. Once the question of the public purpose has been decided, the amount and character of land to be taken for the project and the need for a particular tract to complete the integrated plan rests in the discretion of the legislative branch."

Id. at 488–89.

An additional category of takings cases involves *unconstitutional conditions*. These are also known as *exactions*. These cases basically involve a quid-pro-quo relationship between a property owner's application for a permit for building, and a condition imposed by the government on that property owner in exchange for granting the permit. In *Nollan v. California Coastal Commission*, 483 U.S. 825 (1987), the Nollans were seeking to rebuild a beach front home along the California coast. They planned to rebuild it with a slightly larger home than what was previously on the lot. A permit was issued to them on condition that they allow the public to walk across their property on land abutting the beach. This would allow members of the public to travel more freely between two public parks, one to the north and one to the south of the Nollan property. In placing this condition on the Nollans' permit, the stated rationale for the required public easement was so that people on a nearby highway on the land side of the property could better see the beach and be aware of its existence. The increased opportunity for awareness of the nearby ocean and beach was deemed beneficial to the public. The Court struck down the condition as a violation of the Takings Clause because the rationale given for the condition had little or no relationship to the requirement of providing an easement to the public along the breach front. If the condition had been one of providing a place to park and stand along the roadside for people to see the beach, or if it had been one of locating the house and landscaping in such a way as to preserve a view of the ocean from the road, that might have been another matter, but here there was no connection between the stated government purpose and the condition imposed on the Nollans. The Court held that for a condition to be imposed on the granting of a permit, there must be an *essential nexus* between the stated purpose for the condition and the actual requirements of the condition.

In another exaction case, *Dolan v. City of Tigard*, 512 U.S. 374 (1994), the Court further refined the requirements for constitutional conditions. In *Dolan*, the property owner wanted to expand her hardware store. Her property was partially in a flood zone. At the time of Dolan's request for a permit, the City of Tigard was also working to reduce dependence on automobile usage and was seeking to add bike trails throughout the community. As conditions to issuing a permit to Dolan, she was required to build outside the flood zone and to leave the flood zone open as green space. She also had to permit the green space to be used by the public. In addition, she was required to commit land to a bike trail. The Court acknowledged that the prevention of building improvements in the flood zone had an essential nexus to preventing harm from flooding, and that the addition of a bike trail had an essential nexus to reducing dependence on automobiles.

The issues that arose in *Dolan* involved the infringement on her right to exclude. While setting aside the flood zone as a green space because of flood risks was okay, this did not mean that her right to exclude others from her property was proper. Even if she could not develop that part of her property, she still retained the right to exclude. Likewise, while a bike trail makes sense as a way for a city to reduce automobile use, it was difficult for the Court to understand how bicycle use would reduce automobile trips to a hardware store. Hardware stores typically sell many items that shoppers would not think of transporting by bike. There was little developed evidence as to how much of an impact the bike trail would have on reducing automobile trips to her store. In evaluating the situation, the court held that in addition to an essential nexus there must be *rough proportionality* between the cost imposed on a property owner and the negative impact of the property owner's activity to the public.

If we think of land regulation as trying to control for externalities by making a property owner internalize the full cost of their land use, then we can understand *Nollan* and *Dolan* as trying to make certain that the stated public purpose for the taking is strongly related to the requirements of the condition (essential nexus), and that there is some rough relationship between the costs imposed on the property owner and the benefit derived from imposing that cost on a particular property owner (rough proportionality). In other words, individual property owners should not disproportionately bear the cost and burden of paying for public projects.

In a third case, *Koontz v. St. Johns River Water Management District*, 570 U.S. 595 (2013), there was a requirement that a development permit be conditioned not on making some public use of the property owner's property, but rather on requiring the property owner to contribute monetary funds to a government entity. The government entity would use the funds to engage in activity on other lands that were designed to provide an environmental offset to negative environmental impacts attributed to the property owner's proposed use. The government argued that since these were just monetary fees, they were not subject to the essential nexus and rough proportionality requirements of *Nollan* and *Dolan*. The Court disagreed. In *Koontz,* it held that such fees were subject to the same tests as applicable in *Nollan* and *Dolan*.

A fourth case on unconstitutional conditions, *Sheetz v. County of El Dorado*, 601 U.S. 267 (2024), addressed an additional question regarding conditions on building permits. A theory had developed that focused on *Nollan*, *Dolan*, and *Koontz* as all involving individual property owners seeking permits, and that in each case, the individual permits were issued with specific conditions. Given this, the argument was developed that those cases would not apply to situations not involving individual permits. The argument was that those cases were not controlling when the conditions were imposed by general legislation. Thus, the argument was that local governments can pass general legislation, for example, requiring all builders to contribute money to programs such as efforts to mitigate local traffic congestion, and efforts to enhance affordable housing production, as a condition to obtaining project approval and building permits. Unlike a specific application for an individual building permit, legislation applied to a category of people (developers) and a general classification of activity (residential or commercial building).

In *Sheetz*, the requirement was for payment of a $23,420 impact fee to be paid to mitigate local traffic congestion. This was a condition to receive a permit to build a prefabricated home on the petitioner's land. The court considered these impact fees in terms of exactions. However, unlike in *Nolan*, *Dolan*, and *Koontz*, these legislative requirements were not determined on a case-by-case administrative basis; they applied to an entire category of potential property owners based on legislation. In *Sheetz*, the Court held that even in schemes such as those passed by legislative action, the same tests apply. Thus, these legislative schemes must meet the tests of essential nexus and rough proportionality.

In *Sheetz*, the Court stated:

> In sum, there is no basis for affording property rights less protection in the hands of legislators than administrators. The Takings Clause applies equally to both—which means that it prohibits legislatures and agencies alike from imposing unconstitutional conditions on land-use permits.

Sheetz at 279.

When we assess the general impact of contemporary takings law cases, we can identify an effort to create a somewhat balanced approach to negotiating land development projects between developers and land use regulators. A major consequence of the culmination of these various takings cases is that local governments must be more cautious about taking property for a proposed public purpose, and a little more constrained in the way they approach land regulation. More significantly, local governments are now more careful in preparing detailed analysis in support of projects and regulations so that they can provide better evidence of compliance with the various standards developed in the takings law cases. Establishing compliance with the various elements of the *Penn Central* balancing test and with constitutional conditions requires planning, data analysis, and multiple sources of input. Facts and data must be closely integrated into legal arguments that can be supported under the provisions of the Fifth Amendment. This has created a space for negotiation between developers and local governments as both try to navigate the unclear legal lines that identify the boundary between proper regulation of land use and regulation that "goes too far."

Importantly, it must be remembered that more than real property is protected by the Constitution. Property protected by the Takings and Due Process Clauses include not only real property but also personal property, intangible property, possessory and non-possessory property, and present as well as future interests. Easements and servitudes are also covered; including in some cases negative servitudes such as those that prevent a property owner from blocking another property owner's view. Under real property law, a real estate *purchase and sale contract* creates a property interest in both the buyer and the seller in accordance with the doctrine of equitable conversion. Under equitable conversion, the moment a contract of purchase and sale is fully executed by the parties, title splits. The seller retains legal title, and the buyer has equitable title. The title remains split until the closing of the contract when the title is unified in the buyer as the new owner. While title is split, both the seller and the buyer have protected property rights in the property. These rights are protected against an unlawful taking. Importantly, entering into an *option contract* to purchase real property does not create a property right. An option contract creates a contract right; the right to exercise the option in accordance with the terms of the option agreement. A contract right under an option agreement is generally not protected under the Takings Clause.

Under the Takings Clause, "just compensation" must be paid for a taking. A requirement for compensation for a physical invasion or for a condemnation of property has for a long time been understood. A question that remained for some time, is one of the proper remedy for a regulatory taking. Early cases lacked clarity as to the need to pay damages for a regulatory taking as opposed to simply eliminating the regulation. The idea being that if a plaintiff could make out a case of a regulatory taking, the proper remedy was to prevent the government from being able to continue enforcing the regulation. This allowed local governments to impose regulations that burdened development and then, even if they were found to "go too far," no damages would have to be paid to the injured property owner. This seemed to give an advantage to local government regulators by allowing them to regulate without significant financial costs should they overstep their authority.

The question of awarding money damages for a regulatory taking was clarified in the case of *First English Evangelical Lutheran Church v. County of Los Angeles*, 482 U.S. 304 (1987). *First English* held that even for a temporary taking, not a permanent one, compensation is to be paid. This meant that if a regulation was imposed on a property owner and that property owner successfully won a takings claim, compensation might be due for the time that the property was subject to the regulation. Thus, the regulation would be struck down and in addition, compensation might be due. This requirement actually made regulators more cautious because, in addition to no longer being able to enforce a regulation, they would have a financial cost associated with their unlawful regulatory efforts. The potential cost associated with imposing regulations that "go too far," actually encourages more productive negotiations between property owners and land regulators in the development process.

Qualifications for a temporary taking were further addressed in *Tahoe-Sierra Preservation Council, Inc.* 535 U.S. 302 (1988). *Tahoe* held that communities could place a moratorium on property development for a reasonable time without having to provide compensation even if during that time the value of the property was greatly diminished. The moratorium and its duration had to be reasonable. And, in the case of *Constitution Pipeline Co., LLC v. A Permanent Easement for 1.06 Acres*, No. 14-CV-2112, 2022 U.S. Dist. LEXIS 3023 (N.D.N.Y. Jan. 5, 2022), the court, following earlier case decisions, held that the proper measure of damages for a temporary taking is the fair rental value of the property for the time of the taking. The relief does not include consequential damages.

The takings law cases discussed above all involved some type of administrative or legislative action. An important case that raised the possibility of an additional category of takings was *Stop the Beach Renourishment, Inc. v. Florida Dept. of Environmental Protection*, 560 U.S. 702 (2010). This case raised the question of a *judicial taking*. Unlike the typical takings case that involves a challenge to a legislative or regulatory action, *Stop the Beach Renourishment* suggested that there could be a judicial taking.

In the *Stop the Beach Renourishment* case, the United States Supreme Court reviewed a Florida Supreme Court decision in which the petitioners alleged that the Florida courts changed their common law property rights without providing just compensation. In other words, the claim asserted that a new judicial interpretation of what was argued to be settled law, resulted in the taking of the petitioner's property. Basically, the petitioners believed that their reasonable investment-backed expectations were defeated by judicial action. The opinion of the Court addresses the common law applicable to the claim along with an applicable state statute. The state statute had been enacted to deal with beach restoration projects and was directly applicable to the situation.

The petitioners in *Stop the Beach Renourishment* were a group of land owners with property abutting the Florida Gulf Coast shoreline in the Florida Panhandle. The underlying action in question involved the restoration of the beaches near Destin, Florida. The beaches had suffered from erosion as a result of several hurricanes, and the state was working to restore the beach. This involved dredging sand from further out away from shore and relocating it to the beach to expand the beach front (to restore the beach by providing a wider and bigger beach compared to what was left after the storms).

The case discusses some particularized rules of water law, but the primary consideration for this book is that the case focuses on a judicial decision that allegedly changed underlying common law property rights. This has implications for background common law land use principles as discussed in Chapter

One. The case highlights several sets of common law rules. First, it discusses rules related to *littoral rights*. These are the rights of property owners who own land abutting a lake or an ocean. They are similar to *riparian rights*, but riparian rights relate to lands abutting flowing water such as in rivers and streams. Second, these rights include common law rules regarding *accretions* (additions of sand, sediments, and other deposits to a property arising *incrementally* and *imperceptibly* over time) and *relictions* (when land formerly underwater becomes visible, as in when a lake dries out). Third, the concept of *avulsion*—when a shift in land *occurs suddenly* and attaches to a new property; for example, when large amounts of sand, dirt, or other deposits shift as a result of a hurricane. Fourth, the case also involved the public trust doctrine that gives ownership of land below the mean high-water mark to the state (discussed in Chapter One). In addition, the case involved a Florida statute that established a guideline for setting property lines in situations where, as in this case, it was restoring the beach.

In seeking to avoid some of the complications of the case, we can simplify the facts and the arguments. The basic idea behind some of these common law rules can be illustrated with an example. Assume Robin owns lot #1 and Maggie owns lot #2 on the coast abutting the ocean, and that each of their properties has 100 feet of sandy beach on the seaward side of their lots (distance from their house to the mean high water line). In a state with littoral rights, as owners of the lots, Robin and Maggie would own the beach out to the mean high-water line, and they would have a right to have their *seaward property line touch the water*. Any accretions, such as sand or other deposits that were washed up on their property would become their property. If, over time, sand is *incrementally* deposited and builds up on the beach in front of their lots in a way that expands the seaward side of their property to 105 feet, they now own five additional feet of beach. Likewise, if water incrementally recedes exposing new lands, then that new land would also go to them. On the other hand, if water and climate conditions *incrementally* wash 75 feet of sandy beach away from their properties, they are then left with only 25 feet of sandy beach front. In other words, with *accretion* and *reliction*, their property line can be changed by incremental changes of the waterline over time. In contrast, if the change in water line is caused by a *rapid change* (avulsion) from something like a hurricane that suddenly washes away a large portion of the beach, or by a dredge and fill operation that suddenly restores the beach, Robin and Maggie's property line does not change.

Under the Florida statute addressing dredge and fill activity to restore the beach in this case, property lines for restoring a beach were set at a government determined line that related to the property lines as they were before beach restoration commenced. That is, they were set in relation to the mean high water line prior to the avulsion.

As explained in the case:

> In Florida, as at common law, the littoral owner automatically takes title to dry land added to his property by accretion; but formerly submerged land that has become dry land by avulsion continues to belong to the owner of the seabed (usually the State). Thus, regardless of whether an avulsive event exposes land previously submerged or submerges land previously exposed, the boundary between littoral property and sovereign land does not change; it remains (ordinarily) what was the mean high-water line before the event. It follows from this that, when a new strip of land has been added to the shore by avulsion, the littoral owner has no right to subsequent accretions. Those accretions no longer add to *his* property, since the property abutting the water belongs not to him but to the State.

Stop the Beach Renourishment, at page 709.

> Once a beach restoration "is determined to be undertaken," the [state Trust Fund] Board sets what is called "an erosion control line." It must be set by reference to the existing mean high-water line, though in theory it can be located seaward or landward of that. Much of the project work occurs seaward of the erosion-control line, as sand is dumped on what was once submerged land. The fixed erosion-control line replaces the fluctuating mean high-water line as the boundary between privately owned littoral property and state property. Once the erosion-control line is recorded, the common law ceases to increase upland property by accretion (or decrease it by erosion). Thus, when accretion to the shore moves the mean high-water line seaward, the property of beachfront landowners is not extended to that line (as the prior law provided), but remains bounded by the permanent erosion-control line. Those landowners "continue to be entitled," however, "to all common-law riparian rights" other than the right to accretions.

Stop the Beach Renourishment, at page 710.

In the case, the petitioners argued that two important elements of their littoral property rights were taken by the Florida courts when they decided in favor of the state. These were the common law rights to receive accretions and to have their property line extend to the water's edge. The counter argument to this was that the case did not involve accretion but rather avulsion. This fact coupled with the state's traditional ownership of subsurface lands indicated that the common law already provided a basis for this result. Therefore, the decision of the Florida courts did not amount to a taking.

While not finding a taking in this case, the Court's opinion left open the possibility of a judicial taking by including language to the following:

> Our precedents provide no support for the proposition that takings effected by the judicial branch are entitled to special treatment, and in fact suggest the contrary.

Stop the Beach Renourishment, at page 713–14.

> In sum, the Takings Clause bars *the State* from taking private property without paying for it, no matter which branch is the instrument of the taking.

Stop the Beach Renourishment, at page 715.

Having left open the possibility of a judicial taking, the Court failed to articulate a clear set of standards for determining when a judicial taking might occur. From a land use perspective, the case reminds us that court decisions play an important role in land regulation and in the determination of property rights. This is particularly true in cases such as *Stop the Beach Renourishment,* when the courts are asked to mediate conflicts involving public regulations and actions that are in tension with common law property rights. Thus, it is important to think about common law background rules and how they continue to play a role in contemporary land planning and regulation.

CHECKPOINTS

- **Police power limitations.** Land regulations limiting property rights find justification in the lawful exercise of the police power. This requires that the police power be asserted to protect the public health, safety, welfare, and morals.

- **Going too far.** Regulation of property rights is permissible so long as it does not "go too far." There are several legal safeguards that facilitate determination of what it means to "go too far."
- **Due process.** There are two parts to due process—substantive and procedural. Substantive due process protects one's right to property, whereas procedural due process addresses the requirements for regulating property rights.
- **Under substantive due process**, a property owner has the right to use property for any lawful use so long as no harm is done to others. While property rights can be limited and constrained by land use and zoning regulations, the extent of the regulation is subject to limitations under the Due Process Clause. This requires us to continually strike a balance in our analysis of property rights relative to changing social, political, economic, and cultural norms so that we might persuasively argue that in a given case a regulation does or does not go too far.
- **Equal protection.** Equal protection guarantees emanate from both the Fifth Amendment and the Fourteenth Amendment to the United States Constitution. This requires that land regulation and zoning be rational and that similarly situated properties and people need to be treated in a similar way.
- **Similarly situated properties and parties must be treated the same.** Equal protection requires distinctions to be made when rendering decisions wherein the outcomes differ as among properties or owners who might otherwise appear to be similarly situated.
- **Equal protection** requires that all properties within the same zoning district or zone must be subject to the same regulatory requirements.
- **Discrimination.** Discrimination is a violation of equal protection. There are three methods of demonstrating discrimination.
    - **Disparate Treatment.** Factors to consider in making a case of intentional discrimination include: 1) the discriminatory impact of the governmental decision; 2) the decision's historical background; 3) the specific sequence of events leading up to the challenged decision; 4) departures from the normal procedural sequences; and 5) departures from normal substantive criteria.

- **Disparate Impact.** To establish a prima facie case under this theory, the plaintiff must (1) identify an outwardly neutral policy or practice, and (2) show a significantly adverse or disproportionate impact on persons of a protected class produced by the defendant's facially neutral policies or practices. This requires a comparison between groups and the demonstration of an adverse impact on the protected class as evidenced by statistical or other social science methods. The relationship must be robust. Once a plaintiff establishes its prima facie case, "the burden shifts to the defendant to prove that its actions furthered, in theory and in practice, a legitimate, bona fide governmental interest and that no alternative would serve that interest with less discriminatory effect."
- **Denial of a Reasonable Accommodation or Modification.** People with disabilities are a protected class under the Americans with Disabilities Act (ADA), Fair Housing Act (FHA), and the Rehabilitation Act (RHA). They are entitled to a reasonable accommodation or modification of rules and regulations when they satisfy the established criteria.

- **Takings.** The Fifth Amendment to the U.S. Constitution protects private property from government confiscation or from what we more commonly refer to as a "taking." The wording of the Amendment is as follows:

  > No person shall ... be deprived of life, liberty, or property, without due process of law; nor shall private property be taken for public use, without just compensation.

- **There are two categories of per se takings.** The first involves a physical invasion. The second involves a regulatory taking that eliminates all of the economic value of the property.
- **Regulatory takings** that do not eliminate all of the economic value of the property are evaluated under the *Penn Central* balancing test that considers: the character of the government action, the diminution in value of the property, the property owner's reasonable investment-backed expectations, the whole parcel, the average reciprocity of advantage, and the extent to which the regulation is designed to prevent harm or confer a benefit.

- **A separate class of takings cases involve unconstitutional conditions, also known as exactions.** These arise when government permission or the granting of a permit is granted on a condition. An exaction must have an essential nexus (*Nollan*) between a legitimate government purpose and the condition imposed on the property owner, and it must bear a rough proportionality (*Dolan*) to the impact caused by the requested use of the property by the property owner.
- **The essential nexus and rough proportionality tests** apply to monetary exactions as well as to conditions placed on the use of the land itself (*Koontz*).
- **Legislative conditions** may also be subject to the same essential nexus and rough proportionality tests (*Sheetz*).
- **Judicial takings.** The Supreme Court has acknowledged the possibility of a judicial taking but is yet to provide clear standards for determining when such a taking has occurred.

CHAPTER 7

Limitations on Zoning Regulation—Tension with Other Fundamental Rights

ROADMAP

- Speech (Including Sign regulation)
- Family
- Religion (RLUIPA)
- Disability

In addition to determining when regulations "go too far," it is important to consider when regulations pose special concerns in relationship to other fundamental rights. The regulation of land can cause tension with other important rights because the regulation of land involves putting limitations and restrictions on the places and spaces in which community life is lived. This gives rise to friction among competing claims of rights and the protection of the public health, safety, welfare, and morals under the exercise of the police power. In this chapter, we examine tensions between land regulation and other fundamental rights, such as those related to speech, religion, family, race, and disability.

a. Speech (Including Sign Regulation)

The First Amendment of the U.S. Constitution provides that "Congress shall make no law ... abridging the freedom of speech, or of the press...." This raises important considerations in land use and zoning in several ways. It can have implications for the regulation of such things as signs, flags, architecture, art, and adult entertainment.

One step in an analysis of speech regulation involves classifying the speech in question as commercial speech, political speech, or something else. The regulation of commercial speech has a lower standard of review than some other categories of protected speech. This means that planning and zoning officials have more room and discretion for exercising regulatory control over commercial speech and informational signs than they do for forms of political speech. A second step in analyzing the regulation of speech involves classification of the character of the regulation in terms of it being either *content based* or *content neutral.* In all cases, the regulation of speech involves a higher level of review than that of the rational basis standard that is typically applied in land use and zoning cases. The two higher standards of review that must be considered are intermediate review and strict scrutiny review.

The regulation of commercial speech is subject to intermediate scrutiny. *See Central Hudson v. Gas & Electric Corp. v. Public Service Comm'n,* 447 U.S. 557 (1980). Commercial speech can involve such things as commercial advertisements, promotional signs, billboards, storefront messages, shopping center signs, law office and other professional signs, going out of business sales signs, and sidewalk displays like those often used by restaurants and cafes to inform people of their various offerings. Local communities often seek to regulate this type of speech. The regulation of commercial speech is evaluated in terms of four criteria. First, in order to be protected, the commercial speech (for example, advertising) must concern a lawful activity and not be misleading. Second, there must be a substantial governmental interest in regulating the speech. Third, the regulation must directly advance the asserted government interest. Fourth, the regulation must not be more restrictive than necessary to advance the asserted interest. When a regulation restricting commercial speech is challenged, the government has the burden of demonstrating the constitutionality of the regulation. This means that the government has the burden of demonstrating that its regulation withstands intermediate scrutiny when applying the four stated criteria. The most common application of this analysis in zoning involves the regulation of signs, a topic discussed separately in the pages that follow.

Additional considerations with respect to speech involve the categorization of the government regulation as either being *content based* or *content neutral.* Starting with content neutral regulations; these seek to restrict speech in terms of *time, place, and manner* and do not discriminate or regulate on the basis of the content or viewpoint of the speech. For zoning, time, place, and manner regulations must be pursuant to a proper exercise of the police power and thus must serve the public health, safety, welfare, and morals. Content neutral regulation addresses the *secondary effects* of the speech. For example, large and brightly lit advertising billboards at a busy traffic intersection might be distracting to drivers or block a driver's view of the intersection. In such a case, the type of sign, its size, shape, lighting, and location could be regulated to protect the public safety. These types of regulations are not focused on the content of a sign but rather on the sign's impact on the public health, safety, welfare, and morals.

With content neutral regulation, there are five criteria to consider. First, it must be focused on secondary effects and not on the content of the speech. Second, the regulation must be as to time, place, and manner. This is a type of how, when, and where regulation. Third, the regulation must be pursuant to a substantial or compelling government interest. Fourth, the regulation must be narrowly tailored to accomplish the stated government interest. Fifth, there must be other available avenues of communication. Content neutral regulation is subject to intermediate scrutiny, and the government has the burden of demonstrating its constitutionality. This means the government has the burden of explaining and justifying the regulation based on addressing the five criteria.

Content based speech regulations are subject to strict scrutiny review standards. This is the highest standard of review, and these cases are difficult to win from the government perspective. Content based regulations are aimed at the subject matter of the speech. In zoning, this can include regulation of signs, posters, flags, and other forms of expression. As examples, this might include the regulation of certain political signs or messages such as "Impeach the President," "Black Lives Matter," or the flying of a Confederate flag. When the regulation is directed at the content of the message rather than the secondary effects, it is subject to strict scrutiny review. Content based regulation is presumptively unconstitutional. The government has the burden of overcoming this presumption and of carrying the day on each of the criteria.

The key for reviewing content based regulation includes three criteria. First, the purpose and motivation of a regulation must be very closely reviewed to determine if it appears to be content based. If it is content based, it is subject to strict scrutiny review. Second, there must be a substantial and compelling government interest in regulation. Third, the regulation must be narrowly tailored and constitute the least restrictive means for accomplishing the government's legitimate purpose. Each of these criteria must be established with specificity and with detailed findings.

Applying these criteria to a few standard examples will illustrate how they come into play in a typical land use and zoning environment. First, consider adult entertainment. These places can involve live performances, movies, pictures, magazines, adult toys, and other forms of expression and speech generally related to sexual activity and to human genitalia. Many zoning codes devote multiple sections to simply trying to define and explain what they mean by adult entertainment of various types.

Two classic cases are *Young v. American Mini Theatres, Inc.*, 427 U.S. 50 (1976), and *City of Renton v. Playtime Theaters, Inc.*, 475 U.S. 41 (1986). Each of these cases involved the regulation of adult entertainment, in particular adult movies. In the *Young* case, the city had a zoning ordinance that sought to concentrate adult entertainment activities of various types into specific zoning districts. The idea being that it would be easier to police such activities if they were confined to designated areas. In contrast, the *Renton* case involved zoning that sought to separate and diffuse various adult entertainment activities to lessen their impact on any given neighborhood. The zoning regulations in *Renton* established specified distances that adult entertainment had to have between its venue and that of such places as schools, churches, parks, and single-family and multi-family residential uses. These restrictions dramatically limited locations available for adult entertainment uses.

The dispute in each case was one of first determining if the regulation was aimed at the adult content of the activity or simply directed at the secondary effects of the activity. One argument raised by the theaters was that they were being regulated and zoned differently than other theaters. Theaters showing Disney movies and children's movies were not restricted to the same zones as adult entertainment. Thus, it was argued that the regulations were content based and not sustainable under strict scrutiny review. In response, the cities argued that the regulations were not based on the content of the movies that they displayed but on the secondary effects associated with establishments catering to customers of adult entertainment. Based on detailed studies and police reports, the cities argued that crime and other illicit activity was higher in and around adult entertainment venues and that based on such information, the regulations and restrictions were necessary to protect the public health, safety, welfare, and morals. They made the case that the primary focus of the regulation was on the secondary effects and therefore sustainable under intermediate scrutiny. Having established that the regulation was properly focused on secondary effects, they then established the other criteria related to content neutral regulation.

Two things of note in *Renton*, first, the city did not do its own studies of secondary effects but rather relied on a study done elsewhere by another city. The Court said this was acceptable as long as local city regulators thoughtfully reviewed the other study and determined the relevance of that study for their own community. Evidence of this type of deliberative review is an important fact in supporting its use in a community that is simply borrowing from the study done of a different location.

In addition to the above points, the courts may allow regulations and restrictions on legally permitted speech, but they will generally require that lawful speech have some location where it can be heard. In other words, zoning should not be used to prohibit a full category of legal speech, even if that speech might properly be limited in terms of time, place, and manner. This issue was addressed in the *Renton* case.

In *Renton*, the owner of the proposed movie theater challenged the regulation prohibiting its theater at the owner's desired location on the grounds that there were no other currently available locations for adult movies fitting the distance specification of the zoning code. It argued that locations were not readily available for sale or rent that met the restrictions of the code, and, thus, it should be entitled to a location that was available. In response, the city demonstrated that there were multiple properties that could satisfy the zoning requirements. To this the theater owner responded by showing the difficulty of identifying, for rent or for sale, properties meeting the zoning requirements. On this point, the Court concluded that what is required under the First Amendment is not that an actual location be readily accessible for purchase or rent, but that there are potential locations that can serve as alternative venues of expression. Applying the city's distance regulations to properties within the jurisdiction, it was shown that a number of properties could meet the zoning requirements. The fact that none of these properties were currently for sale or rent, or that petitioner might not be willing or able to pay the asking price, was not the focus of the protection under the First Amendment. Given that a number of locations in the city were zoned to permit such a use, it was up to the theater owner to enter the market and find a willing seller within an appropriate zone for its intended use. This is all that is required. The zoning restrictions were upheld.

Sign regulation is also an area that raises tension with the First Amendment. There are many types of signs. There are road signs, business signs, company signs, restaurant signs, billboards, digital billboards, 3D billboards, lighted signs, neon signs, monument signs, directional signs to guide traffic flow, political signs, signs mounted on poles, and signs painted on a business window or displayed inside but visible to viewers outside. Signs can be made of various materials and come in different shapes and sizes. Many aspects of signs are regulated. One thing that local communities cannot regulate on commercial signs involves *a business's trademark*. Under *section 1121(b) of the Lanham Act*, local zoning ordinances cannot require alterations to federally registered trademarks. They can, however, regulate how it is displayed—for example, restricting the size of the sign.

In general, political signs are evaluated under strict scrutiny, and commercial signs are evaluated under intermediate scrutiny. More specifically, one must determine if the challenged regulation is content based, or content neutral and focused on time, place, and manner. Traffic signs, directional signs, constructions signs, and signs with local information concerning parks and civic venues are typical of signs that are used to ensure traffic safety. These signs assist people in driving and getting safely to and from a given destination. They are content neutral. Political signs supporting candidates for office or advancing particular positions on matters of political debate are typical of signs that raise questions of regulating based on content.

An important case addressing the regulation of signs is *Reed v. Town of Gilbert*, 576 U.S. 155 (2015). In *Reed*, the Court addressed the regulation of temporary signs that provided people with information on local religious meetings. The Town of Gilbert required a permit for the posting and erecting of all signs. At the same time, it identified 23 different exceptions to the regulations. It also categorized signs into three different classifications, each with its own rules. These classifications included "ideological signs" (communicating a message or idea for non-commercial purposes that is not a construction signs, a directional sign, or a temporary directional sign for a "qualifying" event); "political signs" (signs designed to influence the election of a candidate or to influence an elective body); and "temporary directional signs" (signs that are temporary and designed to guide people to a qualifying event such as a meeting of a not-for-profit organization).

Clyde Reed was pastor of a church that had no fixed location and met in different places each week. He posted temporary signs around town to inform people of where their Sunday service was being held for the week. Reed and his church were cited for violating the temporary sign code by leaving the signs up too long, and for failing to include specific dates on each sign. Reed sued and argued that the Town's sign regulations violated his right to free speech because the zoning ordinance was content based and unable to hold up to strict scrutiny. The trial and appellate courts held that the sign ordinance was not content based. They held that the ordinance established general categories and definitions that could be readily administered without delving into the content of expression contained in the signs. In other words, all temporary directional signs would be treated in a similar way, just like all political signs, without regard to the expression conveyed by the sign but simply by its categorization. Given their conclusion that the ordinance was content neutral, the Court held for the Town of Gilbert.

In the U.S. Supreme Court, the decision was different. While there were multiple opinions offered by the Justices in the *Reed* case, the general holding was that, if a sign has to be read and interpreted in order to classify it within one of the various categories of the sign ordinance and one of its 23 exceptions, then it is content based regulation. In other words, if the content must be read and evaluated in order to apply the appropriate regulation, it is content based. This meant that the ordinance had to be reviewed under a standard of strict scrutiny and not an intermediate standard. Under strict scrutiny review, a content based regulation is presumptively unconstitutional. It is up to the government to overcome this presumption based on the established criteria. According to *Reed*:

> ... Because strict scrutiny applies either when a law is content based on its face or when the purpose and justification for the law are content based, a court must evaluate each question before it concludes that the law is content neutral and thus subject to a lower level of scrutiny.
>
> The Court of Appeals next reasoned that the Sign Code was content neutral because it "does not mention any idea or viewpoint, let alone single one out for differential treatment." It reasoned that, for the purpose of the Code provisions, "[i]t makes no difference which candidate

> is supported, who sponsors the event, or what ideological perspective is asserted." ...
>
> ... But it is well established that "[t]he First Amendment's hostility to content-based regulation extends not only to restrictions on particular viewpoints, but also to prohibition of public discussion of an entire topic." ...
>
> Thus, a speech regulation targeted at specific subject matter is content based even if it does not discriminate among viewpoints within that subject matter.

Reed at 228–30.

Consequently, the Town had to justify its sign ordinance by demonstrating with specificity and detail that it advanced a compelling government interest, that it was narrowly tailored, and that it was the least restrictive means for achieving a legitimate government objective. The Town argued that the signs were not aesthetically pleasing and that they posed a safety risk for drivers. However, the Town was not able to establish that the temporary signs at issue in this case were either aesthetically less appealing than other signs of a similar style, size, and make, or that they posed a greater traffic safety risk than other signs. The various opinions issued by the Justices in the case described all types of signs and how they could be regulated. They explained that signs can be limited in size; controlled for lighting and color; restricted near roadway intersections; controlled for certain standards of style and font size; and more. However, distinctions based on a need to read and interpret the sign goes beyond content neutral regulation of time, place, and manner, and triggers strict scrutiny review. In *Reed*, the regulation as written did not pass the strict scrutiny standard of review.

Flags and banners are treated similarly to signs. This means that their regulation has to be evaluated to determine if it is content based or content neutral. If content neutral, an ordinance is then evaluated in terms of time, place, and manner. Generally, flags and banners can be regulated in terms of size, placement, lighting, and such. For flags, the height of the flagpole is also a matter typically addressed in local zoning ordinances. Displaying of the American national flag cannot be prohibited by a zoning code ordinance or even by a Home Owners Association (H.O.A.) in a common interest community. *See* Freedom to Display the American Flag Act, Pub. L. No. 109-243, 120 Stat. 572 (2005–06). However, reasonable size and location regulations may be permissible.

Artwork and sculptures may also be subject to zoning regulations. Again, inquiry must be made into the nature of the regulation—content based or content neutral. If content neutral, artwork regulations can be upheld if they are properly drafted to address legitimate time, place, and manner concerns. Some zoning codes attempt to regulate artwork and sculptures separately whereas other ordinances may treat them as signs.

It may be difficult to determine if something is a sign or art. In the case of *Young v Town of Conway*, No. 23-cv-00070, 2025 U.S. Dist. LEXIS 95364 (Dist. N.H. May 20, 2025), the Town of Conway, New Hampshire, sued the owner of Leavitt's Bakery for having an improper sign on its business. It was improper because it was much larger than the code permitted for business signs. The complaint concerned the fact that the bakery had both an authorized business sign over its entranceway and, in addition, it had a large mural on the front of its building. The Town said that the mural was also a business sign, and the mural far exceeded the size limitation for signs. The mural was painted by art students from the local high school and depicted the White Mountains of New Hampshire. It included some whimsical elements of doughnuts and pastries as part of the mountains. Inasmuch as Leavitt's Bakery sold doughnuts and pastries, the Town said that it was a sign for its business and not art. The local zoning code provided that any communication of the goods and services provided at a business location was a "sign" subject to various restrictions and limitations. The bakery challenged the Town on the grounds that the enforcement action violated the owner's First Amendment rights to free speech and expression. The Town admitted that the mural could be okay under its code if there was a way to paint over or remove the doughnuts and pastries from the mural. They also suggested that the mural, as painted, could be permitted if it was located on a different building. As an example, they noted that the mural might be fine on the side of a barn, but that when painted on the bakery it simply acted as a larger than permitted business sign promoting the commercial activity conducted at the property.

In rendering a decision, the court carefully reviewed the town's justifications for the regulation of the mural as a sign. It was noted that the Town permits murals depicting a variety of images to be painted on buildings, and only limits murals that include depictions of available goods and services at the location. The court pointed to the Town's admissions that the mural would be fine if the doughnuts and pastries were painted out of the mural, or if the mural was located on a building that did not sell those items. Thus, the court concluded that it was not the mural that was objectionable but the content of the mural. Consequently, the court held that the content based regulation in this case was unsustainable and the bakery was permitted to keep its mural on its building.

In some situations, signs, artwork, and sculptures may also come within regulations related to accessory structures. For example, a flagpole or a sculpture in a front yard might be considered a structure if it is attached to the ground. Most zoning codes regulate structures on a property. Without getting into the question of art or expression, the object could be regulated the same as other structures in terms of its size, height, location, and placement. Furthermore, a zoning board might contemplate the nature of the object and make a finding that it is an *accessory structure*. Accessory structures typically have specific requirements. To be an accessory structure, it must be both *customary* and *incidental* to the primary use of the property. Since many properties have flag poles and art, the object might qualify for treatment as an accessory structure.

Architecture also presents a potential tension between free speech and expression, and local planning and zoning regulations. Some communities regulate building design under the guise of protecting the public health, safety, welfare, and morals. This is a proper area of government regulation in as much as contemporary zoning considers aesthetic regulation a proper exercise of the police power. In many cases, a zoning code regulating design often contains regulations establishing an architectural review board to implement the provisions and to consider design plans and requests for building approval. In some situations, a property owner, builder, or architect may challenge a design regulation on the grounds that it violates the First Amendment right to free speech and expression. *See, e.g., Burns v. Town of Palm Beach*, 999 F.3d 1317 (11th Cir. 2021).

In the case of architecture and building design, before one can apply a First Amendment analysis, it must first be determined that speech is involved. There are two approaches that might be used in considering the speech function of architecture and building design in the relationship between the First Amendment and architecture in the zoning context. These two approaches are the *Johnson* test (established in the case of *Texas v. Johnson*, 491 U.S. 397 (1989)), and the *predominate purpose test* (set out in *Mastrovincenzo v. City of New York*, 435 F.3d 78 (2d Cir. 2006)).

In applying the *Johnson* test, it must be determined that 1) an intent to convey a particularized message is present, and 2) the likelihood is high that the message will be understood by viewers. The *predominant purpose* test is slightly different. It has three parts—1) the owners subjectively intend to communicate a message with their design, 2) the predominate purpose of the structure is to communicate, and 3) a reasonable observer is highly likely to understand that the structure is predominantly communicating a message. In both approaches, it is implicit that the structure must be observable in order to communicate with others. Thus, it is unlikely that a structure will meet either test if the structure is a building obstructed from view by walls, or tall hedges and trees.

b. Family

Zoning deals with matters of family in several ways. At the outset, all zoning codes regulate single-family and multi-family residential uses. This requires some working definition of family. There are also issues that arise with adjacent living arrangements such as boarding houses, dorms, fraternities and sororities, group homes, convents, and monasteries. All these varieties of living arrangements pose the question of if the people in these relationships meet the definition of a family for zoning purposes. Some of the issues that arise include the question of if couples need to be married; if all the people in the home must be legally related by marriage, blood, or adoption; how many generations of a family can live in one structure or dwelling unit; and must all or at least some of the people residing in the home be domiciled there as well.

A key case on this subject is *Village of Belle Terre v. Borras*, 416 U.S. 1 (1974). The Village of Belle Terre is located on Long Island, NY and is near the State University of New York at Stony Brook. The case addressed the constitutionality of a Village zoning ordinance that prohibited groups of more than two unrelated people from occupying a residence. This restriction did not apply to people who were related by blood, adoption, or marriage. In this case, the two owners of a home along with their three unrelated student tenants challenged the zoning ordinance on the grounds that it established different classifications between households based on the relationship of the inhabitants in violation of the Equal Protection Clause of the Constitution.

The majority opinion held that the ordinance was a proper exercise of the police power and was subject to rational basis review requiring a showing of a rational relationship to a legitimate governmental interest. It found this relationship in terms of protecting neighborhoods, avoiding overcrowding, and controlling traffic. The case included a compelling dissent that has had influence on the development of law in this area. In his dissent, Justice Marshall said:

> In my view, the disputed classification burdens the students' fundamental rights of association and privacy guaranteed by the First and Fourteenth Amendments. Because the application of strict equal protection scrutiny is therefore required, I am at odds with my Brethren's conclusion that the ordinance may be sustained on a showing that it bears a rational relationship to the accomplishment of legitimate governmental objectives.
>
> I would ... agree with the majority that local zoning authorities may properly act in furtherance of the objectives asserted to be served by the ordinance at issue here: restricting uncontrolled growth, solving traffic problems, keeping rental costs at a reasonable level, and making the community attractive to families.... But deference does not mean abdication. This Court has an obligation to ensure that zoning ordinances, even when adopted in furtherance of such legitimate aims, do not infringe upon fundamental constitutional rights.
>
> ... Zoning officials properly concern themselves with the uses of land—with, for example, the number and kind of dwellings to be constructed in a certain neighborhood or the number of persons who can reside in those dwellings. But zoning authorities cannot validly consider who those persons are, what they believe, or how they choose to live, whether they are Negro or white, Catholic or Jew, Republican or Democrat, married or unmarried.
>
> My disagreement with the Court today is based upon my view that the ordinance in this case unnecessarily burdens appellees' First Amendment freedom of association and their constitutionally guaranteed right to privacy. Our decisions establish that the First and Fourteenth Amendments protect the freedom to choose one's associates. Constitutional protection is extended, not only to modes of association that are political in the usual sense, but also to those that pertain to the social and economic benefit of the members. The selection of one's living companions involves similar choices as to the emotional, social, or economic benefits to be derived from alternative living arrangements.
>
> ... The right to "establish a home" is an essential part of the liberty guaranteed by the Fourteenth Amendment.... The choice of household companions ... involves deeply personal considerations as to the kind and quality of intimate relationships within the home. That decision

> surely falls within the ambit of the right to privacy protected by the Constitution.

Village of Belle Terre, at 13–16.

Belle Terre was followed by the case of *Moore v. City of East Cleveland*, 431 U.S. 494 (1977). In *Moore*, the City of East Cleveland had a zoning ordinance that limited the occupancy of a dwelling unit to members of a single family. It also provided a definition of family. The definition did not include permitting Mrs. Moore to live in the same dwelling unit as her son, and her two grandsons. The two grandsons were cousins and not brothers. The East Cleveland zoning code made distinctions among categories of relatives and defined who could and who could not count as a family member permitted to live in one dwelling unit. The Court held that the zoning ordinance violated the Due Process Clause of the Fourteenth Amendment and infringed on a right to privacy and a right to formulate one's family in diverse and personal ways. In response to an argument that the Court should enforce the zoning ordinance based on its earlier ruling in the *Belle Terre* case, the Court distinguished *Belle Terre* from *Moore* in that *Belle Terre* involved regulation of the living arrangements of unrelated individuals, whereas in *Moore*, East Cleveland regulated the living arrangements of related individuals. Consequently, the decision in the case of *Belle Terre* that supported the local zoning regulation was not controlling in the situation presented by the facts in *Moore*.

The decision in the *Moore* case, and the arguments raised by Justice Marshall in his dissent in *Belle Terre*, have resulted in many communities enacting zoning ordinances that attempt to carefully define family in terms of living arrangements rather than in terms of relationships of marriage, blood, and adoption. For example, a zoning code may speak in terms of unrelated people who share expenses, meals, and household chores as "living as a family." These codes also try to limit the number of unrelated people in a household based on some form of objective standard such as the number of bedrooms, square feet of living space, or number of legal parking spaces per unit. All of these efforts are designed to have the zoning ordinance pass the test of a higher standard of review than that of a rational basis.

There is, nonetheless, a distinction in many of these situations. A zoning ordinance cannot limit the number of related family members in a house. For example, a person could have 2, 4, 6, 10, or even 12 children living in one house, whereas unrelated people living as a family may be restricted in number based on a set of criteria such as number of bedrooms, and square feet of living space.

Group homes present another area of dispute. Many group homes try to establish a family living environment for the residents. Depending on the makeup of the residents, they may or may not all share in the expenses, chores, and activities of maintaining the household. Often, the home is owned or run by a not-for-profit that is paid to provide the housing services for the residents. These arrangements raise the issue of the extent to which group homes can be regulated as to location (single-family residential zone) and as to how best to limit the number of people in the home while staying within constitutional boundaries. With respect to people with disabilities, group homes will be discussed in more detail in a later part of this chapter.

c. Religion (RLUIPA)

Zoning ordinances often deal with religious uses. These can include places of worship and related activities such as religious schools, soup kitchens, thrift shops, and housing for certain people involved in the religion. The government cannot favor or disfavor any particular religion, so the zoning regulations must be written and administered with this in mind. The most important federal legislation supporting the First Amendment freedom of religion in the zoning context is the Religious Land Use and Institutionalized Persons Act, 42 U.S.C. § 2000cc et seq. ("RLUIPA" pronounced "Ruh-lou-pah," rhymes with Chalupa).

RLUIPA addresses a specialized area of land use regulation focused on religious liberty. In general, RLUIPA provides protections for places of worship, faith-based social service providers, religious schools, and individuals using land for religious purposes. More specifically, RLUIPA restricts land use regulation by providing:

- Protection against substantial burdens on religious exercise.
- Protection against unequal treatment for religious assembles and institutions.
- Protection against religious or denominational discrimination.
- Protection against total exclusion of religious assemblies; and,
- Protection against unreasonable limitations of religious assemblies.

The language of RLUIPA provides, in pertinent part, as follows:

> No government shall impose or implement a land use regulation in a manner that imposes a substantial burden on the religious exercise of a person, including a religious assembly or institution, unless the … imposition of the burden … is in furtherance of a compelling governmental interest; and … is the least restrictive means of furthering that compelling governmental interest.

In the context of land use and zoning, a substantial burden is one that causes the person or institution to change its behavior. Once a prima facie case is made for the violation of RLUIPA, the burden shifts to the government to demonstrate that its regulation is in furtherance of a compelling government interest and that it is the least restrictive means for accomplishing this purpose.

Zoning regulations that raise tensions with RLUIPA are subject to strict scrutiny review. *See Mast v. Fillmore Cnty.*, 141 S. Ct. 2430 (2021) (a case applying RLUIPA to overturn a denial by local authorities to an Amish community that did not want to upgrade their waste water treatment facility by employing new technologies). *See also, Church of the Rock, Inc. v. Town of Castle Rock*, No. 24-cv-01340, 2024 U.S. Dist. LEXIS 245286 (D. Colo. July 19, 2024) (applying RLUIPA to overturn a zoning decision denying a permit for a church to operate a temporary shelter on its property as part of its ministry); *Midrash Sephardi, Inc. v. Town of Surfside*, 366 F.3d 1214 (11th Cir. 2004) (applying RLUIPA to overturn a zoning decision in order to permit two small Orthodox Jewish synagogues to operate in a zone where they had been excluded but where other "nonreligious" assemblies and institutions were permitted to operate under the zoning ordinance).

d. Disability

Disability presents a major issue in land planning and regulation. It is estimated that 20–25% of Americans have a disability of some type. Within this population, some 20% of American families have a family member with some type of mobility impairment. This means that disability effects many more people than is typically understood. Oftentimes, perceptions are clouded by the fact that the iconic image associated with disability is a wheelchair, when only about 1% of Americans outside of institutional settings use a wheelchair.

Disabilities, and in particular disabilities related to mobility, make it difficult for some people to easily and safely navigate the built environment. Thus, planning and zoning officials must affirmatively account for accessibility across the built environment so that everyone can participate in the activities of everyday life no matter what the venue. As part of this, it is important to understand that land planning and zoning involve disability and access issues that go beyond the realm of fair housing. Land planning and zoning address a range of issues that relate to accessible infrastructure that enables people of different abilities to fully participate in their communities. Therefore, land use and zoning professionals need to understand disability law so that concerns can be addressed by focusing on the correct requirements and criteria. One cannot just address this area of law by discussing human rights, fairness, or disability rights. The analysis of issues at the intersection of land use and disability have specific evidentiary requirements, and the legal discussion in this area must address specific and integrated legal criteria that may not be familiar to some professionals working only in the field of either zoning or disability.

To get an understanding of disability law and its intersection with land planning and zoning, it is important to appreciate the general requirements of our major disability laws. First and foremost, disability law is modeled on civil rights law and primarily addresses the prevention of discrimination against people with disabilities. It seeks to prevent discrimination against people with disabilities as they move through the places and spaces where everyday life is lived. In general, our disability laws require that all *new construction, and alterations* of existing structures must be accessible to the *greatest extent possible.* The only defense to lack of accessibility for new construction or alterations is *structural impracticability.* In making this claim as a defense, the high cost of making something more accessible is not, in itself, a determinant factor in finding structural impracticability, nonetheless, extremely high costs relative to anticipated benefits might be a consideration in an actual case.

In addition, all *programs, services, and activities of state and local government* must be accessible to people with disabilities; and programs, services, and activities expressly include all the actions and activities of planning and zoning offices and officials. Defenses to claims for greater accessibility include demonstrating that providing greater accessibility to programs, services, or activities would impose an *undue financial or administrative burden* on the state or local government. In order to support the defense of undue financial or administrative burden, one needs to look at the finances and the budgeting of the local government in order to evaluate the burden imposed. One must also assess the reasonableness of the financing and budgeting plans to ensure that the local government is doing what it can to make achieving greater accessibility less of a difficulty.

Physical barriers to accessibility can be interior or exterior with respect to a structure. When considering the interior of structures, one must evaluate barriers to safe and easy movement for people with disabilities. This can include stairways, the height of counters and light switches, and the size of bathrooms. As an interior issue, it is likely to be governed by a building code and not a zoning code. However, structural barriers can be an issue outside of a structure. For example, landscaping, exterior entrances and pathways, and streetscapes may all present various barriers to safe and easy navigation. Presently, existing barriers in or near older buildings must be removed in order to make older buildings more fully accessible to people with disabilities. This requirement is distinct from the requirements associated with new construction and alterations. Consequently, buildings with structural barriers to accessibility do not have their barriers protected by a "grandfather" provision as would be the case with many non-conforming uses under regular zoning law principles. Instead, these barriers must generally be removed unless the removal is *not readily achievable*. The not readily achievable standard might be a result of structural and design problems, or because of high costs.

Finally, planning and zoning regulations must be adjusted and exceptions provided for a person with a disability. This is required if the person with a disability affirmatively requests an accommodation or modification, and the request *is reasonable*. The reasonableness of the request for an accommodation or modification is not determined by the person with a disability but by the person or officials charged with enforcing the regulation. In order to evaluate reasonableness, three criteria must be considered and balanced.

- First, *the request must be reasonable* using a cost and benefit analysis. This means that it should not impose an undue financial or administrative burden.
- Second, *it must be necessary* using a "but for" test—that is, but for the accommodation or modification the person cannot have an equal opportunity to participate in or benefit from the program, service, or activity. In the housing area under the Fair Housing Act, it means that, *but for* the requested accommodation or modification, the claimant is unable to enjoy the use of her home in a similar way to others without a disability. The "but for" test means that there must be

a strong nexus between the requested accommodation and the ability of the accommodation to address the actual disability of the claimant.

- Third, if granted, *the accommodation or modification must not fundamentally alter* the program, service, or activity in question.

When dealing with petitions for a reasonable accommodation or modification, these are the criteria that one must address and on which evidence must be presented. Each of the various requirements of our disability laws and the possible defenses to them have implications for land planning and zoning, and all are the subject of litigation.

Disability laws are intended to protect people with disabilities from discrimination and provide them with an equal opportunity to access and enjoy life in their communities. The primary sources of federal regulation with respect to disability law are identified below.

- *Architectural Barriers Act of 1968*, Pub. L. No. 90-480, 82 Stat. 718 (codified as amended at 42 U.S.C. §§ 4151–4157 (2016). The Architectural Barriers Act (ABA) requires that buildings and facilities designed, constructed, altered, or leased with certain federal funds, after September 1969, must be accessible to and useable by people with disabilities. It addresses construction-based standards of accessibility for new and renovated buildings, rather than the services or programs being provided in such buildings. Private market construction of single-family housing is not covered by the ABA. Removing barriers from an older building may not be required if a property owner can demonstrate that doing so is *not readily achievable*—that is, it raises engineering issues as well as cost considerations. Zoning for historic preservation may also confront issues under this Act. Barriers to access such as stepping up into an elevated entranceway and narrow doorways may make a building inaccessible to some people with a disability. These barriers generally need to be eliminated unless the very reason for preserving the location (its unique design or architecture for example) is undermined by such alterations.
- *Section 504 of the Rehabilitation Act of 1973*, codified in Section 794 of the United States Code as amended by the *Rehabilitation Act of 1978 (RHA)*, 29 U.S.C. § 794 (2016). Section 504 prohibits discrimination based on disability in any *program* or *activity* receiving federal financial assistance. New construction and alterations must be ac-

cessible. To the extent that Section 504 applies to housing, it covers housing programs receiving federal funding and not privately funded single-family residential housing. To the extent that federal funds are used to construct or alter roadways and adjoining sidewalks, zoning must be consistent with disability law requirements. This means that sidewalks receiving federal funds must be ADA compliant in terms of measurements and permitted usage (placements of signs, bus stops, benches, and crosswalks). Federal funds provided by the Federal Emergency Management Agency (FEMA) for rebuilding private single-family housing after a disaster, may provide for adding accessibility features to a reconstructed home that did not originally have the requested accessibility features. These requests have to be applied for by individual application and are governed by FEMA rules.

- *Fair Housing Amendments Act of 1988* (FHAA), Pub. L. No. 100-430, 102 Stat. 1619 (codified as amended at 42 U.S.C. § 3601 (2016), amending Civil Rights Act of 1968, Pub. L. No. 90-284, Title VIII, 82 Stat. 81 (codified as amended at 42 U.S.C. § 3601 (2016)). The FHA prohibits discrimination in housing on the basis of race, color, religion, sex, national origin, familial status, and disability, and it applies to private housing, as well as publicly supported housing. *Id.* § 3601. Activities covered include selling advertising, leasing, and financing of housing. The FHA uses the term "handicap" rather than disability (the addition of language to the FHA to protect people with a handicap was added by the FHAA). The FHA defines handicap in the same manner as the ADA and RHA define disability. Zoning is also covered by the FHA. The FHA requires property owners and zoning officials to make reasonable exceptions to policies and practices to afford people with disabilities an equal opportunity to obtain housing. The focus is on providing an equal opportunity to obtain housing. This may require zoning officials to grant a variance or an exception to a zoning requirement, if the person with a disability can show that doing so is a reasonable accommodation and that it is necessary for the person to be afforded an equal opportunity to obtain housing. A "but for" test is used, which requires the person seeking the accommodation to demonstrate that, without the variance or exception ("but for the variance or exception"), he or she will not have an equal opportunity to obtain housing. The FHA also provides mandates for all new multi-family housing to meet specific inclusive design standards, including guidelines for common areas, entranceways, hallways, light switches, grab bars, spacing to accommodate use of a wheelchair, and other design elements. The FHA also requires that the treatment of group homes, and the definition of "family" do not treat people with disabilities in a discriminatory way. Rules regulating group homes may have to be modified to accommodate the needs of people with disabilities (for example the maximum number of people permitted in the home).

When dealing with private housing and private land regulations such as those arising in leases, deed restrictions, covenants running with the land, or restrictions enforced by private home owner associations (H.O.A.s), the FHA is applicable. ADA Title II applies to programs, services, and activities of local government (not private land regulations); and ADA Title III applies to privately owned places of public accommodation (e.g., restaurants, retail stores, hotels, and other places open for business to the public). Consequently, most private housing arrangements will be covered under the FHA.

- *The Americans with Disabilities Act of 1990 (ADA)*, Pub. L. No. 101-336, 104 Stat. 327 (codified as amended at 42 U.S.C. § 12101–12213 (2016)). The ADA prohibits discrimination against people with disabilities in employment, state and local government services, public accommodation, and telecommunications. *Id.* 42 U.S.C. § 12101. The ADA requires accessibility, and accessibility guidelines are published by the U.S. Access Board as the Americans with Disabilities Act Accessibility Guidelines (ADAAG). U.S. Access Bd., Americans with Disabilities Act Accessibility Guidelines (2002), *available at* http://www.access-board.gov/guidelines-and-standards/buildings-and-sites/about-the-ada-standards/background/adaag#2. The DOJ also has a detailed publication in relation to the 2010 ADA Standards for Accessible Design. *See* U.S. Dept. of Justice, 2010 ADA Standards for Accessible Design (2010). *Title II* prohibits discrimination based on disability in *programs*, *services*, and *activities* provided or made available by public entities. All activities of planning and zoning boards are covered under this Title. This not only includes accessibility to meetings and meeting venues, it also includes a requirement to make reasonable accommodations and modifications to various planning and zoning requirements. *Title III* prohibits discrimination based on disability in the provision of goods, services, facilities, privileges, advantages, or accommodations of any *place of public accommodation* by any person owning, leasing, or operating a place of public accommodation. Private entities and property owners are considered to be operating places of public accommodation when they are open to the public. Places of public accommodation are not government owned or operated; as places of public accommodation they are covered under Title III. A partial list of examples of places of public accommodation, for illustrative purposes, includes the following: hotels, restaurants, auditoriums, shopping malls, concert halls, retail centers, and banks. Various commercial facilities are also covered under Title III. Commercial facilities are slightly different from places of public accommodation, and while they must comply with the new construction and alteration requirements, commercial facilities do not come within the barrier removal requirements. A commercial facility might be a factory or an office building where the employees are the only people allowed in the facility, but if the facility offers tours to the public or to the extent it has areas open to accommodate a range of people, it will then be subject to the full requirements of a place of public accommodation. Private clubs are not covered by Title III, unless the club makes its facilities available to nonmembers. *See* 42 U.S.C. § 12187; 28 C.F.R. § 36.102(e). A single-family residential house is not considered a place of public accommodation, but if there is a business operating out of part of the house, that part of the building is covered by Title III. *See* 28 C.F.R. § 36.207. A mixed-use hotel development project with an area devoted to residential housing and an area with rooms let out as hotel rooms is subject to Title III with respect to the hotel rooms but subject to the FHA with respect to the residences. *See* 28 C.F.R. § 36 App. C. A day care center or senior facility run by a church is covered by Title III, but the actual church itself has a religious exemption. *Id.* Title III requires facilities to be accessible following ADA Guidelines. This means that buildings and facilities need such things as ramps, lifts, accessible bathrooms, automatic doors, and readily accessible entranceways. Local planning and zoning regulations must be consistent with these requirements. For facilities and structures that predate 1992, barriers to accessibility need to be removed to the extent that doing so is *readily achievable.* When older buildings are altered, they must then be accessible to the *maximum extent possible.*

Many of the provisions of our disability laws address structures, places, and activities. Different rules apply in different circumstances. Many of the issues that arise are design and construction matters related to how to comply with rules intended to make our built environment more accessible. Some of these are issues for designers and architects. At the same time, distinct lawyering issues arise in assuring compliance with these rules and in dealing with the legal interpretation of their requirements. Lawyers must examine and evaluate the legislative language, history, and the various administrative and court decisions interpreting these requirements. Most importantly, lawyers must deal with the meaning and application of such terms as: accessibility to the greatest extent possible; structural impracticability; facilities and alterations; programs, services, and activities; undue financial and administrative burden; barriers; readily achievable; reasonable accommodation; reasonable modification; and what it means for a request to be reasonable, and necessary, while not fundamentally altering a program, service, or activity.

In dealing with disability law issues, it is important to understand who is protected by our disability laws. An individual receives no protection from the ADA if the individual's disability falls outside the statutory definition. The broad definition of disability employed by the ADA is applicable to all Titles of the ADA, and it is essentially the same under the FHA and the RHA. In each case, the term "disability" means, with respect to an individual—

> (A) a physical or mental impairment that substantially limits one or more major life activities of such individual;
>
> (B) a record of such an impairment; or
>
> (C) being regarded as having such an impairment.

42 U.S.C. § 12102(1).

For a person to be covered by our disability laws, she must show that 1) she has a disability, 2) the disability affects at least one major life activity, and 3) the disability substantially limits the named major life activity.

The ADA identifies a non-exhaustive list of major life activities including: "caring for oneself, performing manual tasks, seeing, hearing, eating, sleeping, walking, standing, lifting, bending, speaking, breathing, learning, reading, concentrating, thinking, communicating, and working. These activities are considered essential to daily life."

While many of the disability issues in the land use and zoning context are related to design and construction compliance, several issues fall within the heading of seeking a reasonable accommodation or modification. A request for a reasonable accommodation or modification is similar to seeking a variance, and it is often a petition made simultaneously with, or as an alternative to, seeking an area or use variance. Much like a petition for a variance, a request for a reasonable accommodation or modification seeks an exception or adjustment to the rules and requirements that otherwise apply under the planning and zoning ordinances.

For example, a person may want to add a ramp, deck, or pool to their property but doing so violates a variety of lot requirements for the zone. Perhaps the proposed project comes too close to a property line. The person can ask for an area variance or, if he has a disability, he can also ask for an accommodation. Similarly, a person may want to use a given property for a use not permitted under the zoning code, such as for a drug rehabilitation center in a retail zone. The person could seek a use variance to permit the drug rehabilitation center, or she could ask for an accommodation to permit the use. Generally, the request for a reasonable accommodation or modification is directed to the decision-making body with authority to decide the matter, but in some cases, a local government may designate a particular office to handle a variety of requests for accommodations and modifications.

Unlike a variance, the approval of a reasonable accommodation or a reasonable modification does not run with the land. As a consequence, a local planning and zoning authority might approve a request for an accommodation or modification and condition it on the property being rehabilitated to its original condition when the person being accommodated is no longer located at the property, or is no longer in need of the accommodation or modification. While these conditions are presumptively valid, they are subject to review. They may not be enforceable if the court believes that rehabilitation requirements are so costly and burdensome that a person entitled to protection might not request an accommodation or modification. *See Austin v. Town of Farmington*, 826 F.3d 622 (2d Cir. 2016). The court in the *Austin* case considered a condition on an accommodation allowing a property owner to build a therapeutic swimming pool where no pools we permitted, on condition that the pool be removed when the property was sold. When the owners went to sell the property, they did not want to pay the rehabilitation costs to return the property to its former state. They challenged the condition, and the court reasoned that conditions could be placed on accommodations but that the court needed to consider the actual impact of how these conditions might affect the free exercise of one's right to a reasonable accommodation under the law.

Reasonable accommodations and modifications must be provided to a person with a disability. Consider, however, the situation of a person, Paul, who does not have a disability but who has a good friend, Ann, who uses a wheelchair for mobility. Paul may like to seek permission to add a wheelchair accessible ramp to the front entrance of his house even though construction of the proposed ramp may violate the zoning code. Paul wants the ramps so that Ann might easily and safely visit him at his home. Paul may seek an area variance for the ramp, but he cannot seek a reasonable accommodation. Ann could ask for a reasonable accommodation for her property, but Paul cannot qualify for one on his property because he does not have a disability. This raises a question as to how best to improve the accessibility of the broader community.

As to a person with a disability, failure to provide a reasonable accommodation or modification, when requested and appropriate, is actionable discrimination under federal law. This means that a planning and zoning office must make a determination as to the merits of a request by applying federal disability law criteria. They must do this independent of state law requirements applicable to a determination for a standard zoning variance. Moreover, a denial of a request for a reasonable accommodation or modification raises a cause of action for discrimination that can be appealed directly to federal court without exhausting state and local remedies.

There are three methods of demonstrating discrimination under the ADA, RHA, and FHA: (a) disparate treatment; (b) disparate impact; and (c) the denial of a legitimate request for a reasonable accommodation or a reasonable modification. The ADA and RHA prohibit discrimination in the programs, services, and activities of public entities (this includes planning and zoning). Both Title II of the ADA and section 504 of the RHA prohibit discrimination by a public entity based on a disability. Title II applies to state and local government, and section 504 applies to the federal government. The FHA extends this to include access to public and private housing, and applies to zoning and to regulations applicable to a common interest community (such as a subdivision, or condominium with a Home Owners Association—H.O.A.).

The diagram below outlines the three methods of demonstrating discrimination against people with disabilities—disparate treatment, disparate impact, and failure to provide a reasonable accommodation or modification. It also shows the criteria for a reasonable accommodation and modification—a request must be reasonable, necessary, and not fundamentally alter the program, service, or activity for which the accommodation or modification is requested.

Diagram 7.1 Three Methods of Demonstrating Discrimination

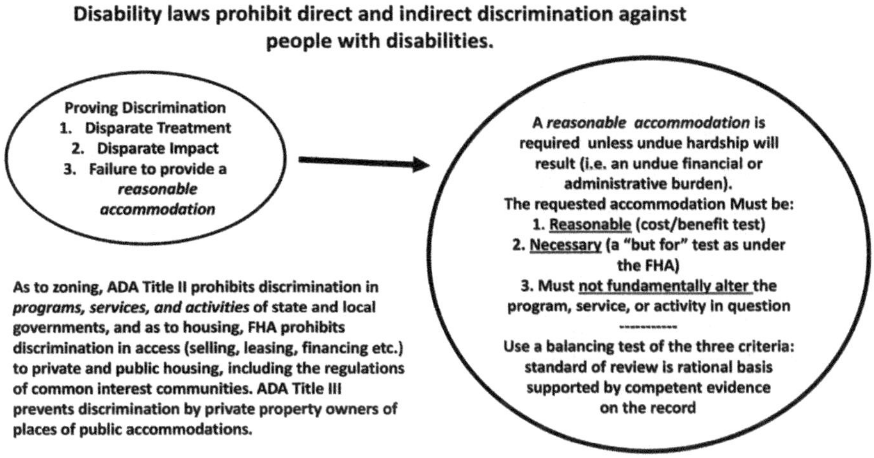

Disparate treatment and disparate impact analysis have already been discussed earlier in this book. Therefore, discussion will focus on criteria for a reasonable accommodation and a reasonable modification. Accommodations and modifications require the same three factor analysis, but accommodations relate to changing rules and regulations, whereas modifications generally relate to changes in the physical environment.

Quoting from the opinion in *Cinnamon Hills Youth Crisis Centers, Inc. v. Saint George City*, 685 F.3d 917 (10th Cir. 2012):

> A claim for reasonable accommodation ... does not require the plaintiff to prove that the challenged policy intended to discriminate or that in effect it works systematically to exclude the disabled. Instead, in the words of the FHA, a reasonable accommodation is required whenever it "may be necessary to afford [a disabled] person equal opportunity to use and enjoy a dwelling." 42 U.S.C. § 3604(f)(3)(B).
>
> What does it mean to be "necessary"? The word implies more than something merely helpful or conducive. It suggests instead something "indispensable," "essential," something that "cannot be done without." ... What's more, the FHA's necessity requirement doesn't appear in a statutory vacuum, but is expressly linked to the goal of "afford[ing] ... equal opportunity to use and enjoy a dwelling." 42 U.S.C. § 3604(f)(3)(B). And this makes clear that the object of the statute's necessity requirement is a level playing field in housing for the disabled. Put simply, the statute

> requires accommodations that are necessary (or indispensable or essential) to achieving the objective of equal housing opportunities between those with disabilities and those without. *See Bryant Woods Inn, Inc. v. Howard County, Md.*, 124 F.3d 597, 605 (4th Cir. 1997); *Schwarz v. City of Treasure Island*, 544 F.3d 1201, 1227 (11th Cir. 2008).
>
> Of course, in some sense all reasonable accommodations treat the disabled not just equally but preferentially. Think of the blind woman who obtains an exemption from a "no pets" policy for her seeing eye dog, or the paraplegic granted special permission to live on a first floor apartment because he cannot climb the stairs. But without an accommodation, those individuals cannot take advantage of the opportunity (available to those without disabilities) to live in those housing facilities. And they cannot because of conditions created by their disabilities....
>
> But while the FHA requires accommodations necessary to ensure the disabled receive the same housing opportunities as everybody else, it does not require more or better opportunities. The law requires accommodations overcoming barriers, imposed by the disability, that prevent the disabled from obtaining a housing opportunity others can access. But when there is no comparable housing opportunity for non-disabled people, the failure to create an opportunity for disabled people cannot be called necessary to achieve equality of opportunity in any sense. So, for example, a city need not allow the construction of a group home for the disabled in a commercial area where nobody, disabled or otherwise, is allowed to live.

Cinnamon Hills, at 922–24.

Requesting a reasonable accommodation for financial feasibility reasons does not qualify as a necessary accommodation. The fact that a person with a disability may prefer to conduct a use of property in a less costly way (e.g., build a cheap ramp rather than an expensive one), or that a given project would be more economically feasible if done on a larger scale (e.g., putting more residents into a group home to enhance revenue to better cover costs), does not make the use necessary for FHA purposes.

When a planning board or a zoning board of appeal is presented with a claim for a reasonable accommodation it must make specific findings. First, it should make an assessment as to the application of the various disability laws to the applicant raising the claim. (That is, determining that the applicant is a person protected by the various federal laws addressed herein.) Second, it should proceed to evaluate the request based on the criteria for accommodation by determining: 1) whether it is reasonable; 2) whether it is necessary; and 3) whether it fundamentally alters the planning and zoning scheme. To make this assessment, applicants will have to reveal certain information about their disability so that the proposed accommodation can be evaluated against the criteria. In considering these three criteria, there is no one factor that is determinate in evaluating if the request is to be granted. Thus, findings should be made on each of the criteria and then a balancing test should be applied. Importantly, the person with a disability is not entitled to the specific accommodation or modification requested, even if an accommodation or modification is to be granted. A decision-making body can provide an alternative if it deems an alternative to be appropriate. In addition, conditions may be placed on the execution of the accommodation and modification. For example, a claimant may be granted permission to add a ramp to the front of their house, but conditions can be placed on the design and construction of an approved ramp. A condition might require construction and design that matches the materials, color, and style of the house. This condition may cost more than a cheaper approach to a ramp, but if structural additions generally have this requirement under the code, they can be imposed on the accommodation and modification. The person with a disability is not being treated differently than others in the same zone when asked to conform to standards such as matching construction materials, housing styles, and colors. Ultimately, a rational decision must be made that is supported by substantial competent evidence on the record. Reasons and justification for the approval or denial of a request must be included with a decision.

Importantly, third parties have standing to weigh in on the consideration of a requested reasonable accommodation or modification made to a planning or zoning board. Third parties typically include neighboring property owners and property owners within a certain established distance from the property being considered. The extent of notification is established by the general zoning code. Planning and zoning board meetings are open to the public. The public can comment on and present evidence to inform the decision maker in determining if a given petition is reasonable. Moreover, if a planning or zoning board grants a reasonable accommodation to an applicant, third parties with standing can challenge that decision on appeal.

A reasonable accommodation, unlike a variance, does not run with the land. It is personal to the person who is granted the accommodation or modification. This means that a board can limit the duration of a zoning accommodation to the time for which it is needed, as in the time during the occupation of a structure by the person with the disability. It also means that reasonable conditions for rehabilitation of the property may be attached to the granting of the accommodation or modification. When an accommodation is no longer needed, the property owner may be required to return the property to its original state.

There is a similar duty to make a reasonable accommodation under both the FHA and Section 504 of the RHA. There is no express language of a reasonable accommodation requirement stated in *Title II of the ADA*, but the language of a reasonable modification is used in the Act, and courts have interpreted the requirement for a reasonable modification as the same as a reasonable accommodation. In addition, the courts have located a duty to accommodate in the statute generally. Thus, all Titles of the ADA require a reasonable accommodation or reasonable modification when appropriate.

A reasonable modification is treated in a similar way as a reasonable accommodation. In practice, courts have treated modifications as changes to the physical environment, such as modifying an entranceway by making it wider and by eliminating a step-up at an entranceway. In contrast, an adjustment in a rule or a practice is often treated as a reasonable accommodation. However, one does sometimes encounter discussion that references making a reasonable modification to a rule or a practice, rather than limiting that phrasing to physical changes to the environment. It is possible that a person may be requesting both a reasonable accommodation and modification at the same time. Requesting a reasonable accommodation or modification for financial feasibility reasons does not qualify as a necessary accommodation.

Some zoning codes regulate how many and what types of animals or pets can be kept at a property location. The ability to regulate in this area can be limited by disability law. For example, a person with a disability may be entitled to maintain a miniature horse on their single-family residential property even if the zoning code prohibits having farm animals on property in the zone. *See Anderson v. City of Blue Ash*, 798 F.3d 338 (6th Cir. 2015).

In regulating with respect to animals, one must be knowledgeable of two categories of animals under our disability laws. First, *service animals,* and second, *emotional support animals* (ESA). Under the ADA, only dogs and, under special criteria, miniature horses are service animals. A service animal must be trained to do work or perform tasks that assist the owner with a disability. Service animals are not pets. If the service animal is housebroken and under the control of the owner, it is permitted to go wherever the person with a disability can go. Under the FHA and the RHA, service animals include emotional support animals. ESAs may be pets, and they do not need to be trained to do any specific task. They may be any type of animal. However, they must be controllable by their owner and not pose a threat to others. Using a reasonable accommodation analysis, the ESA may go where the owner goes. Thus, service animals under the ADA are allowed to go with the owner, but as to an ESA, we must evaluate them in terms of the criteria used for a reasonable accommodation.

CHECKPOINTS

- **Speech.** There are limitations on land regulations that affect speech and expression.
- **The First Amendment** provides that "Congress shall make no law ... abridging the freedom of speech, or of the press...."
- **Implications.** This raises important considerations in land use and zoning in several ways. It can have implications for the regulation of signs, flags, architecture, art, and adult entertainment.
- **Classifying speech.** The general structure of analysis focuses on classifying speech as commercial, political, or something else.
- **The regulation of commercial speech is subject to intermediate scrutiny.** The regulation of commercial speech is evaluated in terms of four criteria. First, the commercial speech must concern a lawful activity and not be misleading. Second, there must be a substantial governmental interest in regulating the speech. Third, the regulation must directly advance the asserted government interest. Fourth, the regulation must not be more restrictive than necessary to advance the asserted interest.
- **Content based or content neutral.** With respect to speech, one must categorize the government regulation as either being content based or content neutral.
- **With content neutral regulation, there are five criteria.** First, it must be focused on secondary effects and not on the content of the speech.

Second, the regulation must be as to time, place, and manner. This is a type of how, when, and where regulation. Third, the regulation must be pursuant to a substantial or compelling government interest. Fourth, the regulation must be narrowly tailored to accomplish the stated government interest. Fifth, there must be other available avenues of communication. Content neutral regulation is subject to intermediate scrutiny, and the government has the burden of demonstrating its constitutionality.

- **Content based speech regulations are subject to strict scrutiny review standards.** Content based regulation is presumptively unconstitutional. The government has the burden of overcoming this presumption and of carrying the day on each of the criteria.
- **There are three criteria used to evaluate content based regulation.** First, the purpose and motivation of the regulation cannot be content based. Second, there must be a substantial and compelling government interest in the regulation. Third, the regulation must be narrowly tailored and constitute the least restrictive means for accomplishing the government's legitimate purpose. Each of these criteria must be established with specificity and with detailed findings to pass strict scrutiny review.
- **Family.** All zoning codes regulate single-family and multi-family residential uses. This requires some working definition of family.
- **Defining family** for zoning purposes can raise constitutional tensions with the Due Process Clause of the Fourteenth Amendment and the rights of privacy and of association.
- **Religion (RLUIPA).** The most important federal legislation supporting the First Amendment freedom of religion in the zoning context is the Religious Land Use and Institutionalized Persons Act, 42 U.S.C. § 2000cc et seq. ("RLUIPA" pronounced "Ruh-lou-pah," rhymes with Chalupa).
- **The language of RLUIPA provides,** in pertinent part, as follows:

  > No government shall impose or implement a land use regulation in a manner that imposes a substantial burden on the religious exercise of a person, including a religious assembly or institution, unless the … imposition of the burden … is in furtherance of a

compelling governmental interest; and ... is the least restrictive means of furthering that compelling governmental interest.

- **Disability**. In general, our disability laws require that all *new construction and alterations* of existing structures must be accessible to the greatest extent possible. The only defense to lack of accessibility is *structural impracticability* wherein high cost is not a determinant factor.
- **In addition, *all programs, services, and activities* of state and local government must** be accessible to people with disabilities (this includes all land use and zoning activities). Defenses to a claim for greater accessibility include demonstrating that it would impose an *undue financial or administrative burden* on the state or local government to make a program, service, or activity more accessible. Evidence on financial and administrative burdens is critical for all sides in such claims.
- **Fundamentally alter**. Likewise, the state and local government may not need to make an accommodation or modification if doing so will *fundamentally alter* the program, service, or activity in question. Evidence of what it means to fundamentally alter must be established.
- ***Barriers***. In older buildings, barriers must be removed in order to make older building more fully accessible (meaning that they are not "grandfathered" in) unless the removal is *not readily achievable*. Evidence of cost and structural difficulties must be provided.
- **Accommodations and modifications**. Planning and zoning regulations must be adjusted and exceptions provided for a person with a disability but only if the person affirmatively *requests an accommodation or modification* and the request *is reasonable*. Each of these requirements and the possible defenses to them have implications for land planning and zoning, and all are the subject of litigation.
- **There are three criteria to balance in evaluating a request for a reasonable accommodation and modification**. 1) Is the request reasonable using a cost and benefit analysis (will it impose an undue financial or administrative burden)? 2) Is the requested accommodation necessary to alleviate the consequences of the disability (using a "but for" test)? 3) Will the requested accommodation fundamentally

alter the program, service, or activity—that is, fundamentally alter the land use plan or zoning code? Developing evidence supporting each criterion is important.

- **Disability with respect to land use regulations related to animals and pets.** Dogs, and in some cases miniature horses, are service animals under the ADA. They can be with their owner. They are not treated as pets. Emotional support animals (sometimes referred to as service animals in the FHA) can be with the owner based on a request for a reasonable accommodation.

CHAPTER 8

Contemporary Zoning Issues

ROADMAP

- Housing
  - Inclusionary Housing—Affordable Housing
  - Homelessness and Squatting
- Climate change—Solar, Wind, EVs
- Sustainability and Growth Management
- Accessibility Planning
- "Smart" Communities
- Critically Sensitive Areas

Many contemporary public policy concerns are addressed in land use and zoning regulations. Key areas to be aware of are discussed in this chapter.

a. Housing

Housing is an issue that concerns many communities. Housing costs represent a large part of most people's budget. In many communities, the average wage worker finds it difficult to afford a home. High costs affect the accessibility of both home ownership and rental properties. Local land regulations can drive up the cost of housing by imposing requirements that extend construction time and limit density. For example, single-family housing typically costs more than multi-family housing because of land costs, and many communities zone a significant part of their jurisdictional territory for low density, single-family residential housing.

i. Inclusionary Housing—Affordable Housing

Land regulation and zoning can add to the cost of housing and make housing unaffordable for some people. This may make it difficult for low-income people to find housing near where they work, or perhaps at all. When zoning results in making housing unavailable or unaffordable to a number of people, it is sometimes referred to as *exclusionary zoning*. This is because the zoning practices make it difficult for low-income people to live in these communities. Exclusionary zoning can be influenced by current owners who use the political process to promote zoning that protects their property values and keeps cheaper housing options out. A counter movement in response to this practice is identified as *inclusionary zoning*. As the name implies, inclusionary zoning seeks to make housing options more accessible and affordable based on adjusting zoning regulations and creating incentives for lower cost housing opportunities.

Two important state court decisions have shaped much of the conversation and law involving inclusionary zoning. These two cases are: *Southern Burlington County NAACP v. Mount Laurel Township*, 67 N.J. 151, 336 A.2d 713, *cert. denied*, 423 U.S. 808 (1975) (*Mt. Laurel I*), and *Southern Burlington County NAACP v. Mount Laurel Township*, 92 N.J. 158, 456 A.2d 390 (1983) (*Mt. Laurel II*). In general, even though these cases were state court decisions under state constitutional law, they promoted a nationwide movement to advance affordable housing, and to require every community to plan for and provide its fair share of the affordable housing needed in a given region. These cases influenced the development of the general law of inclusionary housing.

Mount Laurel I established a requirement mandating that all New Jersey communities plan for affordable housing. In particular, communities were required to plan for and provide for their fair share of a region's affordable and low-cost housing needs. Local land use regulations needed to be adjusted to create realistic opportunities for the construction of this housing. Individual communities could not zone out affordable, low-cost, or subsidized housing in an effort to maintain a certain economic and social status as an "exclusive" community. *Mount Laurel II* reinforced this mandate by extending the mandate beyond newly developing communities to include communities that were well established. It also expanded the mandate's effectiveness by providing a "builder's remedy" allowing developers to sue municipalities that prevented low income and affordable housing to be built.

The policy considerations supporting the *Mount Laurel* decisions have been adopted by many states and have generally been incorporated into national thinking regarding zoning and the need for greater inclusion in housing. In an effort to encourage the development of more affordable housing, many communities have employed *incentive zoning* techniques to encourage more inclusive housing opportunities. In addition, some communities have developed zones permitting so called "tiny houses" that are compact at under four hundred square feet and built with efficiency and low cost in mind. Some of these tiny houses are no bigger than a backyard shed measuring sixty square feet (the smallest proclaimed tiny house is under twenty square feet). These tiny houses can be mobile (on wheels) or on a foundation. Some communities have also eliminated protected single-family residential zones. This permits higher density use of already existing lots and structures, with the goal of reducing housing costs. For example, higher density can be achieved by allowing a tiny house to be placed on the same lot as an existing single-family home.

In seeking to provide affordable housing, many communities have adopted *incentive zoning* that consists of several common practices and policies. Incentive zoning can involve streamlining the planning and permitting process to encourage construction of desired development projects. For example, developers willing to build affordable housing or housing for senior citizens might get a *"fast track"* process for approval and permitting. In some cases, this might reduce the wait time by as much as one third, one half, or more. Reducing the approval time for a project can dramatically reduce risk and cost. A second incentive structure involves the granting of a *density bonus*. Assume that a zoning code requires that all housing units must be built on one acre lots. A community seeking to encourage the building of additional affordable housing might provide a developer with a right to build two or four units per acre based on agreeing to construct a certain number of low-cost dwelling units. The density bonus might also work in terms of the height of a structure. For example, instead of being limited to a one-story apartment building or condominium, the density bonus might come in the form of permitting extra stories to be added to the project so that more units can be built. This increases the density of permitted housing units and lowers the land cost per unit. The developer gets to build and sell more homes, increasing the potential profit on the overall project.

Incentive zoning programs are sometimes part of a *linkage program* to facilitate affordable housing production. Complying with the specific requirements in the jurisdiction is a condition to obtaining a development permit. These programs typically require developers to add to the stock of affordable housing in a community in one of three ways. First, they may require that a developer build and set aside a certain number of units within a proposed housing development to be sold at a below market rate. This means that they will be priced below the market price. These units will only be available to buyers who meet certain defined income requirements that qualify them for affordable housing. Second, there may be an option for the developer to get approval for one project in a given location while agreeing to build affordable units somewhere else. Third, developers may be required to contribute money to an affordable housing fund. The amount required to be contributed is based on a formula established in the legislation. The typical formula requires a set fee based on the size of a developer's project. Size may be measured by number of units in the entire project or by total square feet in the project, depending on the exact terms of the legislation. The money is then paid into a fund, and the fund is used to subsidize affordable housing in locations identified by public officials. These payment schemes are often applied to commercial properties as well as residential properties. The theory is that commercial activities require workers and workers need a place to live. Thus, commercial developers are often required to participate in these programs. Linkage programs are subject to takings law analysis and must meet the essential nexus test of *Nollan v. California Coastal Commission,* 483 U.S. 825 (1987); and the rough proportionality test of *Dolan v. City of Tigard,* 512 U.S. 374 (1994). For examples of the disputed application of linkage requirements, see *Home Builders Ass'n v. City of Napa*, 108 Cal. Rptr. 2d 60 (Cal. Ct. App 2001); *Holmdel Builders Ass'n v. Township of Holmdel*, 583 A.2d 277 (N.J. 1990).

Another way of adding to affordable housing is an incentive program based on eliminating single-family residential zones. The idea is that instead of protecting single-family homes, additional housing can be built on already developed lots. That is, where there is already a single-family home in a single-family only zone, people are allowed to add an additional dwelling or more, based on the size of their lot. This may include converting a garage space into a dwelling space as well as adding a new structure. By eliminating the protection of a single-family only zone, zoning officials cannot prohibit people from adding second dwelling units to their lots. The typical scenario is that a state will prohibit the protection of single-family zones and thus, prohibit local zoning officials from preventing "infill" development that increases density. The opportunity to increase density on existing built-out lots raises the potential to add some more affordable housing to the housing stock.

Early adopters of this strategy include California, Oregon, and Washington. By permitting duplexes, triplexes, and other forms of housing on traditionally protected single-family lots, more housing can be produced per acre lowering the per acre cost of development. In addition to the potential for lower housing costs, the development of more units per lot increases density and might potentially add to the viability of mass transit in certain zones.

ii. Homelessness and Squatting

A continuing problem for many communities is that of dealing with a homeless population. There are many causes of homelessness, and the people who find themselves homeless make up a diverse population. For some people, being homeless is a temporary situation, for others it is a chronic condition. From a land use and zoning perspective, the issue centers around the question of where the homeless have a right to be, given that they seemingly have no legal right to be anywhere. In a country based on private property with a fundamental right to exclude others, those without property must rely on charity and the kindness of others for permission to occupy a space and a place. The homeless may have no property, but do they have a right to be somewhere; and if so, where should that be? This raises fundamental questions for land use and zoning.

One set of issues deals with charitable efforts to assist and house the homeless. Typical of the issues that arise in this context include zoning disputes concerning the location of soup kitchens, health services, and homeless shelter facilities. Related to this is the problem of determining the best locations in a community for these types of uses. When a zoning code does not expressly provide for these uses, there may be a dispute as to how they should be categorized within the types of uses permitted by the code, or they may be permissible using the variance process. The complexity of the problem increases when a number of the homeless people being served are also people with disabilities. This is because disability law adds additional legal rights and considerations to the zoning issues that otherwise must be addressed. These considerations become even more complicated when the charitable group providing services to the homeless is a religious organization, in which case one must also consider implications of the First Amendment protection of religious freedom and exercise, and the Religious Land Use and Institutionalized Persons Act (RLUIPA, discussed in Chapter 7). Both the First Amendment and RLUIPA may work to limit the options available to local planning and zoning professionals when attempting to address the problem of homelessness.

A second set of issues in dealing with a homeless population is that of homeless people occupying private space owned by another. Private property owners have the right to sole and exclusive possession and use of their property. They can exclude others. These private spaces and places can include many property types such as farmland, housing lots, corporate office buildings, private parking lots, and private beaches. When the homeless occupy the private space of another, there is a violation of property law and certain civil and criminal legal actions may be maintained for trespass and adverse possession. From a planning and zoning perspective, the goal is to minimize and avoid such conflicts and confrontations.

A third set of issues involves homeless people occupying public spaces such as parks, sidewalks, and public beaches. Here, there are no private property owners with the right to exclude others. Public lands are controlled by public officials. When the homeless occupy public space, they may be classified as loiterers, vagrants, or trespassers and can confront fines and jail time. When the public provides inadequate shelter and housing, where can the homeless rest, sleep, and live? And with no place to call home, where can they store any personal belongings such as spare clothing, a radio, or a bicycle? Likewise, without adequate shelter or housing, the homeless have nowhere to shower and go to the bathroom. This results in unsanitary conditions. In an effort to avoid confronting the difficult problems of trying to provide shelter and housing to the homeless, some communities just stopped enforcing laws against occupying public spaces such as sidewalks, beaches, and parks. In these communities the homeless were generally not removed from the encampments they were setting up in these public locations.

While homelessness may not seem directly related to zoning, it is within the confines of land planning and regulation, and controlling homelessness and the related sanitation issues is within the scope of protecting the public health, safety, welfare, and morals. Regulating the use and occupation of public spaces can sometimes lead to intense conflicts among people. For example, two recent cases involved lawsuits against cities for not removing homeless encampments from public sidewalks. *See Hood v. City of Sacramento*, No. 23-cv-00232, 2023 U.S. Dist. LEXIS 180812, 2023 WL 6541870 (E.D. Cal. Oct. 5, 2023); *Tozer v. City of Portland*, No. 22-cv-01336, 2023 U.S. Dist. LEXIS

214497, 2023 WL 8295886 (D. Or. Nov. 30, 2023). The lawsuits were brought by disability rights groups who argued that the encampments deprived them of access to the community because they needed the sidewalks to safely navigate the neighborhood. Blocking of the sidewalks deprived people with disabilities of their protected rights of access. The cities involved in these two lawsuits were concerned that they might have an obligation to allow the homeless to remain in public spaces given that the cities did not have adequate housing or shelter for the homeless. This resulted in a conflict between the rights of the homeless and the rights of people with disabilities. The concern over the rights of the homeless was based on the case of *Johnson v. City of Grants Pass*, 72 F.4th 868 (9th Cir. 2023). This case indicated that the homeless could not be removed from public places unless and until a community had adequate shelter and housing for all their homeless. At the same time, disability law protected the rights of people with disabilities to access these public spaces and places, and the homeless encampments were blocking the sidewalks. The matter was clarified on appeal to the U.S. Supreme Court in *City of Grants Pass v. Johnson*, 603 U.S. 520 (2024). In the opinion of the Supreme Court, it was held that cities can remove homeless people from public places such as sidewalks, alleyways, beaches, and parks, and even fine them or sentence them to time in jail. The takeaway from this case is that communities need to develop ways of addressing homelessness by providing shelter and services and not by simply surrendering public spaces and places to the homeless.

Related to the problem of homelessness is *squatting*. Squatting involves occupying a property, land, or space in a building, without the permission of the true owner. The problem presented is one of determining the legal status of the squatter. Under basic property law, a squatter is an adverse possessor and can acquire an interest in the property over time if certain conditions of state law are met. At the same time, if a squatter moves into a home or dwelling while the owner is temporarily absent, the squatter may acquire rights as a presumptive tenant. In jurisdictions that treat the squatter as having presumptively legal possession under a lease, the police cannot remove the squatter without a court proceeding brought by the party asserting to be the true owner. This can surprise some owners who return from a vacation and find someone else living in their home. These court proceedings can be quick or might last months, depending on the jurisdiction and the specific facts. While the matter is being determined, the squatter might be protected by landlord and tenant law.

b. Climate Change—Solar, Wind, EVs

Concern over climate change has caused many states and communities to regulate to promote green development and to reduce the negative impact of development on the environment. State and local regulation supplements federal regulation that is also directed at ameliorating the perceived negative consequences of climate change. In the mix of multi-jurisdictional efforts to regulate land uses that impact on climate change, we deal with two concepts discussed in Chapter 2, preemption and the Dillon Rule.

Preemption involves the hierarchy of jurisdictional authority. As between multiple layers of government, federal, state, and local, whose laws apply to a given topic, and in the event of a conflict, whose law controls? In general, federal law controls over state and local law unless it intrudes on powers reserved to the states. At the state level, state law controls over local law because local governments exercise regulatory powers by virtue of delegation from the state. If the federal government expresses supremacy or is such that it totally occupies the field, then it will generally be said to preempt state and local efforts to regulate in an inconsistent way. State and local governments may nonetheless supplement federal regulatory efforts. For example, the federal government regulates to protect wetlands and prohibit development near protected areas, *see e.g.*, Clean Water Act § 404; 44 C.F.R. § 9.5; Coastal Zone Management Act, 16 U.S.C. § 1451; Coastal Wetlands Planning, Protection and Restoration Act, 16 U.S.C. § 3951–3956; and the Coastal Barriers Resource Act, 16 U.S.C. § 3501, et seq. Even with federal regulation, states and local governments may supplement this regulation by expanding the designated areas protected. They cannot, however, unilaterally reduce the federally protected wetland zones.

At the state level, a state can expressly preempt local government regulation or take over the field and implicitly preempt local regulation. This might be the case if a state passes legislation in support of wind farms and provides that no county or municipality can prohibit the development of wind farms meeting certain state established criteria. This might be done to encourage wind farm development and to prevent local communities from engaging in NIMBY politics (the politics of "not in my back yard," meaning that the political process is used to keep undesired projects out of a given neighborhood).

At the state level, these conflicts trigger disputes centered on the tension between the Dillon Rule and Home Rule authority. The Dillon Rule provides that local governments may only retain and exercise authority that is: (1) expressly granted by the state legislature; (2) necessarily implied by the expressly granted powers; or (3) essential, not simply convenient, to the municipality's objectives and purposes. *Hawkeye Foodservice Distrib. v. Iowa Educators Corp.*, 812 N.W.2d 600, 611 (Iowa 2012); *Kole v. Faultless*, 963 N.E.2d 493, 495 (Ind. 2012). On the other hand, Home Rule authority takes a much more expansive view of municipal power, stating that a local government has broad ability to act unless either the state constitution or statute prohibits it or expressly confers such power to another entity. *Town of Cedar Lake v. Alessia*, 985 N.E.2d 55, 60 (Ind. Ct. App. 2013); *Bd. of Appeals of Hanover v. Hous. Appeals Comm. in Dep't of Cmty. Affs.*, 294 N.E.2d 393, 407 (Mass. 1973). States are split on which rule they follow. Some states expressly designate certain municipalities as Home Rule cities; other states may grant all municipalities Home Rule powers.

Even with this tension between the Dillon Rule and Home Rule, many local jurisdictions are exercising authority to implement green zoning. In some jurisdictions, this includes zoning for solar and wind farms. *See, e.g., Frederick County v. LeGore Bridge Solar Ctr. LLC*, No. 1249, 2020 Md. App. LEXIS 1140 (Md. Ct. Spec. App. Nov. 24, 2020) (addressing regulatory conflicts between state and local regulators with respect to solar arrays). Typically, alternative energy development is regulated at the state level, but often local authority is exercised within parameters established by state legislation. For example, a state may require communities to permit alternative energy facilities within their jurisdiction (they cannot be zoned out) but may leave it to the local jurisdiction to address a safe and appropriate location for such a facility. This would be consistent with the traditional exercise of the local police power to protect the public, health, safety, welfare, and morals.

In some states, local governments are authorized to establish *green development zones*. As an example, Virginia provided for this by statute. *See* Va. Code Ann. § 58.1-3854(B) (2024). In Virginia, local governments can designate green zones and offer tax incentives and regulatory flexibility to businesses engaged in green development or operating energy-efficient buildings. A green development business is defined as "primarily engaged in the design, development, or production of materials, components, or equipment used to reduce negative impact on the environment." Va. Code Ann. § 58.1-3854(A) (2024). Regulatory flexibility includes streamlining approvals and permitting leeway with otherwise applicable planning and zoning requirements.

Some communities are planning for rising water levels and other consequences of changes in weather patterns due to climate change. This can involve zoning to expand flood zones or to regulate development in areas anticipated to be subject to water level rise in the future. It may also include zoning for enhanced protection of shorelines, as water levels are anticipated to rise and water-based storms become more unpredictable and more severe.

Climate concerns have also been the basis for incentivizing a move away from fossil fuels and a drive toward electric vehicles (EVs). From a zoning perspective, this requires land planners and zoning professionals to consider the availability and location of EV charging stations. For instance, when setting parking requirements for various uses (offices, shopping centers, apartment buildings), what zoning requirements should be set for the number of charging stations within each of these uses? Do charging spaces even count as parking places? And what steps must a property owner take to ensure that no one vehicle occupies a charging station for an inordinate amount of time? Should streetside parking include EV chargers?

A combination of zoning and building code regulations need to address power availability at residential housing. Homes need to be built and equipped with sufficient power connections for fast charging of vehicles and for the replacement of many current uses of natural gas with electricity. Some states, such as Washington, require the construction of EV infrastructure for various property uses in communities of over a certain population and located near major roadways. This includes battery charging facilities. Wash. Rev. Code Ann. § 36.70A.695(1)(a), (b), (c) (2024). "Electric vehicle infrastructure" is defined as structures, machinery, and equipment necessary to support electric vehicles, including battery charging stations, rapid charging stations, and battery exchange stations. Wash. Rev. Code Ann. § 36.70A.695(5)(c) (2024). In Delaware, municipalities over a certain size population must implement an ordinance permitting residents to obtain a permit to install EV charging stations on property zoned for residential use abutting a residential street. 22 Del. Code Ann. § 119(a)(2) (2025). There are also requirements for a minimum number of charging stations for multi-family residential uses, and a requirement that a minimum number of charging stations be accessible to people with disabilities. 16 Del. Code Ann. § 8005(a)(1)–(2) (2025), 16 Del. Code Ann. § 8005(d) (2025). Connecticut and Oregon provide additional examples of states requiring municipal mandates for a required number of EV charging spaces for various uses such as commercial, multi-family, and mixed-use developments. Conn. Gen. Stat. § 4b-77(c) (2025), Or. Admin. R. § 918-460-0200(2)(a), (b), (c) (2025).

Climate change regulations often overlap and supplement *sustainability zoning*. One example of this involves the granting of density bonuses or streamlined permitting for developers who make their properties meet certain standards established for a Leadership in Energy and Environmental Design (LEED) certification. LEED is a certification system developed by the U.S. Green Building Council. There are multiple certification levels including, from lowest to highest, Certified, Silver, Gold, and Platinum. The system is based on points, with points awarded for such things as how the development deals with water, energy, carbon, materials, transportation, waste, health, and indoor environmental quality. The goal is to produce more efficient buildings using environmentally favorable materials and technologies to support healthier environments. These efforts support sustainability and work to address climate change.

c. Sustainability and Growth Management

Related to efforts to respond to climate change are land use and zoning practices directed at sustainability and growth management. Sustainability aims to maintain the quality of life in our communities, and growth management is one way of achieving this goal. Key elements of a strategy for sustainability and growth management include: comprehensive planning; consistency; concurrency; performance zoning; and moratoria.

Comprehensive planning can occur at the local, regional, and state levels. As the term implies, these plans are developed and coordinated in the planning department, not the zoning office. Comprehensive planning requires periodic review of current land development matters in a jurisdiction and consideration of projections for future development. These plans will look at demographic information and address such elements as the need for current and future housing, transportation and traffic circulation, water, utilities, schools, parks, open space, agricultural needs, shopping, entertainment, cultural needs, historic neighborhoods, landmark buildings, density, and access to healthy food and medical services. The plans will be thoughtfully prepared and based on carefully accumulated data. There is usually an opportunity for public comment in the planning process before a plan is adopted by the local government. A similar process may be used at the regional and state levels. The plans will include policy objectives for each of the elements covered and mapping information indicating locations for implementation of various aspects of the plan. Once a plan is legislatively adopted, a zoning ordinance will be adopted or amended in order to implement the plan. As such, zoning is said to be done pursuant to a plan. In this way, zoning carries out the plan and expresses an inherent rationality and coherence.

In order to maintain the rationality and coherence of zoning, it should be done in a manner consistent with the plan. And while it is often times stated that zoning must be done pursuant to a comprehensive plan, it remains unclear across different jurisdictions as to what it means for zoning to be done consistent with the plan. Some jurisdictions have a strict standard of *consistency* while other jurisdictions pay little attention to the matter. *See, Pinecrest Lakes, Inc. v. Shidel*, 795 So. 2d 191 (Fla. Dist. Ct. App. 2001) (discussing in part that Florida applies the strict scrutiny standard when assessing consistency of a local zoning board decision with the applicable Comprehensive Plan); *but see City of Chicago Heights v. Living Word Outreach Full Gospel & Ministries*, 196 Ill. 2d 1, 749 N.E.2d 916 (Ill. 2001) (Illinois Supreme Court case holding that a comprehensive plan was not binding, it was merely advisory and could not override a zoning ordinance which deemed churches as a compatible use in the zone at issue). Strict scrutiny standards of review in zoning, such as that applied in Florida, limit the discretion of a zoning board when enforcing a zoning ordinance pursuant to the plan. In a similar way, some states require that local comprehensive plans be consistent with mandated regional plans and state plans. *See* Fla. Stat. § 163.3194.

Zoning *concurrency* is a mechanism used to manage new development and growth within a comprehensive plan in such a way as to not overburden existing public infrastructure and services. This usually involves controlling the issuing of permits and managing uses in such a way as to have development occur at the same pace as improvements to infrastructure related to water, sewer, power, and roads. It also involves coordinating development with services such as policing and firefighting. Concurrence requirements manage property development in a way that reduces the negative consequences of rapid growth. Incentive zoning tools can also be used to manage growth and adjust density in different parts of a community to ensure a more efficient use of infrastructure.

Related to the idea of concurrency is *performance zoning*. This type of zoning regulates land use based on the potential externalities that may spill over to surrounding properties. Rather than focusing on regulating land uses based on zones dedicated to a list of specific uses, performance zoning sets standards for such things as noise levels, traffic, air quality, and environmental impacts. It limits development based on these performance standards while leaving flexibility as to the types of uses that might be compatible with these performance-based regulations.

Another way to temporarily manage growth is with a *moratorium* on certain aspects of development. For example, a community may experience a sudden influx of people and need time to build infrastructure and pass a concurrence ordinance. Or a community might be presented with a request for a new type of land use for which it is unprepared, and for which it has little expertise. Time may therefore be needed to develop thoughtful regulation. This has been the case with the initial introduction of such things as cell towers, wind farms, and solar arrays. In such cases, communities may take a pause, or pass a moratorium, on issuing building permits for such uses while the matter is studied, and appropriate regulation is adopted. This can be done within reason and on a temporary basis under the appropriate facts and circumstances. The law related to a temporary taking functions as a limitation on the moratorium process.

A moratorium raises the potential for a temporary taking action by the affected property owner. *See First English Evangelical Lutheran Church v. Los Angeles Cnty.*, 482 U.S. 304 (1987); *Tahoe-Sierra Preservation Council, Inc. v. Tahoe Regional Planning Agency*, 535 U.S. 302 (2002). The *Tahoe-Sierra* case involved a 32-month moratorium put in place so that a comprehensive plan could be developed. The moratorium put a pause on a developer's project. The developer sued and argued that it experienced a complete economic loss during the moratorium period. The Court held that it was not a complete economic loss and thus not a categorical taking, because the whole parcel had to be considered. In considering the whole parcel, the Court reasoned that the developer still held the fee and would still be able to develop the property once the moratorium was lifted. Thus, the temporary moratorium during a time when reasonable progress was being made by the government, did not result in a 100% loss of all economic value for which compensation was required.

There are many tools available to manage growth and to promote sustainability. Specific tools for promoting sustainability and growth management may include the development of regulations such as those at issue in several key cases on takings law. These key cases explore the use of various tools and address the limits of these tools as proper exercises of the government power to regulate. Key cases include: *Lucas v. South Carolina Coastal Council*, 505 U.S. 1003 (1992) (coastal land management); *Nollan v. California Coastal Commission*, 483 U.S. 825 (1987) (coastal land development and beachfront access); *Dolan v. City of Tigard*, 512 U.S. 374 (1994) (flood zone management and bike path planning); and *Koontz v. St. Johns River Water Management District*, 570 U.S. 595 (2013) (wetlands protection and restoration). Other tools may include land regulations requiring housing to be built above ground elevation, on stilts, in order to avoid flooding. In many of these cases, thought must be given to careful coordination among planning, zoning, and building codes.

d. Accessibility Planning

Accessibility planning involves prioritizing concerns for accessibility to our built environment for people with disabilities and for those who are seeking to age in place. This should be required in order to make our communities safe and easy to navigate for people of a variety of abilities. Accessibility planning includes preparation of an *Accessibility Impact Report* or an *Accessibility Impact Statement*. The report should assess the current level of accessibility across various uses within the community, and then develop a plan for improving accessibility with reference to planned new development and growth. In the absence of clear and detailed state or local criteria on accessibility planning, reference should be made to requirements and standards established under federal disability law and applicable to the states with respect to avoiding discrimination.

An Accessibility Impact Report should include a logistical analysis of the ways in which people move between and among the places and spaces of community life. This kind of logistical study would inform planners on important elements of connectivity and identify needed enhancements to accessibility infrastructure. These types of studies are already done at many locations such as theme parks, shopping centers, airports, and even large grocery stores. They are also done by federal, state, and local departments of transportation and by other departments and agencies. Evaluating how people move through space and place leads to better planning and improves connectivity across the built environment. Consequently, accessibility should be understood as the outcome of good comprehensive planning and investment in adequate accessibility infrastructure.

Accessibility infrastructure includes curb cuts, ramps, appropriate sidewalks, accessible bus and train transport, accessible buildings, and the use of enhanced technology such as speaking crosswalk controls and the use of hearing loop technology in busy transport stations to assist visually impaired people with directions.

In requiring mandatory accessibility planning, there should be "strict consistency" among local, regional, and state planning offices with respect to achieving the goal of making our communities accessible to the maximum extent possible. Strict consistency tightens up the relationship between planning and the zoning enacted pursuant to a plan. This standard of review is best understood as a standard of strict consistency between planning and zoning, and it could be applied as between federal requirements to provide for enhanced accessibility and local planning and zoning to accomplish this goal. Strict consistency should apply to the requirement that facilities, programs, services, and activities of state and local government be accessible to the maximum extent possible. In other words, there should be strict scrutiny and consistency between zoning and disability law requirements.

Likewise, strict consistency should be applied to assertions that compliance with federal disability law imposes an undue financial or administrative burden. To survive strict consistency review, a community should have evidence that is more than competent evidence on the record; it should demonstrate that it is more likely than not that greater accessibility imposes financial and administrative burdens that substantially outweigh the benefits to be achieved. The calculation should account for social, political, and economic considerations. As part of the proof, the community officials should also be required to demonstrate that they have performed an accessibility impact review of the community and developed a specific plan for continuous improvement of accessibility. Accessibility, in other words, should be a specific element of every community's comprehensive plan, and such planning should include realistic steps for financing all needed improvements.

e. "Smart" Communities

Smart communities employ *smart zoning*. Smart zoning is data and technology driven in an effort to optimize land use and property development. For example, technology is employed to manage availability of parking spaces in a downtown area, to assess and adjust traffic patterns, or to identify optimal density levels for different parts of a community. Smart zoning often focuses development around areas identified as good locations for transportation hubs, and on the connective corridors between these hubs and frequently visited venues.

Smart zoning may be used simultaneously with form-based zoning to permit mixed-use development within what would otherwise be traditional Euclidean zones. Smart zones tend to enhance density while seeking to expand transport options to include; public transit, bicycle trails, and walking pathways. This can improve sustainability while reducing our carbon footprint.

One tool used in smart zoning is *twinning*. This involves creating a virtual mirror image or digital twin of the real community. The virtual twin is an interactive model loaded with data of a community's demographics, terrain, buildings, and infrastructure. The model is then used to predict potential outcomes based on testing different planning and zoning approaches. The twin uses real time updated data for simulations and employs machine learning and AI in reasoning and decision making.

f. Critically Sensitive Areas

Many jurisdictions have zoning to protect critically sensitive areas from over development. These are generally environmentally sensitive areas such as tidal shorelines, wetlands, floodplains, aquifers, parklands, forests, and agricultural lands. Property development in these areas can have negative implications for the environment including damaging plant, fish, bird, and animal habitats.

Permits for development in such areas may have special requirements. There may be a need for additional studies and assessment before approval. There may be density limitations, buffer zone requirements, and rules restricting imperviable surfaces. Regulations may also be in place to control water run-off from adjoining properties.

Zoning and land regulation of critically sensitive areas is often accomplished with the use of overlay zones. In a sense, an *overlay zone* is a type of zoning on top of zoning. Basically, an area is zoned for certain uses or types of development. Then, if some parts of a given zone contain critically sensitive lands, an additional layer of regulation applies on top of the regular zoning. For example, a neighborhood may be zoned for single-family use and some portion of land in the same neighborhood may have wetlands on them. The wetlands regulations would be on top of, or in addition to, the underlying zoning. A property owner must comply with both sets of regulations. This can be better appreciated when one thinks of the entire community that may have wetlands scattered among various neighborhoods. Some of the neighborhoods may have single-family or multi-family residential uses, and others may include commercial, or industrial uses. Most of the lands within these different neighborhoods do not include wetlands. In such a situation, the community might develop a zoning ordinance for various uses in different zones. Then, they might enact an overlay zone with regulations applicable to property in or abutting wetlands. The overlay zone would have regulations applicable to all wetlands in the jurisdiction no matter what zone they are in. The wetlands overlay zone would be connected to an overlay map. The overlay map would be positioned over the regular zoning map and then all the properties with wetlands would be subject to both sets of regulations no matter what neighborhood or zoning districts they were in.

Agricultural lands are another type of sensitive land use in need of protection. Many communities seek to protect the availability of agricultural lands from the progress of land development for non-agricultural land uses. For example, many communities experience a loss of agricultural lands to the development of housing subdivisions, warehouses, data centers, manufacturing facilities, shopping centers, and solar and wind farms.

Agriculture is an important industry and retaining good farmland is necessary for many reasons. Agriculture employs many people and supports domestic production of food and nutrition. In addition, new industries have grown up around what is now called agribusiness, or agricultural tourism. These ventures include apple orchards and strawberry farms where people are invited in to pick their own fruits and enjoy other activities as an outdoor experience. Likewise, we see farms open for pumpkin picking, hayrides, and corn mazes. Similarly, we can enjoy craft breweries and local vineyards. All of these uses add to the quality of life, connect people to the land, and contribute to a sustainable and livable community.

In seeking to protect agricultural lands, many communities enact *agricultural protection zoning* (APZ). This type of zoning typically designates specific areas for the primary purpose of agricultural use. Non-agricultural uses are prohibited or extremely limited. In addition, APZ may limit the density of development abutting agricultural zones and restrict the types of uses that can be made of adjacent properties.

CHECKPOINTS

- **Housing.** Local land regulations can drive up the cost of housing by imposing development requirements that extend construction time and that limit density.
- **Inclusionary Zoning**—affordable housing. Inclusionary zoning seeks to make housing options more accessible and affordable based on adjusting zoning regulations and creating incentives for lower cost housing opportunities.
- **Climate Change**—solar, wind, EVs. State and local regulation supplements federal regulation directed at ameliorating the perceived negative consequences of climate change. Here, we need to deal with issues of preemption and of delegation. Some communities establish local green development zones; zone for alternative energy production (e.g., solar and wind farms); require the inclusion of EV charging stations and infrastructure; and prioritize development of LEED certified buildings.
- **Sustainability and Growth Management.** Sustainability aims to maintain the quality of life in our communities, and growth management is one way of achieving this goal. Key elements of a strategy for sustainability and growth management include: comprehensive planning, consistency, concurrency, performance zoning, and moratoria.
- **Accessibility Planning.** Accessibility planning involves prioritizing concerns for accessibility to our built environment for people with disabilities and for those who are seeking to age in place. Accessibility planning includes preparation of an Accessibility Impact Report or an Accessibility Impact Statement.
- **"Smart" Communities.** Smart communities employ smart zoning. Smart zoning is data and technology driven in an effort to optimize land use and property development.
- **Critically Sensitive Areas.** Many jurisdictions have zoning to protect critically sensitive areas from overdevelopment. These are generally environmentally sensitive areas such as tidal shorelines, wetlands, floodplains, aquifers, parklands, forests, and agricultural lands.

Mastering Land Use and Zoning Master Checklist

Chapter 1 • Common Law Land Regulations—Prelude to Zoning

- ☐ **Common law.** Land regulation was possible under the common law before the development of modern planning and zoning codes.
- ☐ **Trespass.** One way to control land uses under the common law was with an action in trespass. Trespass involves a nonconsensual invasion of the property rights of another. This could involve something very tangible such as walking or building on another person's property, or something more abstract such as suing for an intrusion of dust particles, noise, and light escaping from one's property and interfering with another property owner's right to exclude.
- ☐ **Nuisance.** Land uses were also regulated by the law of nuisance. Nuisance was an action based on the interference with a person's peaceful use and enjoyment of her land.
- ☐ **Private nuisance** involves a use that interferes with one or a very small number of other property owners.
- ☐ **Public nuisance** is a use that interferes with the use and enjoyment of the public at large.
- ☐ **Deed restrictions** also limited and regulated land uses. Deed restrictions were binding on the grantee and the grantee's heirs, successors, and assigns.
- ☐ **Restrictive covenants** regulated land by imposing positive and negative requirements. Restrictive covenants run with the land and are binding

on the heirs, successors, and assignees of the parties to the covenants. When all of the formalities of a legal covenant are not present, the courts sometimes enforce an equitable servitude.

- ☐ **Limitations of the common law.** While the law of trespass, nuisance, deed restrictions, and restrictive covenants provide means for regulating land uses, they are generally inefficient because they are limited in their scope and applicability. They are also not well suited to coordinating and mediating the multiplicity of competing activities and interests in a modern and complex society.
- ☐ **The Public Trust Doctrine** is primarily a state common law matter, but the federal government also protects the environment and natural resources for the benefit of the public. The doctrine identifies certain resources such as air, water, and wildlife as things that are held for the benefit of all people. In order to protect and manage these resources, the state holds them in trust.

Chapter 2 • Introduction to Land Use and Zoning

- ☐ **Planning and zoning** became important with industrialization in the late 1800s and early 1900s. Local governments used planning and zoning to coordinate the location of incompatible uses and to avoid unsafe conditions.
- ☐ **Local governments** (cities and towns) began to regulate land uses under authority delegated to them by the state in which they were located. This authority was identified as the police power. The police power is the authority of a sovereign state to regulate private activities and property rights for the public health, safety, welfare, and morals.
- ☐ **The police power** is held and exercised by the states, whereas the federal government generally regulates under the Necessary and Proper Clause and the Commerce Clause of the federal Constitution. The federal government has police powers in the District of Columbia.
- ☐ **Early planning and zoning regulations were challenged** as unlawful and in violation of both the common law and the Constitution. The breakthrough case on the legality of planning and zoning regulations was *Village of Euclid v. Ambler Realty*, 272 U.S. 365 (1926). In *Euclid*, the Supreme Court upheld a local zoning ordinance that separated uses, regulated permitted uses by districts, and controlled for such things as

density, height and bulk of structures, and building setbacks from identified boundary lines.

- ☐ **Planning and zoning are two different functions.** Planning involves policy, review of property development, preparation of a comprehensive plan, and suggestions on zoning updates. A planning board functions to develop and approve plans for development projects in the community. Zoning involves regulation of land uses, and a zoning board enforces the zoning code requirements on development within the community.
- ☐ **Zoning must be rational and done pursuant to a plan.** This is an important connection between planning and zoning.
- ☐ **The planning and zoning process involves both legislative and quasi-adjudicative functions.** As an example, passing a development plan for a city or town is a legislative function, but enforcing a zoning code regulation against an individual homeowner is a quasi-adjudicative function. There are different legal considerations applicable to each of these functions.
- ☐ **Decisions made by a planning board and a zoning board are subject to judicial review.** This means that they can be appealed. When such decisions are appealed, they are subject to a legal standard of review. There are multiple standards of review that need to be considered based on the nature of the legal question involved.
  - **De Novo Review** is where a reviewing court examines the law and the facts on its own. It gives little or no deference to the local administrative decision rendered by a zoning board of appeal.
  - **There are three categories of rational basis review,** and they are fairly debatable (not arbitrary and capricious), rational (in relation to the legislative intent), and rational as supported by competent evidence in the record.
  - **Intermediate scrutiny** requires a higher burden of proof than rational basis, and by example, it is applicable to zoning that differentiates on the basis of gender, or that restricts commercial speech.
  - **Strict scrutiny** requires a very high burden of proof to show regulatory legality, and by example, it is applicable to zoning that differentiates on the basis of race or that restricts political speech.
- ☐ **Local planning and zoning authority relies on a proper delegation of state police power** from the state to the local government. Delegations

can be read narrowly under the Dillon Rule, or broadly as when a state designates a city or town as a place of Home Rule in planning and zoning matters.

- ☐ **There are situations in which state or federal law may *preempt* local law** on a matter related to land use. Typical examples might include state regulations on cannabis cultivation and commercial sales, or at the federal level, land protected under the federal Clean Water Act, wetlands protection, and lands protected for use by migratory birds.
- ☐ **A Unified Development Code** may be used in a local jurisdiction. It is one comprehensive and unified document that brings together what used to be covered in multiple codes. This often includes regulations related to planning and design, zoning, subdivision of land, and water management.
- ☐ **Downzoning** reduces allowable density and intensity of uses, and **upzoning** increases allowable density and intensity.
- ☐ **Land regulation and zoning are subject areas that intersect with real estate development and transactions.** Zoning is important to the real estate purchase and sale contract, title examination, and to mortgage financing.

Chapter 3 • Procedures and Administrative Matters

- ☐ **State Administrative Procedure Acts** outline the procedures for state agencies and their subdivisions to propose, issue, and adjudicate regulations. These can apply to state land regulation agencies. Generally, local land use and zoning jurisdictions have their own published procedures.
- ☐ **Related State and Federal Regulations.** In a land use and zoning practice there will be many occasions when regulations outside of the planning and zoning codes may have implications for land use decisions.
- ☐ **The Standard State Zoning Enabling Act (SZEA)** includes nine sections. They cover granting local governments the authority to regulate land uses for the purpose of promoting the public health, safety, welfare, and morals of the community; dividing the jurisdiction into districts or zones; zoning pursuant to a comprehensive plan; establishing procedures; provisions for amendments; establishing a zoning authority; enforcement; establishing a ZBA; and a method of resolving conflicts with other laws.

- ☐ **The Standard City Planning Enabling Act (SCPEA)** includes four key elements including developing a comprehensive master plan; developing regulations for control of subdivisions; building controls; and engaging in regional planning if desired.
- ☐ **Zoning and planning decisions often require a public hearing.** These hearings give the public notice of what is pending and provide opportunities for input.
- ☐ **Enforcement actions** can be brought by local governments to enforce the zoning ordinance. Generally, violations of the zoning ordinance are discovered when reported to the planning and zoning office by a neighbor or upon inspection.
- ☐ **Zoning Board of Appeal (ZBA)** deals with interpreting and enforcing the zoning ordinance. A ZBA makes quasi-adjudicative decisions. It renders interpretations, adjudicates area and use variances, and evaluates conditional and special use permits.
- ☐ **Judicial Review of ZBA** decisions is provided for under state law. Review can be limited with deference given to the ZBA, but in some jurisdictions or some situations, review may be de novo.
- ☐ **Standing** is available to a person with a direct and specific injury as a result of a zoning provision or decision.
- ☐ **Standing under disability law.** Under the ADA, FHA, and RHA, a plaintiff must show an injury in fact that meets the following three requirements: (1) concrete and particularized or an actual and imminent injury that is not hypothetical; (2) the injury is fairly traceable to a challenged action of the defendant; and (3) the injury is likely to be redressed by a favorable decision.
- ☐ **Exhaustion.** Generally, a claimant must *exhaust* administrative remedies before appealing to the courts. There are limited exceptions.
- ☐ **Ripeness.** The courts do not like to address hypothetical questions; thus, a matter must be *ripe* before it will be adjudicated.
- ☐ **Rezoning** can be done by amending a zoning map or by amending the text of a zoning code. Rezoning is a legislative act, and it must be done in a way that avoids impermissible spot zoning.
- ☐ **Initiatives and referendums** are two different ways that voters can participate in passing and amending zoning codes and maps.

- ☐ **§ 1983 actions** provide a remedy for property owners who have had their constitutional rights to due process, equal protection, and against improper takings violated.
- ☐ **National Zoning Atlas (NZA)** collects information on zoning districts across the country and identifies by jurisdiction the permitted uses and requirements of zoning districts.

Chapter 4 • Public Regulation of Land—Zoning

- ☐ **Under the Tenth Amendment to the Constitution**, any powers not explicitly granted to the federal government are reserved to the states. This is consistent with the police power authority of the states. The police power is an inherent aspect of state sovereignty. The police power can be used to regulate more than land use.
- ☐ **The police power** must be exercised in accordance with due process. In contemporary jurisprudence, due process involves two different elements: procedural due process and substantive due process.
- ☐ **Euclidean zoning** gets its name from the famous case of *Village of Euclid v. Ambler Realty Co.*, 272 U.S. 365 (1926). This case was the first to present the question of the constitutionality of zoning to the United States Supreme Court. The Court upheld the constitutionality of zoning ordinances (codes) as a valid exercise of the state police powers.
- ☐ **The key elements of Euclidean zoning**, as established in the case include: the demarcation of zoning districts that authorize a local government to manage and coordinate land use; a hierarchy among the permitted uses; cumulative zoning based on this hierarchy; and uses permitted in a zone are "as of right."
- ☐ **The power to zone** is exercised in accordance with the police power and pursuant to a comprehensive plan. When a zoning regulation is passed by a local legislature, it must be rational using a fairly debatable standard of review.
- ☐ **Rational as applied.** When zoning regulations are applied to a particular property, they must be rational as applied. And the drawing of district lines, the categories of uses, and other elements in the zoning code must be evaluated on a rational basis standard.
- ☐ **Accessory uses** are uses that are *customary and incidental* to the primary use that is permitted under the land use regulations.

- ☐ **A conditional use**, or what is sometimes referred to as a special use, is a use permitted in a zone provided that certain conditions are met. A drive-through dining facility and a drive-through bank are prime examples of uses requiring conditional use permits to operate in a zone.
- ☐ **The floating zone** starts out as a zone that is not fixed on a zoning map. Instead, it is a zone approved by legislative act that establishes certain criteria for a land use. Its location is fixed at a later date.
- ☐ **Overlay zones** are anchored to specific lands within a jurisdiction. In essence, they establish multiple zoning districts over the same land.
- ☐ **Aesthetic zoning** is permissive to protect the public welfare, but it must be based on clear criteria and be applied in a way that is not arbitrary or capricious.
- ☐ **Historic districts** and landmark preservation acts are forms of aesthetic zoning. State and local governments may regulate land uses for aesthetic reasons under their police power authority.
- ☐ **Spot zoning** is generally not permitted. Spot zoning happens when one or a few properties are singled out for zoning changes that are not applied to surrounding properties.
- ☐ **Subdivision controls** are usually distinct from the zoning code but relate to the overall plan for community development and land regulation.
- ☐ **The Planned Unit Development (P.U.D.)** provides a mechanism for flexibility and doing mixed-use development.
- ☐ **Site Plan Review** is a process that includes a review of development and construction plans for a project to make sure that the project meets local land planning and zoning regulations.
- ☐ **Alternatives to Euclidean zoning.** A baseline for understanding planning and zoning is our traditional reference to Euclidean zoning. There are, however, newer forms of zoning to be aware of and they include: zoning concurrency, form-based zoning, incentive zoning, mixed-use zoning, network zoning, new urbanism, performance zoning, and transect zoning.

Chapter 5 • Variances and Other Standard Zoning Concepts

- ☐ **Area Variance.** Relief based on a practical difficulty in complying with a land regulation is referred to as an area variance. An area variance involves a request for an exception from regulations covering such things as the setback distance between a structure and a road or a property line, the amount of lot coverage occupied by a structure, and the height of a structure.

- ☐ **Use Variance.** A use variance involves a petition to allow *a use* that is otherwise not permitted by the zoning code. Traditionally, a use variance requires a demonstration by the property owner of an undue and unique hardship resulting from the application of the current code to her property.
- ☐ **Public Utility Variance.** Public utilities are often either exempted or subject to different standards for variances.
- ☐ **Run with the land.** Variances (both area and use), when granted, run with the land and benefit future owners and assignees.
- ☐ **Reasonable accommodations and modifications** under our disability laws are personal. As such they do not run with the land.
- ☐ **Non-Conforming Use.** A non-conforming use is a use that is not in compliance with permitted zoning regulations. Generally, nonconforming uses are not permitted. The fact that a use is non-conforming, however, does not necessarily make it an illegal use. A non-conforming use may continue under a "grandfather" provision but will have limitations on its extent and scope. These limitations may include an inability to expand the non-conforming use or to increase the intensity of the use. It may also limit remodeling and rebuilding in the event of a need to repair.
- ☐ **Origin of non-conforming uses**. A change in a zoning code may make previously permitted uses non-conforming. A property that has been granted a zoning variance or an exception under disability law may be non-conforming based on the exception granted.
- ☐ **Amortization**. A zoning code may establish a rule or a set time at which a non-conforming use expires and must be terminated. The non-conforming use is permitted to continue for a period of time (the amortization period), and this time is supposed to provide the property owner with some reasonable return on their property investment such that a taking does not occur.
- ☐ **Vesting**. Vested property rights are protected by the Fifth Amendment to the Constitution. Developers are concerned that projects that take an extended period of time to build might have the zoning and planning regulations change in the middle of a project. This can result in the need

for costly changes to a project and time delays. These potential problems add to costs and undermine the profitability of the original project plan. Consequently, property owners seek to have clarity and certainty as to when their property rights are fixed (vested) under the applicable set of rules and regulations.

- ☐ **Early Vesting and Late Vesting.** Local governments have developed different rules for determining when a property owner's rights are vested. Generally, early vesting jurisdictions have rules that vest the property owner's development rights in the regulations in place at the time a full application and set of plans are officially submitted to the planning and zoning office showing a project in compliance with the current code. Late vesting jurisdictions generally fix the point of vesting much later. This might be after a building permit is issued or after a certificate of occupancy is issued.
- ☐ **Contract Zoning.** Contract zoning is when developers try to enter into a binding contract with a local government wherein the local government agrees not to change the zoning once the project is approved. In general, courts have not favored contract zoning. It is typically viewed as an effort to forgo the legitimate exercise of the police power in order to benefit an individual property owner.
- ☐ **Development Agreements.** While similar in many ways to contract zoning, development agreements are not considered to be contracts and are not governed by contract law. They do, however, seek to accomplish a similar objective. They "freeze" land regulation as of a certain date but also reserve the power of the local government to change the regulation upon a finding of a need to protect the public health, safety, welfare, and morals. Development agreements frequently cover subject matter beyond the freezing of land regulation.

Chapter 6 • Limitations on Zoning—Regulations that "Go Too Far"

- ☐ **Police power limitations.** Limitations on property rights find justification in the lawful exercise of the police power. This requires that the police power be asserted to protect the public health, safety, welfare, and morals.
- ☐ **Going too far.** Regulation of property rights is permissible so long as it does not "go too far." There are several legal safeguards that facilitate determination of what it means to "go too far."

- ☐ **Due process.** There are two parts to due process—substantive and procedural. Substantive due process protects one's right to property, whereas procedural due process addresses the requirements for regulating property rights.
- ☐ **Under substantive due process,** a property owner has the right to use property for any lawful use so long as no harm is done to others. While property rights can be limited and constrained by land use and zoning regulations, the extent of the regulation is subject to limitations under the Due Process Clause. This requires us to continually strike a balance in our analysis of property rights relative to changing social, political, economic, and cultural norms so that we might persuasively argue that in a given case a regulation does or does not go too far.
- ☐ **Equal protection.** Equal protection guarantees emanate from both the Fifth Amendment and the Fourteenth Amendment to the United States Constitution. This requires that land regulation and zoning be rational, and that similarly situated properties and people need to be treated in a similar way.
- ☐ **Similarly situated properties and parties must be treated the same.** Equal protection requires distinctions to be made when rendering decisions that result in different outcomes as among properties or owners who might otherwise appear to be similarly situated.
- ☐ **Equal protection** requires that all properties within the same zoning district or zone must be subject to the same regulatory requirements.
- ☐ **Discrimination.** Discrimination is a violation of equal protection. There are three methods of demonstrating discrimination.
    - **Disparate Treatment.** Factors to consider in making a case of intentional discrimination include: 1) the discriminatory impact of the governmental decision; 2) the decisions' historical background; 3) the specific sequence of events leading up to the challenged decision; 4) departures from the normal procedural sequences; and 5) departures from normal substantive criteria.
    - **Disparate Impact.** To establish a prima facie case under this theory, the plaintiff must (1) identify an outwardly neutral policy or practice, and (2) show a significantly adverse or disproportionate impact on persons of a protected class produced by the defendant's facially neutral policies or practices. This requires a comparison between groups

and the demonstration of an adverse impact on the protected class as evidenced by statistical or other social science methods. The relationship must be robust. Once a plaintiff establishes its prima facie case, "the burden shifts to the defendant to prove that its actions furthered, in theory and in practice, a legitimate, bona fide governmental interest and that no alternative would serve that interest with less discriminatory effect."

- **Denial of a Reasonable Accommodation or Modification.** People with disabilities are a protected class under the Americans with Disabilities Act (ADA), Fair Housing Act (FHA), and the Rehabilitation Act (RHA). They are entitled to a reasonable accommodation or modification of rules and regulations when they satisfy the established criteria.

☐ **Takings.** The Fifth Amendment to the U.S. Constitution protects private property from government confiscation or from what we more commonly refer to as a "taking." The wording of the Amendment is as follows:

> No person shall ... be deprived of life, liberty, or property, without due process of law; nor shall private property be taken for public use, without just compensation.

☐ **There are two categories of per se takings.** The first involves a physical invasion. The second involves a regulatory taking that eliminates all of the economic value of the property.

☐ **Regulatory takings** that do not eliminate all of the economic value of the property are evaluated under the *Penn Central* balancing test that considers: the character of the government action, the diminution in value of the property, the property owner's reasonable investment-backed expectations, the whole parcel, the average reciprocity of advantage, and the extent to which the regulation is designed to prevent harm or confer a benefit.

☐ **A separate class of takings cases involve unconstitutional conditions, also known as exactions.** These arise when government permission or the granting of a permit is granted on a condition. An exaction must have an essential nexus (*Nollan*) between a legitimate government purpose and the condition imposed on the property owner, and it must bear a rough proportionality (*Dolan*) to the impact caused by the requested use of the property by the property owner.

- ☐ **The essential nexus and rough proportionality tests** apply to monetary exactions as well as to conditions placed on the use of the land itself (*Koontz*).
- ☐ **Legislative conditions** may also be subject to the same essential nexus and rough proportionality tests (*Sheetz*).
- ☐ **Judicial takings.** The Supreme Court has acknowledged the possibility of a judicial taking but is yet to provide clear standards for determining when such a taking has occurred (*Stop the Beach Renourishment*).

Chapter 7 • Limitations on Zoning—Regulations in Tension with Other Fundamental Rights

- ☐ **Speech.** There are limitations on land regulations that affect speech and expression.
- ☐ **The First Amendment** provides that "Congress shall make no law ... abridging the freedom of speech, or of the press...."
- ☐ **Implications.** This raises important considerations in land use and zoning in several ways. It can have implications for the regulation of signs, flags, architecture, art, and adult entertainment.
- ☐ **Classifying speech.** The general structure of analysis focuses on classifying speech as commercial, political, or something else.
- ☐ **The regulation of commercial speech is subject to intermediate scrutiny.** The regulation of commercial speech is evaluated in terms of four criteria. First, the commercial speech must concern a lawful activity and not be misleading. Second, there must be a substantial governmental interest in regulating the speech. Third, the regulation must directly advance the asserted government interest. Fourth, the regulation must not be more restrictive than necessary to advance the asserted interest.
- ☐ **Content based or content neutral.** With respect to speech, one must categorize the government regulation as either being content based or content neutral.
- ☐ **With content neutral regulation, there are five criteria.** First, it must be focused on secondary effects and not on the content of the speech. Second, the regulation must be as to time, place, and manner. This is a type of how, when, and where regulation. Third, the regulation must be pursuant to a substantial or compelling government interest. Fourth, the regulation must be narrowly tailored to accomplish the stated government

interest. Fifth, there must be other available avenues of communication. Content neutral regulation is subject to intermediate scrutiny, and the government has the burden of demonstrating its constitutionality.

- ☐ **Content based speech regulations are subject to strict scrutiny review standards.** Content based regulation is presumptively unconstitutional. The government has the burden of overcoming this presumption and of carrying the burden on each of the criteria.
- ☐ **There are three criteria used to evaluate content based regulation.** First, we consider the purpose and motivation of the regulation. The regulation may be directed at secondary effects as a way of showing that it is not content based. Second, there must be a substantial and compelling government interest in the regulation. Third, the regulation must be narrowly tailored and constitute the least restrictive means for accomplishing the government's legitimate purpose. Each of these criteria must be established with specificity and with detailed findings.
- ☐ **Family.** All zoning codes regulate single-family and multi-family residential uses. This requires some working definition of family.
- ☐ **Defining family** for zoning purposes can raise constitutional tensions with the Due Process Clause of the Fourteenth Amendment and the rights of privacy and of association.
- ☐ **Religion (RLUIPA).** The most important federal legislation supporting the First Amendment freedom of religion in the zoning context is the Religious Land Use and Institutionalized Persons Act, 42 U.S.C. § 2000cc et seq. ("RLUIPA" pronounced "Ruh-lou-pah," rhymes with Chalupa).
- ☐ **The language of RLUIPA provides,** in pertinent part, as follows:

  > No government shall impose or implement a land use regulation in a manner that imposes a substantial burden on the religious exercise of a person, including a religious assembly or institution, unless the ... imposition of the burden ... is in furtherance of a compelling governmental interest; and ... is the least restrictive means of furthering that compelling governmental interest.

- ☐ **Disability.** In general, our disability laws require that all *new construction and alterations* of existing structures must be accessible to the greatest extent possible. The only defense to lack of accessibility is *structural impracticability,* wherein high cost is not a determinant factor.

- ☐ **In addition,** ***all programs, services, and activities*** **of state and local government** must be accessible to people with disabilities (this includes all land use and zoning activities). Defenses to a claim for greater accessibility include demonstrating that it would impose an *undue financial or administrative burden* on the state or local government to make a program, service, or activity more accessible. Evidence on financial and administrative burdens is critical for all sides in such claims.
- ☐ **Fundamentally alter.** Likewise, the state and local government may not need to make an accommodation or modification if doing so will *fundamentally alter* the program, service, or activity in question. Evidence of what it means to fundamentally alter must be established.
- ☐ **Barriers** in older buildings must be removed in order to make older building more fully accessible (meaning that they are not "grandfathered" in) unless the removal is *not readily achievable.* Evidence of cost and structural difficulties must be provided.
- ☐ **Accommodations and modifications.** Planning and zoning regulations must be adjusted and exceptions provided for a person with a disability but only if the person affirmatively *requests an accommodation or modification* and the request *is reasonable.* Each of these requirements and the possible defenses to them have implications for land planning and zoning, and all are the subject of litigation.
- ☐ **There are three criteria to balance in evaluating a request for a reasonable accommodation and modification.** 1) Is the request reasonable using a cost and benefit analysis (will it impose an undue financial or administrative burden)? 2) Is the requested accommodation necessary to alleviate the consequences of the disability (using a "but for" test)? 3) Will the requested accommodation fundamentally alter the program, service, or activity—that is, fundamentally alter the land use plan or zoning code? Developing evidence supporting each criterion is important.
- ☐ **Disability with respect to land use regulations related to animals and pets.** Dogs, and in some cases miniature horses, are service animals under the ADA. They can be with their owner. They are not treated as pets. Emotional support animals (sometimes referred to as service animals in the FHA) can be with the owner based on a request for a reasonable accommodation.

Chapter 8 • Contemporary Zoning Issues

- ☐ **Housing.** Local land regulations can drive up the cost of housing by imposing development requirements that extend construction time and that limit density.
- ☐ **Inclusionary Housing**—affordable housing. Inclusionary zoning seeks to make housing options more accessible and affordable by adjusting zoning regulations and creating incentives for lower cost housing opportunities.
- ☐ **Climate Change**—solar, wind, EVs. State and local regulation supplements federal regulations that are also directed at ameliorating the perceived negative consequences of climate change. Here we need to deal with issues of preemption and of delegation. Some communities establish local green development zones; zone for alternative energy production (e.g., solar and wind farms); require the inclusion of EV charging stations and infrastructure; and prioritize development of LEED certified buildings.
- ☐ **Sustainability and Growth Management.** Sustainability aims to maintain the quality of life in our communities, and growth management is one way of achieving this goal. Key elements of a strategy for sustainability and growth management include: comprehensive planning, consistency, concurrency, performance zoning, and moratoria.
- ☐ **Accessibility Planning.** Accessibility planning involves prioritizing concerns for accessibility to our built environment for people with disabilities and for those who are seeking to age in place. Accessibility planning includes preparation of an Accessibility Impact Report or an Accessibility Impact Statement.
- ☐ **"Smart" Communities.'** Smart communities employ smart zoning. Smart zoning is data and technology driven in an effort to optimize land use and property development.
- ☐ **Critically Sensitive Areas.** Many jurisdictions have zoning to protect critically sensitive areas from overdevelopment. These are generally environmentally sensitive areas such as tidal shorelines, wetlands, floodplains, aquifers, parklands, forests, and agricultural lands.

ABOUT THE AUTHOR

Professor Robin Paul Malloy is the E.I. White Chair and Distinguished Professor of Law; the Kauffman Professor of Entrepreneurship and Innovation; and Senior Fellow of the Burton Blatt Institute for Disability Law and Policy at the Syracuse University College of Law. He is a leading expert on property; land use law and zoning; real estate transactions; and on the relationship among law, markets, and marketization. He has pioneered work on the intersection of land use and disability law. He is also recognized as a leading legal scholar on the jurisprudence of Adam Smith. Several of his works on market theory and law are translated into Chinese, Spanish, and Japanese. In addition to this book, Malloy has published twenty books (including four books with Cambridge University Press, two other books with Carolina Academic Press, two books with Aspen Law Publishing and a third Aspen book in process, and several books with other presses). He has also authored over 30 scholarly articles in addition to numerous book chapters and essays. During spring 2026, Malloy served as a Distinguished Visiting Fellow of the Institute for Advanced Studies at the University of Palermo, Italy; and he has been a Sun Life Research Fellow at Oxford University, U.K.; the Dickenson Dees Fellow at University of Durham, U.K.; and for three consecutive summers in the early 1990s worked with the Committee on Legal Education Exchange with China and served as a teaching fellow on transition to a market economy teaching in China at People's University in Beijing, and at Fudan University, and East China School of Politics and Law in Shanghai. He has served on the International Advisory Board for the Law and Economics Program at St. Gallens University, Switzerland, as a member of the Turin School of Local Regulation, Turin, Italy, and for five years as a member of the Working Group on Law and Marketization at the University of Helsinki, Finland.

Malloy is the founder and inaugural president of the Association for Law, Property, and Society. He served on the Board of the National Italian American Bar Association for 20 years, and was Vice Chair of the Zoning Board of Appeal for the Town of DeWitt, NY for 10 years. He has also served on numerous committees of the Association of American Law Schools.

For more than forty-five years, Malloy has been researching, publishing, teaching, and consulting on real estate development, land use regulation, land use and disability, and market jurisprudence. His years of experience provide a rich foundation for this book.

INDEX